THROUGH THE LION GATE

For Annie —
    with thanks for your
encouragement and support —
I hope you enjoy this new venture —
mine into a second publication,
and yours into happy years ahead —
    With much love,
        Eleanor

July 24, 2003
Palos Verdes
California

THE SUQ AL KHAMIS, HUFUF, SAUDI ARABIA ON
MARKET DAY—1958

THROUGH THE
LION GATE

An American woman challenges the traditions
of a veiled society and discovers a daughter

Eleanor Nicholson

To order additional copies of this book, contact:

Xlibris Corporation

1-888-795-4274

www.Xlibris.com

Orders@Xlibris.com

15676

CONTENTS

Dedicated to the family of His Highness, the Governor Of the Eastern Province, Kingdom of Saudi Arabia, 1960s.

NOTE

THROUGH THE LION GATE is a true story.

The events actually took place. To insure the privacy of living characters, their names have been changed and adjustments made to obscure identification.

The Author

ACKNOWLEDGMENT

Full credit goes to Cynthia Castain for the emergence of a manuscript into a book. I am forever indebted to my daughter for her expertise in the field of computers, her devotion to the success of this venture, her endless patience and willingness to give whatever it took that THROUGH THE LION GATE might become a reality.

INTRODUCTION

Thirty years of living in the Kingdom of Saudi Arabia came rushing back, as I returned the telephone to its cradle. All the exciting, unpredictable happenings of those years, the good parts and the bad, had been fused together in memory since I last said goodbye to the sand and the wind, to vast desert vistas, mud villages and oil company towns—to the villas and palaces of the Al Abdullah family, rulers of the Eastern Province where we lived. Now those years returned, obscuring the ocean view from my home in Palos Verdes, California, the green hillsides, the ease of everyday living. My morning on this day of April 20, 1988 had been turned topsy-turvy, leaving me tingling with excitement at the advent of the unexpected.

The telephone's demanding ring had done that, as well as the voice on the other end—a voice I could never forget.

"Mrs. Nicholson? This is Latifa . . . I'm in Beverly Hills. Can you come and visit?"

Latifa . . .

Where do you start to catch up, when you're thrown into the past by a quirk of time? Latifa . . . how many years since I'd seen her—the young princess I called my third daughter? Could it be fifteen . . . twenty, maybe? I turned off the coffeemaker—no need for a cup before breakfast to arouse my day. You think of so many things at once—nothing fits together;

yet all a part of the whole: February 1950 and a TWA Ambassador flight to Rome to meet and marry Russ. We had met at Paramount Pictures, Inc. in Hollywood, California, where we both worked. ARAMCO, the Arabian American Oil Company, recruited him for a job in Saudi Arabia. His acceptance depended upon my willingness to follow him later, when family housing became available. I agreed. A year later I received a cable: "Can you meet me in Rome in two weeks?" I could and did.

Arabia was complete fantasy at first with its living Biblical scenario, until I gave it a chance to become real and to share its uniqueness with me. Latifa had done that.

What would she be like today? How much had she changed since I first met her in 1960—the insecure young bride of a powerful Saudi Arabian Prince? She had renounced personal freedoms and left Bavaria, where her Jordanian family lived, to face the isolation of *hareem* life in a Muslim land. For her, too, Saudi Arabia was a challenge. Marriage to a Prince of the royal family of Al Saud meant being molded into a tradition of seclusion, and for her—loneliness.

"Latifa, you're really here? In Los Angeles?"

Her laugh was reassuring. "Yes—of course. Are you surprised? We're staying at the L'Age d'Or in Beverly Hills . . ."

We? That meant the Prince was with her.

"Can you find us?"

"Of course."

"And you'll come soon?"

"It'll take me about an hour."

Freeways in Southern California were not dependable, always crowded and accident prone—especially the 405 to Beverly Hills.

My morning routine of preparing breakfast, retrieving the L.A. Times from the driveway and finishing dressing was suddenly reduced to one need: what to wear! Flashes of remembering—Latifa in beautiful Arab gowns—the Prince in flowing robes—made me wonder about their choice of dress now.

I hurried into the bedroom. Russ was still asleep. Could I leave him for three or four hours? He was just two days out of minor surgery and was doing well. I felt positive my brief absence would be all right.

A quick search of the closet brought forth a mauve crepe dress with full draped skirt. Its jewel neckline would set off the Persian Gulf pearl and gold pendant she had given me many years before. I hung the dress on the closet door, then reached for a pair of pink shoes. The rustle of tissue paper, as I lifted them from their box, disturbed Russ.

"What's going on, El," he asked.

"Latifa . . ." I said. "She's here!"

"What'd you say?"

"Latifa . . . in Beverly Hills. And the Prince is with her."

A moment's pause. He aroused himself into wakefulness. "You must go, of course."

I walked over to the bed. "She said to come as soon as I could—and have lunch with them."

He turned on his side to face me. "Lunch with the Governor His Highness Amir Mishari Al Abdullah, first cousin of the King, is something you can't miss."

"Sure you'll be okay?"

"Positive." He had a way of giving me everything I wanted.

I fixed a quick breakfast, gave him the Times, smoothed the bed, changed my clothes and was on my way. The 405 cooperated, and the drive to Beverly Hills was uneventful. What would she be like? Her voice was positive—in command—nothing like the insecure girl I had met so many years before. Would she look different? Older, of course, but that wouldn't change her questioning smile, her expressive eyes, the lilt of her speech. I even wondered if her hair still shone with the golden glint of henna paste, like sunlight in a darkened room.

The foyer of the L'Age d'Or, a small exclusive hotel of

elegant suites and furnishings far from the madness of Los Angeles, presented a glittering array of mirrors, crystal chandeliers and gilded furniture. The lobby continued the theme of French artistry in pale green, white and gold. Other than the desk clerks, there was no one around, so I walked into the adjoining arboretum to collect my thoughts, then turned back. And there they were.

I recognized them immediately, as smiling, they walked across the lobby to meet me. Not him at first—for to me most Arab men looked alike in their robes and full beards. This time he was in western dress—a light grey suit and multi-colored tie, his beard closely trimmed, and minus the Arab head cloth, his dark hair curled around his ears. He wasn't as heavy set as I had thought without all those layers of skirts and cloaks and the overwhelming gold braid trim. In fact, he complimented her delicate appearance exactly.

Simple elegance—that was Latifa, down to her black kid slippers. A long straight skirt of dupioni silk—in color, not black but deepest grey. An off white blouse with long full sleeves and a graceful neckline that revealed the curve of her shoulders and skirted the roundness of her breasts—exactly right for the only jewel she wore—a gold chain carrying a perfect black pearl of considerable size. It was her face that held my attention, its openness unrestrained by a veil, its radiance the gift of choice.

And I had returned to the days I knew so well. Impulsive Arab greetings—the touch of lips on each cheek—a rush of questions concerning the family: is everybody well? Did Haifa come with you? How are Fahada and Aysha? All answered in time.

It is not customary for the Saudi Arab to show affection in public, but she held his hand and selected a secluded spot to sit and talk, the way she and I had done over the years. It was special having His Highness a part of our pleasure in being together—the mingling of sexes, once separated.

"Are you sure everything is all right," she kept asking me. "I have missed you so much. Are Linda and Cyndy good, too?"

I reminded her that my daughters were no longer children but married young women and pursuing their own careers. I thought of Haifa, her daughter, the child I had boosted into the branches of a plane tree that she might catch a glimpse of the turquoise waters of the Persian Gulf over the high wall that surrounded her secret garden. Why, the child must be in her mid twenties—most certainly married by now—to a husband arranged for her.

Latifa laughed at my question. There were plenty of suitors, she explained, but Haifa turned them all down. She insisted her opinion be considered in the selection of a husband.

How things had changed! Not so long ago a husband was chosen for you and arrangements were made without your consent. Now, a young woman like Haifa expected to have a voice in her future.

"She is really very busy . . ." Latifa hurried to explain. " . . . so many friends, and she studies very hard."

"Does she go to college?" I asked, aware that higher education was available to women through closed circuit TV and the telephone.

"She wanted to attend in Jeddah, but it was quite impossible to make arrangements—her royal relationship, the need for proper security—to live there." Latifa shuddered at the thought. "She is doing very well at home. Islamic law and culture are important to her—you can't believe how much she studies."

My disappointment for Haifa became aroused excitement, as Latifa continued. "Also, she is very clever. She designs women's gowns—a touch of Paris blended with the Arab style. They are quite unusual, and everybody wants one."

No wonder Haifa hesitated at marriage, I thought. She had shaped a career for herself within the limits set for women. One day she might open her own shop, displaying luxurious fabrics, French laces and trims—even manikins to show off her latest creations. There would be a private office in the rear for consultation with female customers, and a male manager up front to make it all legal. I wanted to hear more, but Latifa directed her attention to the Prince, who engaged her in conversation.

She wore no wristwatch to check the hour. Time was for us to use as we wished, and so she suggested we might have lunch.

"Where would you like to go?" she asked. "There is the Beverly Hills Hotel or the Wilshire. Perhaps you'd like the Bel Air Hotel. I hear it is very nice." Away from the closed walls of her Kingdom, life had opened up for her, and she filled it so well.

"Please—your decision," I said.

"Then—the Bel Air. I shall make arrangements."

She excused herself to His Highness and approached the desk clerk, as though, for her, it was an everyday event to confront a strange male without her veil.

"We have a reservation at the Bel Air, and I have called a taxi," she said upon returning.

We met the cab in the courtyard. There was no indecision about seating. She encouraged the Prince to sit in front with the driver, and I sat with her on the back seat. How different from those days of the *hareem's* selective comings and goings, of black veils on car windows, of women without faces, of red velvet seats in a pale blue Mercedes—the color of preference for royal family cars.

The gateway to the Bel Air Hotel soon came in sight, and at Latifa's insistence the maitre dé seated us at a table in the garden near the edge of a running stream. Blossoming trees and flowerbeds circled our privacy, and Latifa's selection of luncheon was as delicious as these moments shared with them. She leaned to explain her choices to the Prince, and a streak of sunlight touched her hair, setting up a crown of gold. The henna was still there.

After lunch we walked around the garden, then rested on a

wrought iron bench near a low waterfall—the sound of water spilling over rocks a fascination for those who spend their lives on the desert.

"Will you come back to Arabia?" the Princess asked.

" . . . one day. I'd like to," I told her.

"You can't imagine how everything is so different since you left. Dammam and Al Khobar have grown into large cities, everybody picnics along the Corniche, and you can find anything you want to buy in the shops—even Italian shoes!"

Her eyes flashed amusement for a secret we shared, and yesterday intruded: dried brine on a tar encrusted beach, musty rolled up woolen carpets sharing a littered *suq* with bolts of Indian silks and blends of exotic perfumes. Here I had poked through cluttered shelves and crates for some little thing she wanted: a jar of *kohl*, some ribbons, and that special pair of Italian shoes I could never find.

Did I really want to see Al Khobar's physical changes from days well remembered? I would like to visit my friends and see for myself the opportunities offered to women. A promise of that had been evident at Princess Fahada's wedding.

"I would love to spend the afternoon with you in your Dollhouse . . ." I said. That is what her home was to me—a priceless jewel behind high walls and tucked away in the gardens of the old Amirate Palace, seat of government for the Eastern Province. It seemed important to linger longer with those days.

"I'd like that, too . . ." she said.

I hesitated. "The guards would never let me pass. I'm sure they thought I was unsuitable as a visitor to the royal family—arriving in a taxi—unveiled and no male escort."

"Was it really that bad—getting past the gate? Yes, I know it was." She sounded almost apologetic. "It's worse now. People try to reach the Governor through me. Really, no one is allowed in . . ."

Listening, understanding, the Prince engaged her in conversation. She turned to me. "My husband wants you to know there will be no problem—that he was always pleased when you came to see me."

"When Haifa chooses a husband, I will come," I said. "I must be there for her wedding."

Latifa eagerly picked up the thread: "When Haifa gets married, you'll come?"

"It's a promise!" And I knew it was one I would keep.

Back at the L'Age d'Or we said our goodbyes. It was prayer time for them, and I needed to get home to Russ. His Highness leaned toward me and with a broad smile extended his hand. Past favors were not lost. He stepped back, and the gesture offered a moment of privacy. I took advantage of it.

"Latifa, do you remember when you asked me to tell my friends in the States about Saudi families, because newspaper stories made you sad?"

"Yes." Her eyes flashed a moment of concern. "No one understood—nor seemed to care. You did."

"I've started writing about it. Would you object? It's about you, and I would never betray your privacy."

She laughed. "Well—I'd want to read what you have written. Will you send it to me?"

"Of course. It may take me some time to finish. I just wanted to let you know."

"I would like that. I'll phone you from Dammam."

I thought about her reaction all the way home on the 405. It sounded like a go ahead. The thirty years I had waited to tell this story were coming to an end. The Princess Latifa had made her choice and invited the world through the Lion Gate.

A WOMAN OF HUFUF OUT SHOPPING ON THURS-
DAY MARKET DAY—1960

Chapter One
THE WALLS OF HUFUF

It was hot. Too hot for early April. The broad strap of the Hasselblad stuck to my skin where it hung around my neck. I took a chance bringing a camera to this centuries old trading center of Hufuf, Saudi Arabia, heart of Islam. Photography was forbidden, and the *mutaaw'ah*s were on the alert to enforce public morals.

It was difficult to recognize these religious zealots, for their appearance was little different from any other pedestrian on the street. I would have to risk the consequences of getting caught, for the slender white camel and rider emerging from the passageway through the thirty foot thick wall of the Al Kut fortress challenged me to use the camera. A tribal chieftain riding his handsome *dhulul* was something you didn't see every day, even when you lived in the Kingdom of Saudi Arabia.

I dodged the flowing robes of pedestrians and scanned the market area for my two young daughters. The massive Al Kut fortress stood guard along the Suq Al Khamis, main street of Hufuf and center of the Thursday Market area. Two storied mud and limestone buildings paralleled the Fort on the opposite side. Here the girls had lagged behind in the colonnade of the

Qaisariyyah shops cornered by a group of Bedu women hawking heavy silver bracelets.

The dim interior of the Qaisariyyah housed permanent shops. Treasures could be found within the nooks and crannies of the old buildings: brass studded wooden milk bowls and long barrelled rifles, remnants of former desert battles. Today I was concerned with the slow pacing camel swinging through the jumble of shoppers, as the rider came closer into view.

The chieftain's appearance was not unusual. Enclosed within the area of the Al Kut stood the white limestone palace of the Al Abdullah family. His Highness, Amir Mishari Al Abdullah Al Saud, mayor of Hufuf and ruler of the District of Al Hasa, held a weekly *mejlis* and open house for tribal *sheikhs* and petitioners, affording his subjects the opportunity to state grievances to him personally and to benefit from his generosity and justice.

Camels were not a rarity in this desert kingdom. Vast herds sustained life for wandering Bedu. Their ragged coats and weaning belts had no relationship to the richly caparisoned *dhulul*, the purebred white female and pride of a tribal leader. With regal splendor the *sheikh* sat above the crowd. A curly black sheepskin cushioned the high pommeled saddle. Large woolen bags, woven in stripes of black, red and orange, hung from either side, and long red tassels swung in rhythm with the camel's rocking gait.

The *sheikh* appeared to have been well received, for his eyes twinkled above the draped red and white *quttra* that covered his head and lower face. He paid little heed to vendors and donkey carts vying for space along the Suq Al Khamis. Though, from time to time, he reached out with his long bamboo cane, urging pedestrians to allow him passage to the tall outer gates of Hufuf and to the desert beyond.

Most Arab men posed willingly for my camera. They seemed to enjoy the attention. Not so the black robed Muslim women. They shunned twentieth century western women on village streets. This open rebuff made you feel unworthy rather than different, an attitude that voided attempts at friendship and accentuated the difficulties of dealing with a closed society. Even now, veiled figures hurried in and out of shops and down alleyways: women like threatening clouds on a summer's day.

I dismissed further thought of these counterparts and shouted at the girls, now sauntering near the rug merchants. It was a useless gesture, consumed by the screech of wooden wheeled carts and the haggling of bystanders over a flock of sheep looped together in the middle of the market place.

Cynthia, our ten-year-old and younger of our two daughters, caught my frantic wave and hurried toward me. Her blue Italian sandals side-stepped flat baskets of rock salt and cardamom pods a vendor had laid out on the street. I couldn't see my husband, Russ. His six foot two inch height usually towered above the crowd. But, it didn't matter. He enjoyed amazing shopkeepers with his ability to bargain in Arabic. He would find us before long.

We waited for Linda to catch up, then pushed our way closer into the path of the on coming camel. Poised against the hump of his tall mount, the rider peered down at us: an unveiled woman and two bare headed, short skirted girls, shamelessly and brazenly exposed in the conservative Eastern Province, unacceptable by Muslim standards for women in this year of 1962.

The *sheikh* released his *quttra* from across his face. With a wide grin and a flick of his long cane, he brought the camel folding to its knees. Small boys with cries of, "*Baksheesh*!" scattered to get out of the way.

"*As Salaam Alaikum*," I called. The traditional welcome tested his friendliness.

He nodded. I raised the Hasselblad and signaled the girls to move in closer. Cyndy stared at the colorful woolen tassels bobbing above the camel's haughty face. The man laughed and adjusted his cloak. I stepped back for a wider view through the reflex camera. The scene passed all expectations. My finger rested on the shutter release.

"Hold it!" Linda cried. Too late. The mirror clunked, exposing the film at the instant the lens went black.

Scream after scream rang through the market place. I looked up with alarm. Terrified eyes glared at me through slits in a leather mask. With horror, I realized a woman had stepped in front of my camera at the critical moment of releasing the shutter.

The instant of recognition vanished as quickly as it had occurred. Before I could appreciate the enormity of the act, the woman hurried away. One hand pressed the mask against her face. The other clutched her *abbaya,* the black cloak that covered her from head to toe, tight against her throat. Screaming, she ran toward the Al Kut and disappeared into the passageway where the camel had emerged.

Western technology had brought the centuries into my life, and I felt the pressure of the Al Kut settling on my shoulders. This walled area within the walls of Hufuf had been built in the eighteen hundreds by Ali Pasha and his Turkish invaders to protect government and military properties. The massive fortress, with its protruding thirty bastions, now encompassed the rights of the escaping woman, leaving me to shudder at the consequences.

Those screams translated into trouble. More trouble than the picture was worth. Was she a servant of the Amir's *hareem* on a shopping expedition for her mistress? It was enough to have photographed any woman. I needed to put distance between the market place and myself.

At times like this, it was difficult to explain what had brought me to this Kingdom, millions of miles away in time and distance from my origins.

A BASTION OF THE AL KUT FORTRESS ON
MARKET DAY—HUFUF, 1960

The Arabian American Oil Company had hired Russ during a period of expansion. I had joined him a year later, when family housing became available. There was so much to learn about this Kingdom, especially directives that were very clear: do not photograph a mosque, nor a Muslim woman, and leave your camera at home when you go to Hufuf, the heart of Islamic reform.

The Hasselblad had been a gift from Russ. He knew about my love affair with the camera, ever since I had worked in production at Paramount Pictures, Inc., Hollywood, California. It captured meaningful moments time might otherwise steal away. The images on a piece of paper were mine: memories come to life in treasured albums, personal, emotional, like a heartbeat that repeats itself again and again.

Cameras were frowned upon in the early 1950s. You took a chance bringing one into the Kingdom. If the Customs Agent was in a good humor, and you declared you had a camera, it would be logged in a book and a stamp placed on the flip side of the viewer cover to declare its legal entry. The stamp became a treasured possession. The crossed swords and palm tree, insignia of the Al Saud Royal family, entered our lives even to the stamp on a camera. The Kingdom needed foreign expertise to build an empire of oil sealed by a handshake and mutual trust.

Had I broken that trust by wanting to photograph a camel? The thought made me aware that the subject of my transgression had slipped way as uncannily as it had appeared. Self-preservation urged me to leave the area before the certain arrival of the *mutaaw'ahs* eager to enforce public morals. I was a prime target for that. With a daughter's hand clutched in each of mine, the evidence of my guilt hanging on its neck strap, I headed for the alley of the mattress beaters, the nearest path away from the Suq Al Khamis.

I didn't consider the tone of the crowd's reaction, as I made our way through a wall of robes that seemed to encircle us. A sense of guilt could not distinguish whether we were being protected or held for the authorities. I needed to get away. But that was not to be.

The wall parted, and a man pushed through. He appeared to be the least of the citizens of Hufuf. A soiled gown wrapped his thin body, weighted by a heavy leather gun belt. A piled up orange scarf covered the top of his head. Yet, this man brought more concern than the numbers of pedestrians crowded around. A remnant of the Ikhwan, I thought, bent on controlling the streets. His unrelenting stare confirmed I had committed an offense against the Wahhabi tradition forbidding the photographing of Muslim women. I prided my ability to handle situations that arose from living in a foreign country. This instance required a man: a man to deal with men in a male dominated society.

Where was Russ? He could not have missed hearing those screams. Neither his appearance moments later, nor his apology in the classical form of the desert Arab, persuaded the *mutaaw'ah* to overlook the incident. He demanded the camera. I refused to give it up. That meant facing the *qadhi* (judge) at the Police Station.

"Can't we go back to the car?" Linda pleaded. Cynthia agreed, not looking forward to the long walk to the Station.

The unusual never fazed our daughters. The Kingdom of Saudi Arabia was "home", where they were born and went to school. They must be hot and tired after the three hour drive from our home in Ras Tanura on the Persian Gulf. And the Police Station was no place for young girls. Russ had parked the Land Rover near the Palace and the historic Mosque of Ibrahim within the area of the Al Kut. They would not be annoyed by passersby.

Russ agreed. "I'll take them to the car, then join you," he said.

I watched them leave before considering my own situation. Western women were not accountable to these zealots, who often overstepped their self-appointed responsibilities. They might rap our legs with a cane while shopping in local villages, if the *mutaaw'ah* considered our skirts too short. Saudi Government officials somehow transferred safeguards for their own women to cover expatriates who were "Guests of the King".

However, my refusal to relinquish the camera required a visit to the *qadhi*.

The heat seemed to increase, as I walked from the Qaisariyyah to Police Headquarters near the Al Khamis Gate. I didn't feel upset with the *mutaaw'ah*. He was exercising his right as he saw it. No village escaped these men who performed a duty based on the ideology of returning Islam to its purest form. Hufuf was the holdout for remnants of the Ikhwan, the Brotherhood. Ibn Saud had organized the movement to control rebellious Bedu, during the days of uniting the tribes. He gave them a religious purpose, settled them in agricultural communities, and then used them to fight his battles. The Brotherhood took control and overran the local citizenry with demands for purification. They wrought such havoc among the people, that Ibn Saud turned against the Ikhwan to restore moderation and peace. The few who remained still waged a personal crusade.

This I knew of the man who paced some distance behind. My concerns did not include him. The event evolved around a Muslim woman and an American wife. One hapless instant accentuated how differences in religion work against human nature.

I might have said, "I'm sorry. It was an accident." To which she could have replied, "*Ma'laish,—*it doesn't matter". And we would have parted none the worse for the encounter. Nobody asked us what we felt. We were caught in a trap already set. One I wanted to release. At least, I could keep on trying. We didn't have to agree on everything, just answer the need of humans for affinity with each other.

Somehow my spirits lifted, and I shifted the Hasselblad to my shoulder before entering the Police Station. I had no fear of being left to languish in a Saudi jail. The worst that could happen would be losing the camera. I also realized my situation would be resolved on a man-to-man basis. So, I waited on a rickety bench in a windowless room for Russ to appear. The amused stares of the guards reminded me of the risks I took.

But, sometimes defiant irritation prodded me to let my world come through.

The laws of Islam became real to me one day when I went shopping in the Dammam *suq*. A young girl waited outside a shop. We stared at each other, her mother standing by. I tried to make contact, asked where I could purchase an *abbaya*. Her eyes lit up through her mask. The mother signaled me to follow them. There was eagerness in the meeting. I wanted to ask them to visit me and sensed they had similar longings. But there was a distance between us, even as the walls that enclosed their home and the barriers men had built around us. The girl and her mother walked away, foregoing the moment that had brought freedom of choice into their lives.

When Russ appeared, he took the Hasselblad from me and set its case, which he had been carrying, on the bench. The police captain greeted him with enthusiasm, and a voluble conversation in Arabic ensued. I caught snatches of the niceties one expresses in greeting a friend, for Russ could expound them all with grace and sincerity.

He offered the camera to the *qadhi*. The man examined it with interest, for the Hasselblad had a unique mechanism and was regarded as the finest instrument of its kind. I noticed the *qadhi's* pleasure in Russ's knowledge of Arabic, including flowery nuances typical of the language. He returned the camera to Russ, but demanded the roll of film: a fair bargain between men.

I put it back in its case. The situation could have been worse; yet, the heat of my own resentment produced greater discomfort than the closeness of the room. I longed to escape into the bustling Suq Al Khamis, but my hopes faded, when a guard carried in a large tray with brass coffeepot and tiny porcelain cups.

"No!" I thought. "Do we have to wait for coffee.. . . !"— the ritual of Middle Eastern hospitality that preceded any conference and concluded every agreement. I stood up and stared into the glare of the dusty street. How long was this going to take. Unexpectedly, I heard words of departure. Russ was not staying for coffee. How could he offend the *qadhi* with this breach of etiquette, a personal affront to the host?

"*Fiamanillah* . . . goodbye, my friend," Russ said. "May the goodness of Allah be upon you . . ."

"*Fiamanilkarim,*" the man replied. "Go in the name of Allah—the Great—the Just . . ."

I didn't have to witness the final handshake to know that all was well between men. I swallowed hard and clenched my fingers about the broad strap of the camera case. The leather molded to the contour of my damp hand. Frustrations of days past throbbed in my head. It was not easy for a twentieth century American woman to live with traditions of purdah. You could isolate yourself within fenced compounds the Arabian American Oil Company constructed for its employees, saying you didn't care, or look out to the Arab world and live with the difficulties you could do nothing about.

"It's your choice," Russ always said. "We'll stay and enjoy Arabia, or return to the States . . ."

The fact is, I loved Arabia and was proud to be one of the diverse elements in a test tube, which someday might fuse and create a miracle of emergence for an ancient culture. In the process, there had to be times of collision, when the whole experiment seemed to explode.

So far, the reactions in the test tube remained neatly in balance. ARAMCO kept check on western technology suddenly implanted on a culture unchanged for thousands of years. When Prince Abdul Azziz had granted a concession to American businessmen to explore for oil, he imposed restrictions to safeguard his own people. Somehow, in the implementation, American women who followed their husbands to the oil fields became locked in a vacuum without escape, as long as there existed the black masks of Islam.

The gutturals of the *qadhi* interrupted my thoughts, with

final words of parting: "May Allah guide your steps."

I couldn't bear to hear them, to be wrapped in the generosity of Allah, a formal politeness that did not include me. Refuge lay in the Suq Al Khamis. To reach it, I would have to bore a path through a group of men squatting in the only shade the eye could see. Their jeering faces stared at me above homespun robes.

Directly in front of the Station, two posts supported several sagging cross wires from the roof. Strips of tattered matting tied to the wires provided a six-foot square of shade for the duty guard outside. Into this sanctuary crowded the faces: Bedouins mostly, I guessed, from their weathered skin, bottomless black eyes, and gaping grins. Men resting from the heat, while outside the town walls their shrouded women unloaded bundles of desert firewood from complaining camels resisting efforts to be couched.

I dreaded pushing past them. Not for the stale odor of dung smoke and animal sweat that stiffened their wind beaten garments, but for the disapproval in their searching eyes.

I clutched the camera tighter, and behind the security of my dark glasses, pushed through the men and into the dust layer of the street. The word, "*Amrikaniya . . .*" followed me from the faces, along with overtones of "shameful". An angry flush added to the heat hanging low over the *suq*. Twelve years of living in Saudi Arabia could still make me feel like a stranger.

I thought I knew this land, its barren topography and neighboring villages tucked in small oases. We often came to Hufuf. Thursday Market day promised fun and excitement in the historical capitol of Al Hasa, known for its handmade brassware and fine woolen fabrics. Massive mud walls protected this trade center and focal point for caravans heading toward the government capitol of Riyadh, some three hundred kilometers west. Treacherous salt flats reached for it from the sea, and shifting coastal dunes moved in with the winds to reclaim the fortress for the desert. A short distance from Hufuf's barren setting stretched the vast palm gardens of Al Hasa, rich with flourishing crops of dates and gushing springs of sweet water.

Market day brought sea captains from the Persian Gulf to barter their cargoes, villagers with produce from the oases, and tribesmen from the desert to sell firewood, sheep butter and homespun cloth. It also brought hordes of small boys.

"*Baksheesh! Baksheesh!*" A filthy palm lunged at me from the ragged sleeve of a blue striped gown. Insistent tones and darting bodies accompanied this insatiable plea of the Middle East.

"*Imsh!* Go away," I shouted, exercising my right to ignore the third tenet of the Prophet.

I dodged my way to the towering wall of the Al Kut to wait for Russ. The lone figure of a woman blended into the shadow of the rough stones. I stared at her as one awed by the unfamiliar. She squatted and pulled the *abbaya* over her head. I wanted to say something, to escape the vacuum, to be a woman with her. But, what words could reach an anonymous mound dumped amid piles of litter and broken brick.

The brilliant pink of a satin dress rushed to the black mound, as a small girl ran up, a basket of fresh fish swinging from her fingertips. Even as I watched, the child vanished, swallowed up by the woman's voluminous robe now billowing in flight. Sour gall rose in my throat for customs compelling such flight, and for the fragile spark of femininity soon to lose its glow in the dimness of its prescribed future.

How could you outweigh a balance already set, a scale that would not tip ever so slightly to allow a small measure of understanding? My girls would never be brought up like that.

Thinking of my daughters produced an urgency to go to them. I knew they were safe in the car. Yet—I had seen customs of Arabia much different from our own. The more I thought about it, the more anxious I became.

I dodged my way through pedestrians, the camera case slapping at my legs, and looked eagerly for the passageway through the wall, the only access from the Suq Al Khamis to the inner area of the Al Kut—and the Land Rover. I had never been concerned about our personal safety. But, at this moment I needed to feel the girls' arms about me, to know they were all right, and to be reassured our twentieth century had not been consumed by a black cloak.

Chapter Two
THE BAIT AMIR

Several temporary stalls set against the wall compelled me to turn toward the street. Rollicking donkey carts with animated drivers raced over the ruts. I scurried to get out of their way and to keep clear of the men in flying robes who seemed to be everywhere. Their brisk strides accentuated the graceful movement of the cloth, so that the street rippled along like blowing sand. I hadn't gone far, when a hand touched my shoulder.

"Here—I'll take that," Russ said.

He reached down and transferred the weight of the Hasselblad. My taut muscles eased. The blood tingled in my arm and hand. I caught his half smile.

"What's your hurry?"

"We'd better get back to the girls," I said, avoiding his direct gaze.

His silence held me, then, "Is that all you have to say?"

I didn't answer. I hated being made to face myself.

"You should have been more careful," he added without sympathy.

He was right. I must curtail my love affair with the camera. It grew out of years before Arabia, when I worked as a production assistant at Paramount Pictures in Hollywood. Sometimes the Arabian scene appeared to be just another set on the back lot. The actors were all there waiting for the director's touch.

Russ was real. He took my arm and led me away from the street. We walked together against the great height of the fortress wall. Its components of jagged rock and mud plastered rubble defied our presence with the same indifference that had challenged the onslaught of time. The thirty bastions remained invincible, more powerful than the past rulers the fortress had protected. Its immensity augmented to heights of grandeur the feat of Abdul Azziz, warrior Prince of the house of Al Saud. With a handful of tribesmen the Prince had scaled these walls with palm trunks and claimed the district of Al Hasa for his emerging Kingdom.

Only thirty years ago, I thought, as we bypassed the tinkers with their pots and pans pegged to the powdery mortar of the nearest broad based tower. Other vendors had spread straw mats on the ground and piled flat palm baskets, like huge plates, with sticks of sandalwood and fly darkened dried fish. The acrid odor of polished brass and pungency of sour leather attracted my attention. I paused for a quick look at the wide beaked coffeepots of the antique dealer. Instantly, the old vendor leaned close, the bristles of his beard rising and falling with the kneading action of his chin.

"From Makkah, *memsa'b* . . . Sixty *riyals*."

I stepped back from the strong breath. A boy with bangs fringing a brightly colored cap pushed between. The youth stopped, a glint of mischief in his eyes, and spread a fistful of squirming locusts under my nose. I cringed. A laugh gurgled in his throat, locked between teeth clamped on two crusty yellow bodies, spiky legs kicking against the boy's lips.

I ignored his humor in favor of keeping up with Russ. His six-foot-height plus ten-gallon Stetson towered above the shorter stature of the Arabs. He stood close to a small brown donkey. A dried goatskin with stiff upright legs was strapped to the donkey's back.

"Hey, El . . ." The tone was ecstatic. ". . . how about some dates?"

"Not again," I thought, remembering a similar package stuffed with spiced dates Russ had brought home from the gardens of Samha the year he had studied Arabic in Hufuf. The donkey's load recalled a vivid picture of grotesquely angled legs each time I had thrust a hand down the headless neck.

"How about it?" Russ picked black hairs off a sticky mass and popped it into his mouth. "Here—try some." He dug for another sample, as the unkempt vendor stretched the open neck with eager fingers. "Where else can you keep dates for twenty years and have them taste like this?"

My stomach churned. Maybe if I took the camera he would come. We squeezed through several onlookers, for few Arab men could resist conversation with this westerner who spoke their language so well. Nor could they look away from an American wife—not because she was American, but because she did not wear a veil.

The passageway through the Al Kut wall lay beyond the next protruding tower. It would take us to the Amirate Palace and our Land Rover. It also meant a return to the scene of the white camel. Remembrance brought bitterness. I needed to feel a partnership with my adopted country and a friendliness with the shrouded figures—women like myself who must share feelings similar to my own.

Impulsively, those feelings came alive. "I only wanted a picture of that camel."

"You're just being emotional." Russ's tone was flat.

"But you did tell the police it was unintentional?"

"That doesn't make any difference. You know the law."

Suddenly, I was curious. "What did you say?"

"When?"

"Well—when he gave the camera back."

A slight smile curled his lip. "I promised you would never bring it to Hufuf again . . ."

"You didn't!"

" . . . and praised Allah for his protection of women."

I suspected this last remark to be an additive for my benefit. Arab men never mentioned women in the presence of strangers, and Russ would honor that code.

I chose to ignore it. "How come you didn't stay for coffee?"

" . . . reminded him that the girls were alone and a man's duty is to protect the sanctity of his unmarried daughters."

This time he really smiled. I didn't have to be reminded how well any Arab would understand that.

We moved on. The colonnaded Qaisariyyah appeared on our left. The passageway yawned a few steps ahead. I pretended not to see the *mutaaw'ah* strolling by the shops, warning shopkeepers to shut down for prayers and rapping small boys with his stick to clear them off the street. Men saw him coming and took a last puff on a waterpipe, or set coffee cups on rickety tables before hurrying off to the mosque. Vendors stacked dry goods in neat piles and tied them in bundles with blue plastic cloth. Donkeys brayed in hiccoughs, as loaded carts vied for access to narrow alleys, their sharp corners scraping deeper into well worn grooves eating into the mud buildings.

The area in front of the Qaisariyyah cleared. Several Bedu women squatting near a column made no move to pick up their baskets. I paused, impelled toward them.

"This way," Russ urged. He headed toward the opening in the wall.

I made no move to follow. "You go on," I said.

"Hurry," he urged. "We've got to get to the girls."

I pushed the camera on him. "I'll only be a minute."

He took it, his expression one of disbelief. What did I want now? A Pakistani in a purple checked *izzar* (cotton skirt) pushed between us shouting his wares. "*Khubbuz! Khubbuz!*" He hurried away, a trail of flies settling on loaves of flat bread impaled on a stick.

Russ had moved on. I caught sight of his tall frame disappearing into the passageway of the Kut. Most of the vendors had closed shop and gone. Still, the Bedu women made no move to pick up their baskets. I stood in front of them, not knowing why, except to wonder whether the freedom of the desert allowed a feminine response.

A girl joined the women from behind the colonnade. Her hands whirled a slender shaft with a square knob, deftly winding a thread of rough goat hair from a matted mass tucked under her arm. She spoke to the women, and two of them leaned over to collect their wares.

"*La!* No," an authoritative voice commanded. It belonged to the oldest of the group—if one could judge by hands, voice and attitude, for a stocking hood covered her face. She reached into the basket and held aloft a purple and orange cap top stitched with gold thread. "*Khumsa riyals . . .*" The voice addressed itself to me.

I took the *qaffiyah* from her hennaed hand. It rounded my palm with a touch of brightness.

"*Zain.* Very good," the woman encouraged. She dug out more caps in various combinations of colors: blue and yellow, red with orange, dark green and white, all glittering with gold thread. "*Laaszim, khumsa riyals.*" You must pay five *riyals*.

I didn't want them, but I held the caps in my hand. Every boy wore one, and the men, underneath their *quttras*. The colors vibrated, reminding me of the desert after a rain, oleanders in a garden, or a child's pink satin dress. Would she understand that? Could I get through to her—as a woman?

"*Jamila*—beautiful . . ." I began.

Her hands flew to her face. They pressed against the coarse cloth. The contour of the nose dominated.

" . . . orange . . . yellow, like the dunes . . ."

"*Khumsa riyals . . .*" she droned.

A voice—nothing more.

"Do you have children? I have two daughters."

A man's voice breathed in my ear. "Do not bother with them. They are Bedu. They will rob you." He laughed, then went on his way.

I dropped the *qaffiyahs* into the basket, all but two. "I'll take these," I said. "My daughters will like them."

The woman clawed at me. "No!" The voice screeched. "Take all."

I tried again. "I live in Ras Tanura. Where are you from?"

No answer. She deposited my heavy coins into the deep recesses of her robe. What could I know of her? Nothing. Except that she existed on this street, as her sisters had lived among the tents of Abraham centuries ago. Perhaps Hagar had cut her fingers on rough goat hair spinning thread, even as the girl twisted it now.

I made a decision. "I want that," I said, indicating the spindle. "I'll give you ten *riyals*."

They did not respond.

"This . . ." I touched the stick, polished from much usage.

A moment of puzzled silence. Then, they laughed, a blank, empty laugh that carried no recognition of similarity between us. My skin chilled in the heat. Why had I not gone with Russ? I turned to leave. The girl stepped forward. She broke the thread in her hand, then extended the spindle toward me. The length of loose thread dangled from the stick like a severed lifeline. Her eyes, dark rimmed with *kohl*, held no fear. They glistened clean as the sunlight slanting off her calico mask.

"Thank you." I offered her the coins. She shook her head.

"*Ahlan wa sahlan,*" she whispered. What I have is yours: a note of tenderness, a kindness, even a touch of understanding.

I left them and hastened away with my treasure: a tenuous link with their lives and with the tents of Abraham.

A man balancing a floppy mattress on his head nearly knocked me off my feet. I ducked, then headed for the passageway. The clang of iron shutters over rusty rollers incited me to move faster, as permanent shops shut down for prayer.

The muezzin's chant rose from a minaret. The streets cleared, save for the belly groan of a camel and the jangle of donkey bells.

I emerged onto a small square. A wing of the Palace appeared above an inner wall on the north side. At any moment I should see the car. The caps would please the girls. I was glad I bought them.

I walked past the tall palms in the square. Their dull fronds drooped dusty and limp. Stalky oleanders, witnesses to some long forgotten attempt at a central garden, stood thick and brittle baked to a distortion of their original shapes. You could not guess how long they had been planted there, for life withers quickly in a harsh environment. They could not be as old nor as steadfast as the tamarisk trees, whose sparse, grey-green tops stared above the Amirate wall. Several tall bay windows showed along the third floor of the Palace. Their carved wooden shutters of interlocking scrolls allowed a minimal view of the street. The *mushrabiyyah*, *hareem* shutters, afforded the Muslim woman her only glimpse of the world outside her comfortable apartments.

The final notes of the call to prayer wafted over the square. Like a thing alive, the sound took shape. It hung above the villages and over oases gardens. It called to the sands and rocky plains, to the high escarpments and lava plateaus. It swelled above the seas and moving dunes, until over Makkah it converged with the call to prayer to all the faithful from every part of the Muslim Empire.

"There is no God but God, and Mohammed is the Messenger of God."

No one lingered near to see me. I wanted to get off the square. The silence following the benediction denounced me for what I was: an unbeliever. My own world held fast on this street, too: the Land Rover. I hurried ahead toward the Mosque.

The Land Rover. Where was it? I scanned the street. No sign of the car.

BEDU WOMEN SELLING CAPS, SUQ AL KHAMIS,
HUFUF-1960

This was the correct place. I recalled my concern for parking
too close to the historic Mosque of Ibrahim and to the Palace.
A rush of guilt engulfed me. I should have come right back.
Where would I begin to look?

Almost immediately, Russ appeared from a side street, his
long strides indicative of uneasiness. His words trumpeted
through the emptiness.

"The girls aren't with you?"

The idea was incredible!

"No. Of course not. They're in the car." Then, "Where is
the car?"

"Had to move it from the Mosque."

" . . . and the girls?"

" . . . not in it."

The silence was an awful void through which my heart pounded. It couldn't be. It just couldn't be. I glanced around, expecting their laughter to ring out at any moment. But the square held only the flapping of palm fronds from the dying garden. I struck out at the most illogical. How well did I know the Arabs? Not at all, really. And their cloaks . . . How easily they swallowed up a child.

"Russ—you don't think. . . ?"

"No, I don't." How quickly he read my mind. "You're just being emotional." He raised the broad Stetson and wiped the sweat from his brow. "They're not babies—probably got tired of waiting and wandered off."

" . . . maybe shut up in a shop during prayer call." That sounded reasonable. My panic abated. "Of course. There's a bookstore over there." I started to take off.

"Don't waste your time," Russ said. "I've already looked. They're not anywhere on this square."

The finality of his words descended like a dreaded truth. Our daughters were gone. Everything would be closed now: the police station, the *baladiyyah* (city hall). We couldn't just stand there. I looked toward the main gateway of the Palace. A pair of curly headed plaster lions gazed at each other from each side of the iron gate. Did they know? Would they tell?

As if in answer, the laboring grind of revolving rusty hinges scraped through the stillness. I followed the sound to observe a second smaller gate higher up on the square. An old man, bent over from the weight of his robes, strained against the grillwork of a small door set in the solid planks of the gate. He stepped through to hold it open, eyes directed toward the ground.

A girl wearing a short print skirt, one blue Italian sandal clutched in her hand, walked into the street. A second figure followed dressed in denim skirt and red cowboy boots. Black

45

silk veils enveloped their heads and shoulders. They backed a few steps, and the old man pulled the gate shut. A flash of shimmering blue fluttered behind the grillwork. The girls waved. They looked up to the carved shutters and waved again. Turning, they ran toward us across the square.

Russ reacted first. "Hurry . . ." he ordered. His long legs in motion, he met the girls half way and herded them down a side street. By the time I caught up with them the engine was running and my door open.

"Get in!" he shouted.

I did. He reached over and slammed my door shut. The car shot out, then swung sharply into the first opening between buildings, away from the Al Khamis Suq and the road out of Hufuf. I knew better than to ask why. He had had enough of feminine wiles for one day. The girls, too, sensed their father's displeasure, as he raced to put distance between the square and us. They sat quietly, now and again glancing at each other with suppressed giggles. I reached back and snatched off the veils.

"Oh, Mom."

Their cheeks were damp and flushed. Strands of hair stuck to their foreheads. The eyes were alive with the excitement of a shared secret. But they said nothing. And I didn't ask, not while we all hung on for dear life, as the car wound in and out of narrow alleyways.

Russ slowed the car. "This ought to be the place . . ."

"What are you looking for?" I asked. "And why are you driving like a madman?"

"To find the rear entrance to the palm gardens and escape the police. I used to live here, remember? "

"The police? What for? Why don't we go back to the Al Khamis Gate?".

Intent on his landmarks, he didn't answer.

"How come you're so angry, Dad?" Linda ventured to speak.

"I told you to stay in the car."

Now I plunged in. "What were you doing inside the Palace gate?"

"Listening to Elvis Presley records," casually from Cynthia. "You what. . . ?"

"It's true, Mom. What do you think we were doing?"

I grabbed the handrail, as the car swung into a sharp left turn and righted with a jerk. We followed a rutted trail that led to a palm garden and the blessed comfort of deep shade. Irrigation ditches wound through the palm trees, bypassing plots of alfalfa and vegetable gardens. A roof of palm fronds showed above a crumbling wall, the tumbled bricks patched with beaten out rusty oil drums. I could sense Russ relax, for his grip on the steering wheel loosened, and our speed slowed. He pulled the car off the trail and came to a stop. An opening through the palms allowed a view of the Al Khamis Gate and the main road to the oil towns of Abqaiq and Ras Tanura.

"I'm sorry, Dad," Linda said. "We didn't mean to do anything wrong. It—just happened."

Her tone of voice accepted her father's concerns. To her life was a storehouse of discovery and learning. She enriched it with insight and compassion to be shared with those less fortunate than herself.

"What did you expect us to do?" piped up Cynthia. "Golly, you were gone such a long time." She toyed with the veil on her lap.

"Consider yourselves lucky," replied their father, " . . . with no guard at the gate and the religious committee in the Mosque."

"But, there was a guard." Cynthia insisted. "Amsha made him come inside."

"Amsha . . ." I hesitated before repeating the name.

"Sure. The girl who let us in." Cynthia's tone was a bit flip.

"Because you were banging on the gate, I suppose."

I couldn't blame Russ for being irritable.

"No. It wasn't like that at all." Linda's quiet approach grew out of her ability to analyze a situation. "You usually give us credit for using our heads, Dad."

"Linda, you've lived in this country long enough to know the consequences."

"I know."

A PAKESTANI SELLS LOAVES OF BREAD ALONG
THE SUQ AL KHAMIS

"Didn't I just bail your mother out?"

"I suppose so."

"I'll be lucky not to lose my job over this. We could all get returned to the States—that is, if the Company can get us out before the police become involved."

"But, Dad." Linda didn't get a chance to finish.

"The guards will have made a report. Look . . ."

We followed his gaze toward the walls of Hufuf. Three cars were just pulling out: two long black limousines and a jeep with soldiers. They raced down the narrow road horns blaring. Now, I understood why Russ had brought us to the gardens. He knew there would be a search party.

"They'll probably go as far as the Coast Guard Station. We'll wait until they return." Russ reached for his cigarettes on the dashboard.

"Guess we did make a mess of it," Linda said. Then she spoke up with assurance. "But, it wasn't our fault. How could we say 'no' to the Princess, when she came through the gate and asked us to follow her."

"And you know what," mused Cynthia. "She had the latest Elvis Presley record. You know, the one you wouldn't buy me in Rome."

Yes, I did recall something about a record our youngest wanted on our last long vacation. Now, it lent authenticity to a situation completely unbelievable. I needed a second to think, to absorb the reality of their words. I was dying to know the full story of what had happened. My clothes stuck to the seat, as I shifted position and loosened the collar of my shirt. It was wilted and damp. The spindle lay on the mat against my dusty boot. It must have fallen from my lap during that wild ride. I leaned down and picked it up.

"Hey, where'd you get that?" Cynthia asked.

"It's a long story." I took my time rewinding the severed thread.

"Can I see it?" She asked, extending a hand over my shoulder.

"You're not the only one to have adventures," I teased, counting on our youngest's interest in the unusual. Our travels over long vacations had created a budding anthropologist.

"Tell you what, Mom. Let's show and tell."

"As long as you don't leave anything out."

"Okay." Cynthia leaned toward the front seat. "Well—you know how long you were gone—and then there were these men—and a bunch of boys made me lose my sandal—and we had to wear a veil because of the Prince . . ."

"No." Linda interrupted, pulling her sister back by the shoulder. "You're getting it all wrong. I'll tell."

"But . . . that's not fair."

"You can tell the part about the records."

"Well . . ."

"Okay, Cyn?"

"I guess so."

There was a moment of thought, as Linda sought an opening. Then she said, "You may not believe it, but we really did go inside the Palace. We saw the Amir and his family. It was strange sitting in the *hareem* . . ." She paused. "But . . . well . . . I'd better start at the beginning . . ."

Chapter Three

ABDUCTED (Linda relates being abducted by a Princess)

Linda and Cynthia sat alone in the parked Land Rover. It seemed hours since their father's back had disappeared behind the garden in the square that separated the Mosque of Ibrahim from the old Palace.

Resigned to heat and boredom, Cynthia rested her head against the seat. From time to time she rubbed the back of her neck and screwed up her shoulders to relieve the pull of two tight pony braids against her head. Always a good citizen, she acceded to family rules and was prepared to wait, however long, for the return of her parents. Her liquid eyes, soft as chocolate, pleaded with her sister: "What do we do now?" Fidgeting did little to relieve the boredom.

Not so Linda. Realistic to the core, she evaluated her father's warning to keep the windows closed as being unreasonable. She brushed her long hair away from her face, strands curling against her damp forehead. Impatient at her inactivity, she leaned forward and pressed a finger on the window catch. The glass panel slid along its metal runner. A quick movement of air cooled her damp skin, arousing her senses to the odors of the old city locked into the battlements and to the centuries of refuse ground into the streets.

Except for a pleading beggar or jovial cart driver, the girls had not been annoyed. People who passed through the square did not linger within the shadow of the Al Abdullah Palace, wherein lived His Highness Amir Mishari Al Abdullah, Amir of Hufuf and brother of Saud Al Abdullah, tyrannical governor of the Eastern Province. The guard at the Palace gate with rifle and *kanjar* encouraged all to move on.

From time to time, long bearded elders came and went from the Mosque. They alone paid sharp attention to the occupants of the Land Rover each time they traversed the square. However, the men neither stopped nor spoke, as their fingers clicked yellow beads along circlets of worn string.

Linda nudged her sister. "The guys are back . . . ," she said, while pretending not to notice them.

Cynthia opened her half closed eyes. "Why don't they just go away."

Linda shrugged. "Guess it's their job."

"Yeah . . ." Cynthia sat upright. "Margaret told me that her brother got whacked on the legs by a *mutaaw'ah* because his pants were too tight."

" . . . or your skirts too short," Linda added. She wriggled her denim skirt free of the plastic seat and pulled the cloying cloth from her damp skin.

The men stopped to talk with the guard at the Palace Gate. On impulse, Cynthia yanked at the bright print of her dress that had crawled half way up her thighs.

"Don't worry," Linda said. "It doesn't apply to kids. Besides, we're in the car—not on the street."

Her assurance offered little comfort to Cynthia's frayed patience. "Wish Mom and Dad would hurry. I want to get out of here." She paused to watch, as the patriarchs gathered their cloaks about them and returned to the Mosque.

Linda sighed. "Maybe they'll stay there."

She hated to be stared at, even if it did break the boredom of their confinement. Then, a bright idea. "Why don't we stand outside for a minute. At least our legs won't feel so sticky."

Cynthia welcomed the suggestion for a change of any kind. She dismissed her father's warning for the prospect of relief and wriggled her flowered skirt free of the seat to move closer to her sister. Linda's hand held the door handle, as she cautiously scanned the square. A man walking the Governor's horses in front of the distant stables seemed to be the only sign of activity. She stepped out of the car.

"We should have done this a long time ago," she thought. It felt better than sitting inside.

Cynthia swung her feet out, but before they were firmly on the ground, Linda pushed her back. Cyndy's foot struck the doorframe, knocking one of her sandals into the street. It turned over in the dust and lodged against a front wheel. There was no time to retrieve it before Linda jumped inside and reached for the open door. A group of boys, chasing after a couple of goats, spotted new quarry and raced toward the car. They lunged at the partly open door. Linda kicked out hard with her boot. The pause in the on rush allowed time to slam it shut.

"My shoe," Cynthia wailed, as one of the boys picked it up and swung it around by its delicate strap.

The tormentors climbed on the hood and rapped knuckles against the windshield. They kicked at the tires and made drums of the spare gas cans attached to the front fenders. They pressed noses against the glass with loud shouts and jeers. Such heckling further aggravated the waiting, but Linda knew that to respond in kind would only incite the abusers to more mischief. Unexpectedly, the boys took off.

The patriarchs were back. They didn't stare this time but walked off with long strides. They banged on the doors of shops built against the inner wall of the Al Kut. Shopkeepers dispersed, and dark figures hurried to their homes. Prayer time could not be far off.

"That's just great," moaned Cynthia. "Now I've lost my best sandal."

"I'm sorry, Cyn. Maybe we'll find it on the street."

"Yeah—if ever Dad gets back. What time is it?"

Engrossed in their own miseries, the girls missed the significance of a little drama being enacted at a second entrance to the Palace. A young man appeared behind the grilled door set in the solid planks of the gate. He spoke to the guard, then they both retreated behind the wall. Shortly after, a black robed figure sped swiftly out the gate and across the square. It ran directly to the car, darkening the window like a sudden sandstorm. Shapeless, faceless, the figure spoke, fingers pressed against the glass.

"*Ta'aliy! Ta'aliy.*" Then, in painful English, " . . . please come."

Linda tried to penetrate the face behind the veil, but the newcomer turned her head and gestured toward the Palace.

"What does she want?" Cynthia asked.

Linda hesitated. "I'm not sure."

Her father had warned of disastrous consequences if anyone approached a local woman. But, this one ran to her. What did it mean? What if it was the woman Mom had caught in her camera? What then?

The fingers tapped on the window again. Linda saw a pair of dark eyes through the veil before the head turned to search the square. No one was in sight. Linda slid the window open a few inches. A hand reached through and touched her lightly on the arm. The palm was smooth and golden with henna. A frill of blue satin hugged the wrist.

"Please, come . . ." the voice repeated. Then, the figure hurried away and slipped into the Palace grounds.

"Well. . . ?" Cynthia's eyes opened wide. She looked to her sister for a decision.

"Wonder what she wants . . ." Linda's quick mind juggled the pros and cons. In some ways this new encounter posed more of a problem than the boys. She had never been approached by a Saudi woman. The dark shapes usually disappeared, whenever an American wife showed up on the streets. Now, this one spoke to her. Even pleaded for her to follow.

"What should we do?" asked Cynthia.

"I don't know. I think she's a girl . . ."

"She spoke English, too."

"But, the Palace," Linda added.

"We can't go there." Cynthia was positive.

Linda took a moment to delay the decision. "Did you notice her watch? It's a lot better than mine."

"Bet she's not just a nobody—like a slave or something," deduced Cynthia, to which her sister agreed. But—what to do?

An old man, bent over with age, pushed against the iron gate. It began to close. The Arab girl appeared behind him. She waved anxiously toward the car in a gesture of encouragement. Released from its clutch, the robe slipped from beneath her chin, and the high sheen of a blue satin dress shimmered between its folds. Linda could not refuse such an invitation. In some ways the girl was like herself. Linda loved people and never missed an opportunity to make a new friend.

"Why not," she lilted. "We'll be back before Mom gets here."

"But . . . ," from Cynthia.

"We'll just go to the gate. I promise," Linda said.

It took only a minute to traverse the square. The girls stopped dead, as the wall loomed high above them. It was one thing to place the barrier in its historical significance. Quite something else to think of stepping inside. Did Linda really want to meet this girl? She had never spoken to a Saudi woman before. She didn't count Muna, the little daughter of Khalifa who brought alfalfa to the Ranch for the horses. Muna was about six years old. She didn't wear a veil, only an embroidered hood over her dark hair. What would it be like to know a real Saudi girl?

She took a step forward. The gatekeeper didn't raise his eyes, when the Arab girl pushed past him, grasped Linda's hand, and pulled her through the opening. Not to be left alone, Cynthia followed her sister through the Gate.

The girl hurried them over a tiled walkway toward a lower more graceful wall. Arches and palm trees had been carved into the plaster, and the whole decorated with green and white tiles. Their guide stopped in front of a solid wooden door that stood ajar on its massive post. A garden lay beyond, but a young man blocked the way.

"In such a hurry, my sister?" he said.

Linda knew many Arab men. They worked in the compound where she lived. Mohammed, their gardener, and Ahmed, the houseboy, were like part of the family. Then, there was the taxi driver, Ali. He joked all the time. She liked the guys who ran the snack bar. They were friendly and fun. She helped Khalifa's six sons spread the alfalfa for the horses, when he delivered it every week. They were like school friends.

This one was different, too arrogant, wanting his own way. His tone of voice offended her. She judged him to be slightly older than herself and already exercising his place in a man's world. He made no move to get out of the way but played with the jeweled hilt of a curved *kanjar* thrust through the broad belt at his waist.

"Naiyf," the girl said. "Go. Let me pass." Her attitude suggested some involvement with him.

He refused to leave. Instead, his penetrating gaze scrutinized the Americans. Linda returned look for look. She would not be put down by any man's stare. He smiled appreciatively. Had he ordered the guard's disappearance, she wondered. Mere chance had not brought him to this doorway. In fact, his presence conveyed an act of discourtesy and a reflection on family honor. She knew women had a right to privacy with their friends without male interference.

The girl became impatient with her brother's insolence.

Again she ordered him to leave. Her tone of voice indicated a right to be obeyed. She pushed past him and through the door, urging Linda to follow. A laugh died on the other side, as the Arab girl leaned against the heavy door and forced the bolt into place.

Cynthia had limped through in some distress. She stopped to lean against the rough basin of a small fountain to brush away pebbles imbedded in her bare foot. Erratic jets of water splattered her arm, and spilled over to the jasmine hedge that bordered the walk.

"You said we'd only go to the gate . . ." she whispered to her sister.

The closer view of the shuttered windows seen from the street disturbed her, and she was in no mood to go any farther. Linda's attention, too, focused on the walls. No matter where she looked, the crenellated battlements towered above, ensnaring her own youthful freedoms.

"Let's go back . . ." Cynthia pleaded.

"We can't leave now," Linda said. "It'll be all right—maybe even fun."

The Arab girl sensed their uneasiness. She beckoned Cynthia to follow and headed for a colonnade. It was cool under the shadowed archway. They could not linger, for the girl turned a corner and stopped in front of a second brass-studded door. It was shut tight. A guard of monstrous proportions implanted himself in front of the thick wooden planks, as though the wall had taken human form to impose its will. Linda felt cowed by his fierce demeanor, accentuated by the robe of leopard skin that draped from his shoulders. She didn't understand the brief exchange of Arabic, but with a deference bordering on tenderness, the guard opened the door.

Linda accepted the stark drabness of the desert land she called home. Now she caught her breath at the unexpected glow of life and color that filled a small garden. Low oleander bushes bloomed in pink profusion. Fragrant white jasmine peeped through dark green leaves at the base of tamarisk trees. Colorful rugs and cushions covered the grass in the shade. They might have been exotic flowers themselves, the little girls in long dresses of brilliant satin, shimmering cloth of gold and sequined laces. Like guardians of the treasure, two dark skinned slaves sat on the rugs, intent on the safety of their charges.

Children of the villages sometimes wore dresses of metallic cloth to celebrate the holidays after Ramadan. The color brightened the dun of mud walls, where women and children gathered to watch the men perform the sword dance. But this was different, something she never thought existed within the formidable Al Kut. Maybe it was the open faces of the children that made it so different. Their loose hair fell free of any *bukhnug*, the hood little girls always wore that covered their heads and framed their faces.

A scent of sweetness reminded Linda that she was hungry. Perhaps the thought of food had been aroused by a little girl who ran toward them. She had a half eaten honey cake in her hand.

"Amsha . . . ," the child called.

The guide lifted her to a warm embrace. The child snatched off the veil. It floated to the ground. The exchange of kisses brought a flush to her cheeks. The child laughed as the girl avoided a honey cake being directed toward her mouth.

"*La* . . . No," the girl said. She pushed the hand away that held the cake and set the child on the ground. A slave hurried to take her away.

"My sister," the escort said. "My name is Amsha."

Linda looked into the smiling face of a girl not much older than herself. The very large eyes, outlined heavily with *kohl*, were almost hidden behind thick bangs of dark hair. The directness of her gaze made Linda feel like a curiosity, something her father always warned about when she looked too closely at natives of other countries they visited on vacation.

Had she been brought here to be stared at? She didn't mind being considered different, but not a curiosity.

Amsha's manner seemed quite sincere, as she extended the Arabic greeting, "*Marhaba.*"

For a moment Linda probed her classroom Arabic for a reply. "*Marahib.* . . . I am Linda, and this is my sister Cynthia."

Amsha repeated the words. She looked intently at Linda. What did this girl want with them, Linda wondered. Why had they been brought this far? Cyndy felt uneasy, she could tell, for her sister kept turning for a look at the door they had just passed through. Perhaps Linda better explain that their parents would be looking for them, and they had better go back. Before she could say anything, Amsha headed for an outdoor staircase that ascended to the second floor. It was partly covered to secure privacy from the street.

"Please, Linda . . . come . . ." the Arab girl laughed at her pronunciation of unfamiliar words. She shrugged her shoulders, raised a length of skirt, and ascended the stairs.

They were being taken into the Palace. Why, this was really an adventure. More than her mother could dream up. Cynthia's expression conveyed they had come far enough, but Linda knew they could never get past the guard, so they might as well go on.

A second girl stood at the top of the stairway. She reached out to grab Linda by the hand and guided her into a windowless hallway. Brass filigree lamps hung from long chains and cast a warm glow over the wooden floor, a comfort to Cynthia's bare foot. Amsha and the newcomer stopped in front of intricately carved doors with large brass knobs, and slipped out of their shoes. Cynthia left her sandal by the door, too. It was easier than walking with only one.

Amsha pushed on the brass knobs and the doors swung open. Flying skirts and noisy chatter gathered around the new arrivals, as other girls hurried to greet them.

"Enough," Amsha said, gesturing for her kinswomen to

move away.

Linda wondered what would happen next. She was glad when the girl who had led her here addressed her with respect and friendliness.

"I am Fahada ," she said. "Please come . . ."

One of the relatives stood alone near the door. Her bright yellow dress blended with the sheen of the polished wood. Cynthia had been aware of her, for the girl had not participated in the exuberant greeting. She appeared to focus her attention on the unexpected guest. The girl walked toward Cynthia and gently kissed her on each cheek. Her smile was warm and friendly, as she brushed back a lock of hair that had fallen out of place. Cynthia felt strange and uncomfortable. Nothing like this had ever happened before. She didn't acknowledge the girl's gesture but moved closer to her sister.

"It's all the fault of that old camel," she whispered. " . . . and Mom wanting a picture. Can't we go?"

"They're just girls—like us," Linda said. "It'll be okay."

She followed Fahada and her friends. As if in answer, the girl in the yellow dress invited Cynthia to come. She seemed friendly, Cynthia thought, and her smile made you feel welcome. Still, Cynthia held back. In her mind, friends were special. Not just anybody could be a friend. Since there was no alternative, she dismissed her misgivings and accompanied the Arab girl into the room.

PRINCESS FAHADA
(Linda continues her story)

Linda avoided tripping over the rugs scattered across the wooden floor, as their guide urged them forward. The high beamed ceiling made the room appear larger at first, more spacious than the East Lounge of the Surf House, where she and her friends watched their parents square dance on Friday nights. There the sea breeze wafted in through open windows facing the Gulf, but in this room she felt stifled by perfumed air, stirred and rotated by flat bladed fans. She had never thought much about Arab homes. Hearsay painted one picture, actuality was something else.

Three ladies seated in overstuffed chairs turned to watch her as she passed. Linda took quick note of their colorful long dresses and hair that hung in braids over their shoulders. She felt self conscious at such intimacy, for she had never seen Arab women without *abbayas* and veils. Her faded denim skirt, hiked half way up her thighs, and clunking red boots were out of place in this setting. She wanted to remove the boots in keeping with Arab custom, the way Cynthia had slipped out of her one sandal at the door.

One of the ladies leaned out of her chair to stare at the American girls. Her concentrated gaze made Linda wonder what the woman thought. You could not tell, for the face held no expression like women on the street who have no faces, just an *abbaya* and mask. She was relieved to see Cynthia close behind.

Their guide paused near one of the large shuttered windows—the *mushrabiyyah* Linda had seen from the street. A fleeting moment of recognition gave her a sense of direction, for the Land Rover could not be far away, and perhaps she could find her way back.

Dark skinned servants plumped large cushions on a low divan. The Arab girl dismissed them and invited Linda to sit with her. Linda hesitated. If she sat down, she would have to stay, and she did not want to do that. She hardly knew what to do in this situation and was saved from embarrassment when someone grabbed her from behind, and they both tumbled onto the floor.

"*Ya*,Fahada," greeted a vibrant voice. Its owner pushed herself up and pulled Cynthia down beside her.

"Hussa! When did you come?"

The girl named Fahada leaned forward to greet the newcomer, her loose robes almost smothering Linda. The girls rubbed cheeks together, as men often did on the streets, their laughter expressing delight at seeing each other.

"This is Hussa, my aunt from Buraida," Fahada said.

Hussa's sparkling eyes and good humor helped Linda to feel at ease. Somehow the constant flow of chatter and playful glances did not go with the humility Linda associated with Arab women, even with teenagers like herself. She didn't know why she felt that way, she just did.

Hussa tried to explain a relationship between herself and Fahada, but her loosely piled hair, escaping in flying strands, distracted her thoughts, and hands sped to contain the spilling pins. Who was the aunt and who the niece—or whether they were cousins as well—Linda could not begin to unravel. Relationships were complicated in an Arab family.

Despite the girls' friendliness, Linda felt uneasy. The woman in the green dress got to her feet, her slender fingers nervously adjusting the gold embroidery that trimmed the neck of her gown. Who was she? What if she disapproved of the two Americans?

"Ummi . . ." Fahada said. Then in English, "My mother."

"Oh, you do speak English," Linda said, relieved she would not have to search her limited Arabic.

THE AL KUT FORTRESS, HUFUF, SHOWING
THREE BASTIONS

Fahada shrugged. " . . . only a little." Then eagerly, "But I want to. I want to speak much English."

Servants entered from a side door. They carried large brass trays that appeared to be more round than the servants were tall. They served glasses of hot tea to the women sitting in sofas along the walls. Cynthia eyed them with distrust and nudged her sister.

"How long are we going to stay?" she asked, watching the progress of the trays.

Linda knew her sister did not like the syrupy sweetness of Arab tea. To refuse it would be an insult. They had better leave before that happened. She stood up.

"*Laaszim ruh*—we must go," she said.

Cynthia made a move to follow, but Hussa extended an arm and held her down

"*La!. La!*" Hussa said. Then, with hesitation, "No."

A whirlwind of gestures brought the tea service closer. A young black child hurried over, offering tiny glasses, barely three inches tall with a slender handle so fragile it might break when you picked it up. A palm tree and crossed swords were etched in gold near the bottom of the glass—the insignia of the Royal House of Al Saud. A woman set a low table of inlaid wood before her, while another placed dishes of chocolates, orange fingers, pomegranate seeds and honeyed dates.

"For you," Fahada said. She waited until her guests helped themselves, before staining her fingers with the fruit.

Cynthia frowned.

"Try the dates, Cyn," Linda encouraged. "I'll drink your tea."

The girl who had expressed friendship toward Cynthia watched the scene with interest. She moved quickly to sit on the floor next to Cyndy, offering her goodies from the table.

"I am Hessa," she said. "What is your name?"

Cyndy did not feel like answering so she said nothing.

Amsha dug among the cushions and uncovered a small red phonograph and a stack of records. With great care she selected a record and set the needle. A high whine slowed to a dying groan, and the turntable stopped. Amsha gave the handle a few quick cranks and reset the needle. The jarring rhythm of Stateside rock and roll beat through the room, and the persuasive crooning of a male vocalist bemoaned the faithlessness of women.

"You know—who. . . ?" Hussa asked. Her wide eyes glistened between heavy applications of *kohl.*

Linda was too astonished to reply. Elvis—in this room?

"Sure!" Cyndy cried, sitting up as straight as the cushions would allow. "It's Elvis Presley." She began to sing the words , to the amusement of eager listeners.

Amsha set the pile of records on Cyndy's lap. The jackets testified all Presley songs. His suave face and slick dress beamed into the female assemblage where it meant death to the male stranger who dared to intrude. Such a possibility did not bother Cyndy. She had made a discovery.

"Hey—Lin—look . . . This is the one Mom wouldn't buy me in Rome." She held up a record. "I'm going to play it."

"Say—great . . ."

Where did this Arab girl get it? Certainly not from the local *suq.* Not even the ARAMCO canteen would dare to carry banned items. Customs did not allow anyone—even Americans—to bring these records into the country. Moral censorship did not approve of Elvis. Why was Hussa interested in him anyway? Somehow it didn't fit. Just as she, Linda, didn't belong sitting in this room. She sought for an answer in Fahada's face, but her dark eyes were keeping her relatives at bay with a glance.

Who was Fahada? Why did she bring the Americans in off the street? Why bring them into the Palace . . . of course . . . the home of Mishari Al Abdullah, Amir of Hufuf. More than that, he was first cousin of the King and son of the late Governor Abdullah Al Abdullah, who had fought side by side with Abdul Azziz to unite the tribes and to form the Kingdom of Saudi Arabia. Why—she, Linda—at this moment was part of the *hareem* of the Amir.

Never! Startled at the thought, she looked at the women in the room. Were they all relatives?

Wives—aunts—children? What would it be like to have such a large family? Did Fahada have a lot of sisters? And the women—who were they? All family—that is what *hareem* meant. She, Linda, had one grandmother. She visited her every two years on long vacation.

How different the Arab girl's life was from hers. She had not thought about that until now. She never had the opportunity to know. Nobody talked about Arab families, and women were always covered up on the street. Arab men were friendly enough. She knew those who worked around the bowling alley and snack bar. Khalifa and his children brought alfalfa for their horses. Ahmed, the houseboy, and Mohammed, the gardener, were just like family. The women were something else.

"Have you seen him?" Hussa asked.

"Who. . . ? Oh, well . . . once—in a movie."

"Do you see movies every day?"

This was a strange question. The movies at the Recreation Hall weren't all that great. There were no theatres anywhere else. Besides, friends were more fun. Linda was puzzled. Why were movies so important to this girl? There were no public meeting places anywhere—only shops, the mosques and schools for boys.

"No," she said. "I have my friends." She almost used the word *saadig* everybody did. Her father insisted it was not a proper word, and he knew a lot about Arabic.

Fahada had something on her mind. She took a small dictionary from the pocket of her gown. "My teacher," she explained, thumbing through the pages.

"Don't you have a teacher?" Linda asked.

Fahada shook her head. "I want to go to school in America, *Inshallah*, God willing."

She eagerly pressured Linda for information. She asked to know all about Americans—how they dressed—what did they do—could girls go out alone—why didn't Linda cut her hair—could she talk to a boy—did she drive a car—and how big was New York.

The mixture of Arabic and English could be carried so far. Hussa tormented her niece for translations. The amount of Arabic Linda had learned in school over two years represented a token gesture to satisfy the desire of parents that their children be taught a speaking knowledge of the language. Imported from Beirut in the Lebanon, the popular Huda Sukkari had taught her pupils the Lebanese version of a zoo and the Arabic equivalent of "Oh, Christmas Tree". These were no help in a situation like this. She resorted to gestures and to phrases she had picked up from her father and the Yemini houseboy.

The needle scraped across the record, and the turntable dragged to a stop. Cyndy and Hessa scrambled to get it going again, while Fahada and Hussa concentrated on Linda.

"You have a husband?" Fahada's dark eyes narrowed.

Linda's immaturity was caught off guard. "Oh—no . . ."

Boys offered a never ending topic for discussion among Linda's classmates—but marriage? This girl couldn't be serious. She showed no embarrassment. Arab girls married quite young and often shared a husband with as many as three other wives, so she had heard. Could Fahada be like that?—maybe even have children of her own? Linda felt unequal to this turn of the conversation. She gazed at the shutters.

How long had they been here? What if her mother was waiting? She got up and stood by the window. Through the interlocking scrolls of the shutters, she could see the street. The Land Rover remained parked where they had left it. No sign of the parents.

Linda wished she could be on the street, too. She liked the Arab girls but felt uneasy facing different customs. Their lives were entirely different. Why were they interested in Americans, anyway? You could never get to know each other. She tried for a graceful way to leave.

"My mother will be coming. We must return to the car," she said. She remembered to use the Arabic word for car, "*sayaarah*", and not say hospital. She sometimes got the two words mixed up.

In response Fahada ordered a servant to watch the window. Linda had not expected such strategy, nor Fahada's insistence she pronounce the words in her dictionary. That would take forever. A burst of conversation centered about the women. One of the ladies stood up, commanding the respect of the room.

Amsha shook Linda's arm. ". . . bint Azziza," she whispered. "Amira . . ." (wife of the Amir)

Azziza waited as the quickening silence snatched fleeting chatter and the dying vibrato of Elvis. Linda knew the word *sharif* meant noble, even a descendant of the Prophet, and she sensed the Amira upheld that lineage. Something was about to happen, but what, for two of the girls sat in front of the Americans, blocking them from view.

A woman entered supported by two maidservants. She walked with difficulty, but her bearing commanded more respect than that given to Azziza. Linda could not imagine her ducking into a doorway or squatting on the street. Hussa explained that the lady was the Great Aunt Nura, Matriarch of the family. Linda stared fearfully, as the woman surveyed the salon and allowed attendants to assist her into a high backed chair. A dark skinned companion, equally old, sat at her feet.

The Great Aunt spoke to Azziza, and the Amira directed her gaze across the room.

"What now?" Hussa whispered, for Fahada's gentle nature began to cloud with defiance.

The question required no answer, for servants distributed flimsy chiffon to guests who wished to cover their faces.

"The Amir is coming," a servant whispered, handing Fahada two veils.

THE BAIT AMIR OF MISHARI AL ABDULLAH,
MAYOR OF HUFUF

"My uncle must not know I brought the Americans here."
Fahada said to Hussa, "I thought he had gone to Riyadh."

She gave the veils to Linda and ordered the two young
relatives to sit closer together. Linda could barely see through
the double layer of silk. She disliked its clinging texture and
faint fragrance of sandalwood. Her sense of freedom rebelled.
The game had changed, and she wished to escape. She turned
toward her sister who was helping hide the record player under
the cushions and to cover the gaudy albums with Hussa's long
skirt.

Linda watched a man stride into the room, layers of skirts
rustling as he walked—Mishari Al Abdullah, Amir of Hufuf, a
Prince of the House of Al Saud. She recognized power in his
stance and absolute authority in his commanding gaze. He
greeted Azziza with gentleness and his aging aunt with affection. In spite of such kindliness, it would be easy to fear this

man—with his tight little eyes and black beard—if only because he was the brother of Saud, the dreaded Governor of the Eastern Province.

Everyone in the small Oil Company compound of Nejma, where Linda lived, knew the story of Abdullah Al Abdullah, Amir Mishari's father. He had saved the life of the King, Abdul Azziz, when as young warriors of the desert, they had fought side by side to unite the tribes and to create the Kingdom of Saudi Arabia.

"Why has he come?" Fahada whispered. "Why did he not invite us to visit him?"

"He has signed a marriage contract," Hussa confided. "Didn't you know?"

Linda understood the meaning of a marriage contract. A shiver crawled along her spine. She was glad the veil covered her confusion when the Prince looked her way. Princess Fahada seemed disturbed. Did it concern her? Marriage to a Prince— with all that money—seemed an exciting situation. Not for her, Linda, of course, but still exciting.

Fahada gasped in protest, but Hussa clamped a firm hand on her shoulder.

"*La! No,*" she hissed.

Fahada shook free of Hussa's grip and collected her self control. Linda could not guess why the Princess appeared to be so concerned, as she gathered the dignity of her birthright and standing tall approached the Amir. She showed no fear of this man whom everyone held in awe.

"I have no wish to marry."

The Amir smiled. "The families have agreed. Our daughter's security is assured."

He seemed to accept the challenge. Here was no cringing figure but as much a warrior as her celebrated grandfather.

"Your time has not yet come," he added. "Contracts for your marriage to His Royal Highness Prince Bandar are being considered."

Fahada stiffened. The delicate fabric of her dress could have been carved from marble. Strands of long hair, wafted by ceiling fans, alone indicated life. Motionless, Fahada watched the Amir depart, followed by her mother, the Amira and the Great Aunt. Hussa broke the spell. The servants watching the window had indicated the American parents were on the street.

"You must go," Fahada told Linda. "I shall take you."

Linda did not know how to respond. These events had nothing to do with her. She could not possibly understand all that was happening.

She needed to say something. "The Amir—he really is a Prince?"

Hussa interrupted. "You would like to marry a Prince? " she teased. "You would have much money and jewels." She extended her arm, heavy with gold bracelets.

"I shall never marry," Fahada said. "Not even the King's brother."

Amsha caught up with them half way down the stairs. She held a pair of gold sandals in her hands.

"For you," Amsha said, giving the shoes to Cynthia.

"She really could be a friend," Cyndy thought, slipping the shoes on her feet.

They were at the bottom of the stairs when Linda thought they should thank someone. The children and their attendants had left the garden. Several men washed down the tiles of the courtyard, but they did not look up. The air was still heavy under the colonnade as the girls ran toward the far door. Fahada slipped the bolt and peered out. No one in sight. Naiyf had been a big help. The old gatekeeper was blind and would not tell anyway.

Cynthia stepped out onto the street. Linda paused to face Fahada.

"Look—," she said. "I live in Ras Tanura. Will you come and visit me—and my friends?"

The Princess did not answer. Maybe she did not understand.

Her attention settled on the approaching Naiyf. Quickly she hustled Linda through the gate. The gatekeeper threw the bolt. Linda turned and waved, as both girls ran across the square. Her father wasn't pleased she knew. He hurried them to the car, gunned the motor and swung out, even as the car door closed. Linda hung on to the door strap when the car made a sharp turn. How could she begin to tell her parents all that had happened? And, if she did, would they understand.

I listened to Linda's story without interruption, not knowing what to say. The shadows hung deeper in the gardens, and wisps of smoke from evening fires hung between the ragged fronds, reminders that the day was going, that we were tired, hungry and eager to return home. It had been quite a day—not all of it believable, and so far our problems were more or less resolved. We would be on the road much later than anticipated, but, it could not be helped.

The long, slow desert dusk made driving hazardous with its sameness of light and shadow, the land and sky blending into a monotonous nonentity. Donkey carts and a few battered trucks were leaving the old city, to wind their way back to the hamlets in the palm gardens. Several tank trucks appeared, turning off toward As Saha'ba and the fresh water springs for which Hufuf was famous.

The story of the girls' adventures kept turning over in my mind. It could mean so much or nothing at all. Only time would tell. I was aware of Russ starting the car and moving slowly toward the fringe of the grove. The limousines were returning now. The Jeep had already reached the Al Khamis Gate and turned off toward the garrison headquarters.

Now was the time to go.

I did not ask Russ what he thought about all this, but I could guess. And it was not favorable. He settled himself into his seat and checked the tautness of his safety belt. The tires hummed, as the car reached the tarred road, and we turned left toward Abqaiq and the long way home. I touched his arm, as he took a drag on his cigarette. "We'll have to stop for gas in Abqaiq," was all he said.

But I knew his concern lay deeper than that, for the girls had ventured beyond the fences that kept the twentieth century in check, and who knew how the Al Abdullah family or the Oil Company might react.

Chapter Five

THE LONG ROAD HOME

The dust film on the Rover's windshield cut the glare rising off the oiled surface that unrolled ahead. It was a good road by desert standards, built by American engineers to connect the various installations of the Oil Company. Just wide enough for vehicles to pass, its rough shoulders spawned cart tracks and camel trails meandering toward remote villages. Somewhere beyond, the Bedouins took over, for they alone knew the secret of survival on the Eastern Deserts.

Above the audible vibrations of the car, I could hear the "swoosh" of tires making contact with the slick surface, as softened ridges of tar burst under pressure, and the tread sucked up the jets of sticky sand and oil. I felt a kinship to the metal and glass confines of the car. Here I could identify and find again that sense of belonging away from and beyond the living past. For Saudi Arabia was history, and we Americans who lived there looked upon the Kingdom through eyes far distant in its future.

The thin black line of the road was an intrusion in Time: a fragile course that kept open the barriers of difference. With the help of maintenance camps dug in along the side of the road, it survived a continuous battle against flash floods, sandstorms, and destructive temperatures that daily nagged its permanency. Now and again, the rhythm of sand and pipeline was broken by the intrusion of broad camel crossings—pounded marl and rock piled high over unbroken pipeline that, like the road, connected Oil Company outposts.

"Guests of the King . . ." I told myself. That's what we were, we Americans operating the Oil Company. And that position of honor—a guest—often diverted confrontation with Sharia'h law and Muslim tradition. Would it hold true now? Had not Linda been a guest of the Princess Fahada—unexpected, but nevertheless invited? Still, I experienced apprehension of the unknown, anxious moments shared by all expatriate families, arising from careless attitudes toward local laws and tradition. Russ felt it more strongly than I. A personnel man, he dealt with repatriating offenders when local officials could not "look the other way".

It was not my nature to live behind invisible walls, and more than once I was guilty of transgression. Each time, like today, it seemed the vastness of Arabia, with its collective living generations, concentrated on one vulnerable speck—us— tolerated as long as we kept to the thin, dark line.

Sometimes it seemed difficult to separate actual from imposed barriers. We were there for one reason only: get out the oil, and the Oil Company, otherwise known as ARAMCO, wanted to avoid extra curricular confrontations. Today we had breached something else, a moment, that was all, real not imagined, a touch of human hands that might span the differences. I breathed in this draught of fresh air flowing into the vacuum. Already it eased the burden of our circumstances and gave meaning to frustrations born of patience, our longing for loved ones in the States, our isolation from the familiar: today's threads being woven on the loom of yesterday.

Certain it was, that the heat seemed more tolerable, as it lay upon us like a closely tucked blanket. With distance, the shimmering glaze became an ever-thickening veil that gathered up the yellow walls of Hufuf behind, while releasing its hold on the approaching village of Al Mubarraz. Here the desert came as an intruder on the palm belt, and there were no shades to conceal our flight. We skirted the exterior walls of the town, where the flat roofed buildings made little more than a rise in the same dun colored landscape.

Suddenly, a warning from the back seat. "Dad! A policeman!"

We looked toward a crumbling break in the wall that served as an exit from the town. A shouting Saudi guardsman tried to sort out a tangle of overladen donkeys, large wooden wheeled carts and a string of camels, all squeezing through the narrow opening at the same time. Our fears proved groundless. The man was too busy to notice us. Besides, the noise of the Rover's engine became lost in the bawling of animals, the screeching grind of wooden wheels on wooden axels, as carts twisted and strained through chuckholes to gain the road. Some strung out ahead, their outsized truck tires bouncing along to the jogging step of Al Hasa's famous white donkeys.

"Hi! *Saadig!*" shouted a driver, as he paralleled our car. An open mouthed grin lit up the dark skinned face beneath a checkered head cloth. "You want—*hammi hammi*—a race?"

He leapt to the shaft, standing upright, and beat the donkey's backside with his driver's stick, the only directive to slow, stop or full speed ahead. Russ swerved the car to avoid contact, just as a Kenworth double-trailer pipe transport truck bore down from the opposite direction on its way to the Gahwar oil fields. The donkey cart on our right forced the Rover into the middle of the road. Russ gunned the motor and swung the car toward the far shoulder. It hit the *dibkakha* sand hard, skidded, then jarred to a stop. High above our heads the pyramid of twenty-four inch pipe sailed past at a reckless rate of speed.

"Wow!" Cyndy was both mad and breathless. "Those crazy Arab drivers." She rubbed the side of her head, where it had banged against the window.

"The wheels!" exclaimed Linda, as behind us the trailer swallowed the width of the road. "They're taller than I am."

And we could be under them, I thought.

I didn't blame Russ for not wanting to drive the Company roads. Most American men felt the same way. It was not just the donkey carts. Inexperienced Saudi drivers out on a lark challenged the latest of Allah's gifts. Responsibility did not accompany the arrival of the automobile. Before ARAMCO set up a bus system for its employees, villagers returned home from work by whatever means they could. Some piled into dump trucks, until one trigger-happy finger released a lever, and the men sprawled like so much gravel down the road.

Altercations involving vehicles meant Saudi courts and a Saudi jail. Involved Americans were shipped out of the Kingdom on the first international flight available. This meant commandeering flights, leaving Karachi or Bombay going west, to make unscheduled landings at Dhahran for emergency passengers. I knew such thoughts were in Russ's mind, as he straightened the car and pulled back onto the road. We had survived another miss.

Through the years of commuting between Saudi Arabia and the United States, we had experienced our share of harrowing moments. Once the electrical system of a KLM prop plane shorted out in mid air between Vienna and Istanbul. The engines cut out as though we had hit a brick wall. On another time, we took off with Northwest 707 on the short runway out of Tokyo for Anchorage, Alaska, because an arriving plane had pancaked on the long one. Unlimited offerings of champagne eased passenger concerns of "will we make it". Now, I could offer only distracting conversation.

"You girls won't remember," I said. "But ARAMCO had a trailer so huge it picked up a KLM plane from Amsterdam that had been forced down on the desert due to engine trouble, and drove it to the Dhahran airport."

"A whole plane on a trailer?" Cyndy said.

"How did anyone get past it?" Linda asked.

"You couldn't," Russ said. "The area around Dhahran was blocked off when the trailer came through."

"What happened to all the passengers?" Linda asked.

"Buses with sand tires picked them up."

I didn't tell the rest of the story: that the passengers were put right back on the plane, when it arrived at the airport, and had to sit there in the high summer temperatures while a new engine was flown in from Amsterdam, because nobody had a visa to land in Saudi Arabia.

Ahead now, on our right, rose the dark fringes of the great oasis of Al Hasa, with its endless vista of closely packed palm trees. Some of the finest dates in the world were packed and shipped from its gardens. Donkeys with riders turned toward garden trails that wandered around irrigation ditches and over palm log bridges to hamlets hidden under a sunless canopy of branches.

Many ARAMCO employees lived within the vast oasis of Hufuf. On working days they wore the tight trousers of the westerner and traded loose sandals for high-toed safety shoes. They drove Kenworth trucks, operated lathes, drilling rigs and refinery boilers. They went to training schools to learn English and to improve their professional skills. Five times a day they spread their *quttras* on the ground and kneeling, bowed their heads toward Makkah. ARAMCO constructed prayer shelters in all compounds and between shops and service buildings. Prayer time found Arab men paying homage to Allah in the gardens of family homes, walkways and the sands by the side of the roads.

On Fridays, the Muslim holy day, men donned snow white *thaubs* and *quttras* and went to the mosque. Sometimes a man joined his Bedouin family in the goat hair tents on some distant horizon, there to replenish his soul with freedom and contentment, to sit in the sands around a coffee fire, to enjoy the closeness of family and friends, and to share mutual problems of survival. The *riyals* he earned, the comforts he witnessed about the American camps, made him capable of participating in the new era of prosperity, and he took home transistor radios, refrigerators and automobiles to areas without electricity, or roads, or even houses.

"When will we get to Abqaiq?" Cyndy's patience began to wear thin.

"In about an hour," her father said.

"Can we get a hamburger? I'm starving."

"If your mother says so."

It was all right with me. I was anxious to wash some of the dust off my face and to attend to other matters associated with a station stop in the States. Here, such provisions were just not a part of the scene. Besides, I was mentally enjoying the wonderful "A.C." (air conditioning) of the Abqaiq Recreation Building and couldn't wait to feel the coolness envelop me in sensuous satisfaction.

In reality, the heat seemed even greater in the narrow pass we drove through between the walls of the distorted Shedgum escarpments. They formed weird shapes, wrinkled and wind bitten, the result of centuries of erosion. Soon we would be joining the 'Ain Dar spur to the Gas Injector Plant and the pipeline to the ARAMCO community of Abqaiq.

The late afternoon sun made glints of gold out of the sand spray that blew off the dunes surrounding Abqaiq. Beyond where the eye could see would be black goat hair tents, the *bait ash sha'ar*, home of the nomad Bedouin. I had seen them many times from the air, mere specks in a flowing river of red and yellow sand. How did people survive in this wilderness? Not just men, but women and children—and babies, both human and animal.

The Bedu women in Hufuf, from whom I had purchased the caps and the spindle, belonged to the *bait ash sha'ar*. Periodically they came to town to sell handmade weavings, sheep butter and firewood, and to purchase supplies for their journeys. The women of the desert were no less secluded than their counterparts of the villages. They were more aggressive with concerns vital to survival rather than speculating on a chance meeting with a stranger.

Long before we reached the approach to Abqaiq, an unnatural orange glow veiled the desert sky. Farther on, the twists and turns of leaping flame challenged the sun's right to caress the crests of dunes. Another turn toward the Main Gate, and we were engulfed in searing heat. The Abqaiq flare: a solid sheet of fire, half a mile in length and a hundred feet in height, burning off the various gasses released in the processing of oil. Heat waves cast eerie shadows on the silver spheroids of the Gas Oil Separator Plant that processed the sour crude from the Abqaiq pool before pumping it down the pipeline to Ras Tanura and Dhahran. At night it lit up the sky in all directions, serving as a landmark for aircraft and desert wanderers.

We drove past the native *suq* area and the rows of brick dormitories built for Arab employees, past fenced in storage yards that reclaimed vehicles of all types and sizes. An endless variety of scrap materials littered the ground, including stacked pipe, rigging, lumber and bathtubs for houses. The high cyclone fence continued on to surround the whole Abqaiq camp, where American men, women and children endeavored to create a familiar lifestyle long since left on shores half the world away.

The flare's shimmering heat waves created a false corona about the lowering sun. Our life here in Arabia was like that: unrealistic in the technological age the rest of the world faced. No unemployment within this fence, no economically or educationally deprived, no crime, no fear. Nor were there grandparents to spoil the children, to ease their hurts, and to bake Thanksgiving pies. We had no youth beyond ninth grade, except when high school students returned for the summer from boarding schools in Europe and the States.

My former days in Hollywood had faded into the lavender

haze hugging the base of a chain of dunes. The Roads I once traveled with Bing Crosby, Bob Hope and Dorothy Lamour to Singapore, Zanzibar and Morocco, had sent me alone on the Road to Arabia. A detour they never caught up with.

"Where are you going, dear?" Bob had asked at a Paramount farewell party in my honor.

"I'm following the road to Arabia—without you."

Could that have been twelve years ago? This static desert existence deprived us of advances in our own country. I could never pick up where I had left off. But one day we would have to catch up with our future, as now the Saudi Arab looked anxiously at his.

Chapter Six
THE DATE PIT

We entered the lounge of the Recreation Building. The juke-box blared, and the American kids were shaking down the walls. We dodged flailing arms, legs and flopping hair as we headed for the "Date Pit".

"Hi! Mrs. Nicholson . . ." Dark brown eyes and a big smile shook free of a cascade of blonde hair. "Linda with you?"

"Getting a hamburger, Judy. How's your mother?" Judy's family had just returned from three months of long vacation.

"Great. See ya later . . ."

The blue-jeaned legs shook on down the hall. I noticed the laced sides to the jeans, the latest fashion from the States. Besides crates of clothes, furniture and household needs—including a two-year supply of gifts for birthdays and Christmas—each vacation brought back the newest hit records (sometimes sneaked through customs) and the latest gyrations of the dance floor. Every summer, when our high school students returned from boarding schools out of the Kingdom, our vocabularies changed: new words added and others deleted, or given a different association so that we had to learn all over again. Words took men to the moon. Words cried out for civil rights and rebellious youth, situations that never touched us.

At the "Date Pit" we observed our girls bolting down hamburgers and passing bleeding French fries to a group of long haired peers. Separated by two hundred kilometers of desert, friendly rivalry raged between the American communities of Abqaiq, the Sand Dune City, and the Resort Town of Ras Tanura.

"Bring your bed roll and spend the weekend," Linda told one of the girls. "Any of you guys . . ."

" . . . maybe you could fix us up with a Prince, huh?" her friend replied.

" . . . and some of the *hareem*. That's something I haven't seen." The speaker swept his arm around a snug sweatered figure, her wrists draped in gold bangles, and pushed her toward the door. "Come on you guys . . . roll it, man . . . roll it!"

Others joined them, and they all swung out of the "Date Pit". A blast of the Beach Boys set dishes rocking on the tables. Linda made signs of following her friends.

"Just a minute, young lady . . ." Russ sat down with that even all-of-a-piece movement of his, eyes holding his daughter's face.

"What gives?"

"A word."

"So. . . ?"

"Well, we're not out of the woods yet," said the parent voice. A momentary silence. A puzzled look. "Now, what'd I do?"

The Arab waiter greeted us at the table, and we ordered.

"Please, Dad . . ." an anguished voice. "I hardly ever get to see these kids."

"Don't get all worked up. This won't take a minute. I just think you use bad judgment. You talk too much."

Her mouth tightened, accentuating the droop of one corner of her lip. Then, " . . . what about?"

"The Amir's family in Hufuf. It'll come back, you know."

Linda squared her shoulders. Her eyes gathered depth and penetration. "What'd I do wrong?"

"Nothing—except, I just wouldn't spread the word around."

"Look—it wasn't my fault she crashed the gate . . ."

"No. But you could have used better sense."

"Like what?" The chip teetered dangerously. "Say no?"

"I told you to stay in the car."

This was no place for discussions, so I interrupted. "I don't think I could have refused . . ."

Russ glared his disapproval. "You've lived here long enough to know better than that." He didn't like me taking sides when he laid down the law. He held responsibility for all family problems.

I had to say it, even though my retort included every day situations. " . . . and by now things should be more realistic than they are."

"That's got nothing to do with it. If you've had enough, just say so, and we'll all go back to the States."

"Oh, Russ," I blurted. "That's not fair."

"Fair or not, that's how it is."

What could I say? I lived with it every day. ARAMCO didn't need women and children to explore, refine and ship oil. It needed men. We were the extravagance on the budget that insured contented living conditions for employees and thus long time employment. The Company bent over backwards to avoid any incident that might offend its host country. By mutual agreement, they tried to prevent the twentieth century from crashing down on the ancient culture of the Arabs. The high cyclone fence about the American towns protected us from wandering camel herders and from the curious eyes of village boys. It also served to establish social limits. ARAMCO training schools taught the male Arab English and the American employee Arabic. There were no provisions for dependent women to learn either language. Ignorance of language and custom proved to be more effective than the American fences and the purdah of the Arab.

"Dad . . ." Linda's analytical mind took over. "It was just

kids. How can you say kids could ruin all the Saudi women?"

I had to smile. Put like that, it did sound ridiculous.

"Look, sweetheart," Russ played the guiding father now. "We may understand and see nothing wrong, but those cars and the soldiers were no mirage."

"I bet it was just the brother—Naïyf, or something like that," Linda said. "If a guy wants to see a girl, he's going to figure out a way." Her analysis sounded reasonable.

" . . . and I bet Saudis are no different from anyone else I've met anywhere in the world."

How true, I thought. I could recollect any number of instances. There was Bobby—I'd forgotten his last name—the extremely handsome Indian receptionist at the Grande Hotel in Calcutta. He had danced with Linda one night after dinner when minors were not allowed in the public rooms. After that, he got the day off to take the girls to see the white tigers at the zoo. And Steve. Sophisticated Steve of the Raffaello, who invited her up to first class, so they could dance to the best combo on board. I had to include Mike, the British educated Thai in Bangkok. He followed us to the klongs and showed up with baskets of luscious fruits and small pink striped sacks of sweet banana chips. Then, there was Italy. Ah, Italy! "Madame, you have such a beautiful daughter!" called a gondolier from across the Grand Canal, and I thought his bow would overturn the boat and toss him into the water.

Was it so unusual, after all, that youth, seeking its own kind, should be the first to open the door to the *hareem*?

"But, the family of the Amir . . ." I said. "You really started at the top."

"Could I help who she was?"

"Run along," her father said, ending the conversation. "But don't leave the lounge. We'll be on our way in ten minutes."

Russ signed out, as we left the Main Gate, and drove the short distance to the junction with the Dhahran-Hufuf road. It was quite dark now, and the leaping flare was a dance of *jinns*, feverish and gesticulating, spreading unnatural shadows on the crescent dunes caught within its ring. The man made oasis of Abqaiq, its lawns and trees, its swimming pool and movie theatre, its school and family store, disappeared into the darkness. Ahead lay the desert, two hundred kilometers of blackness, known only to the thin oiled road and to the interruption of the Coast Guard Station about twenty kilometers ahead.

The military jeep that had passed us earlier was parked at the Coast Guard Station of Al Jadidah. We pulled alongside the stop sign in front of the shutterless and crumbling building. Four men sat on wooden boxes within the dim glow of an oil lamp that sputtered with darting insects. The quiet emptiness pounded in our ears, as we waited to be accosted. The men barely looked up from their game of drawing circles in the sand. We sat in silence, until a hand waved us on, and we jumped out into the night and the stars.

* * * * *

Ras Tanura, the beautiful Seaside City with its wide white beach and turquoise waters of the Persian Gulf, had been home for ten years. We enjoyed all the physical comforts that trips around the world and generous shipping allowances could provide: rosewood and rugs from Hong Kong, silver and crystal from Denmark, lacquered ware from Kashmir, Rosenthal from Germany, silks and brassware from Damascus and nicknacks from almost every country in the world.

To take care of all these and to clean up after spring *shamaals* blew red dust into every corner of the house, we hired houseboys in white uniforms and colorful caps called *qaffiyahs*. Every day they bicycled back and forth from dormitories in the nearby township of Rahima. We wrote them "chitties" to cover all their needs, and before departure at night, they filled plastic containers with "sweet water" from our special faucet in the kitchen. In the morning they returned with the latest news from the outside world. The Arabs always had it first, and from Ahmed I would learn of the assassination of President Kennedy.

Each of the three Oil Company districts had its own reason for existing. Dhahran was the administrative headquarters where lived the President and CEO. Here policy, operations and government relations were formulated and carried out. Abqaiq was the drilling center and site of the largest oil pool yet discovered. Ras Tanura's existence depended on the ever enlarging refinery, where crude oil was processed into sweet and gasoline refined for local use. If "all roads lead to Rome", then, all pipelines terminated at Ras Tanura. Here the government coffers were filled, as oil flowed over the piers and sea islands and into tankers that yearly shrank the depth of the Gulf.

Life in ARAMCO communities might be termed idealistic, unnatural and lacking in reality. American children born and reared in Arabia grew up knowing very little of their birthplace or the country of their citizenship. Our way of life lacked the basic structure of society. It had no strata. Each employee represented the best of his profession or craft. Linda often reminded me that everybody was rich because ARAMCO had all the money.

The Company provided services normally paid for by employees. There were no coin boxes on local or district buses. Utilities and home maintenance came with your house. Young teens sent away to school met with rude awakenings and dealt with problems never faced before. They confronted bad situations alone. Communication between Saudi Arabia and the rest of the world was limited.

Several months passed since that eventful day in Hufuf. Russ's fears proved to be groundless. We faced no repercussions from the Amir. Perhaps Linda had been right, and we had overestimated the possibilities. Whatever the outcome might have been, we relaxed and celebrated another birthday for Linda. Before Christmas that year, we took a short vacation to Beirut in the Lebanon, and on to Lugano in Switzerland, where Linda would be attending boarding school at the close of ninth grade. She would have a month of summer vacation, then depart for Zurich.

As parents, we had raised her to be self-sufficient and to make sound judgments in anticipation of this change. My days would now be filled with preparations, such as sewing, mending, packing and completing shipping forms for her trunks. I quite forgot the day in Hufuf—hid it away in my own resolutions not to become involved—until one day in April at the swimming pool, where I sat reading, while the girls sunned on towels, deepening their golden tans.

" . . . imagine all those slaves waiting on you." Linda sighed with envy.

"We've got Ahmed," Cyndy replied.

"Oh, Cyn, that's nothing." Linda rolled over on her back and contemplated the translucent roof above the blue recreation pool. "And all that money. The clothes I'd buy."

"You'd probably expect to have a whole ER number all to yourself." Cyndy did not yet appreciate the magic of clothes, but she understood that shipping numbers were hard to come by.

"So—what if I did?" Linda turned up the transistor radio. The Company station was playing the song of the hour.

"I wonder if they go to school," Cyndy said.

"Of course not. Did you ever hear of Arab girls going to school? . . . especially a Princess."

"Then, what do they do?"

"You saw . . . just be elegant and royal and give orders." A trace of envy colored Linda's voice. "I wonder what it would be like to marry a Prince . . ."

"You couldn't wear jeans."

Linda sat up suddenly. "Say, Cyn, I sure am going to give everybody an earful about Arabia when I get to Switzerland. It'll be great."

Cyndy shrugged. "I'm going home. Wonder what Mom's got for dinner. You comin'?"

"Nope. I'm going to have a little chat with Charlie."

I watched her gaze follow a deeply tanned youth about to spin off the diving board.

Cyndy rolled up her towel and put on a yellow beach robe. She shook out her long hair, still wet from the pool, and brushed it off her forehead. I was up and waiting for her by the pool entrance, and together we walked along the wide white beach, the warm waters of the Gulf lapping at our toes. Two years difference in age, the interests of the girls had not yet crossed. Linda was always eager to leap ahead and happily accepted our reference to "thirteen going on sixteen" on the occasion of her recent birthday. Now, I suspected, Cyndy foresaw, that in time all too short "home" in Arabia would no longer hold a place for her..

The flagstone walk between houses bordering the beach led to our *jareed* fence, a native construction of dried palm spines tied together with parallel rows of rope. I lifted the heavy latch and pushed open the solid wooden gate ornamented with large brass studs. Cyndy washed down the sand from her feet with the garden hose and yelled when the water poured out hot.

The full blast of the A.C. hit me when I entered the laundry. I reached for a sweater folded on the dryer and slipped it over my shoulders. Ahmed was at the stove preparing dinner. Small of stature but quick on foot, he bustled about in his polite way with all the extra movements of the industrious and eager to please.

"The man from Housing bring these, *memsa'b*," He said, handing me a manila envelope.

"Thank you, Ahmed. It's papers for Linda's trunk." I made a mental note to get after them right away, if the trunks were to be shipped four months in advance. "Did you get the dresses ironed?"

"Yes, *memsa'b*. I put them in Linda's closet."

I set the envelope on the embroidered cover of the rose-wood buffet. Above it in gold frames hung the hand painted pepul leaves we had bought in Agra on a trip to India. Next to them I had suspended our special treasure: a long necked lute splendid with Persian miniatures hand painted every inch of its surface, even the pegs. It had been covered with dust in a *suq* in Isfahan.

I went to the girls's bedroom. Signs of change showed everywhere: clothes laid out on the bed for labeling and mending, new dresses needing hemlines raised, the footlocker half packed, the desk a hopeless jumble of posters, phonograph records, snapshots and stuffed animals. I heard the back door slam and Ahmed's voice, as he followed Cyndy into the dining room.

"You get a holiday from school next week."

"How come?" Cyndy was interested.

"The King—he comes next week . . ."

"How do you know?"

"I know."

And when Ahmed said he knew—he knew. The King had visited the Eastern Province only twice, and each time he had declared a holiday for all employees. This included school children, since teachers were also employees. Later, when Linda learned of the impending arrival, she thought of Princess Fahada.

"I wonder if the Amir's family will be seeing him," she asked her father.

"It would be in Hufuf, if they did."

"Wouldn't they come to Dhahran, or Dammam?" she asked. Dammam on the Gulf was the provincial headquarters of the Saudi Government.

"I doubt it. There's been no official confirmation that he's coming."

Linda doodled the head of an Arab woman in the center of

her math problem. "I was just thinking. I did ask her to look me up . . ."

Russ contemplated his daughter. "Don't count on it," he said.

"How come?"

"The Amir wouldn't allow it, and I don't want any of you involved."

His tone of voice was conclusive enough. And I agreed. I didn't want to be responsible for a Princess sneaking out the gate, particularly if her father found out. I wasn't best pleased that Linda had brought the subject up again. In retrospect, the incident in Hufuf took on a different outlook. It could have been the result of a dare for the amusement and entertainment of ladies whose cloistered lives held little excitement or change. I might even be indignant at the abduction. Nevertheless, there nagged the probability that the young Princess had made a gesture I wanted to match, and that behind the veils beat hearts and desires no less human than my own.

No. It would be better to forget that day in Hufuf. I was almost glad that Linda would soon be removed from the scene, though already the pangs of separation were growing.

Chapter Seven

TEA PARTY FOR A KING

True to Ahmed's predictions, His Majesty King Saud Ibn Abdul Azziz Bin Abdul Rahman Al Faisal Al Saud arrived in the Eastern Province, and Cynthia had her holiday. I received my official confirmation of the event at approximately 3:07 PM, along with a shower of math and science papers.

"Guess what. . . ?" Cynthia cried, bursting through the front door. "No school tomorrow."

"No school?"

"Sure. The King gave us a holiday."

Then, it fluttered into my hand, as she dashed down the hall, a slip of paper bearing the signature of the president of the Arabian American Oil Company:

> "His Majesty King Saud has arrived in the Eastern Province from Riyadh and has declared tomorrow a holiday for all employees."

On official visits to ARAMCO executives in Dhahran, word of His Majesty's impending arrival came directly from the Royal Palace in Riyadh. Then intercoms on polished desks buzzed, and those in authority prescribed protocol down to the least significant members of our community.

Other times, the wandering Bedu had the news first. Their system of communication across the formidable desert was faultless, and the word spread from tent to hamlet to village. Houseboys picked it up, and the news hovered around the back doors of our neat little houses and over the dusty jasmine hedges. Custodians swept it from mail carrier to secretary, until finally it raced through the corridors and pounded on the door of the president.

The word of the Bedouin tribesman was true. In no time, a shining green and silver plane descended to the Dhahran airport, and the King of Saudi Arabia stepped forth, the fact of his arrival as magnificent as the emergence of an iffrit from Aladdin's lamp.

Ahmed knew the King had arrived long before the Company issued its official announcement. A small brown skinned man, alert to every facet that might stimulate a spark in an otherwise drab existence, Ahmed was the soul of discretion, propriety and respectability. He spoke good English and in many ways was a product of the British occupation of South Arabia. They had set him up as a hotel bartender in the Yemen. His word of mouth information never failed to be true. From him I learned that U. S. Marines had landed in the Lebanon in 1958, and in later years, that President Kennedy had been assassinated.

A tirade of indignation followed his announcement of the King's arrival. The Bani Khalid tribe, that claimed parts of the Eastern Province as their territory, had inundated our neighboring township of Rahima with tents, flocks and families.

"Allah! Allah!" he intoned. " . . . you see this thing that happens—you won't believe, *memsa'b*, but I swear on my God it is true."

I was in the kitchen, fingers dripping with the residual contents of cracked eggshells, as Cyndy's breakfast spattered in the pan.

Cynthia swallowed a bite of toast. "What's that, Ahmed?" she asked. "Sounds interesting."

"Now, Cyndy, you not go anywhere. Everybody crazy— *wajjid* big tea party for the King!"

A BEDU WOMAN DRESSES IN HER FINERY TO
GREET THE KING

"Hmmm . . ." Cyndy mused. "A tea party for the King—in Dhahran, I suppose."

"No—Rahima.."

"Rahima? You mean, he's coming to R.T.? You going?"

"Allah! Not me!" Ahmed threw up his hands. "I don't want anything to do with these people. When the King comes on Thursday, I stay in my room." He plunged his hands into the sudsy dishwater, as if to cleanse himself of contact with Saudis.

A bite of scrambled eggs fell from Cyndy's fork. "Thursday! What happens about the new horse?" she cried. "Dee's riding it up on Thursday. Dad said so."

Thursday, formerly known as Saudi Pay Day, when Arab employees lined up at the cashier's window to collect their silver *riyals*, and Friday the Muslim holy day constituted our weekend. About a dozen horse lovers in our community had organized a self directed group known as the Ras Tanura Ranch Association. We had planned to bring up a mare, recently purchased from a Bedouin family.

"You know Dad won't go anywhere with the King's entourage racing down the roads." She wiped a sudden tear.

"Look, sweetheart," I said. "Let's talk about it tonight. Right now you better eat your breakfast and be on your way, or you'll be late for school."

When morning activities quieted down, and Ahmed had tidied up the house and gone home, I reflected on the King's visit: an exciting event for all his subjects, and one I could not share.

I longed to see the hastily erected wooden arches spanning narrow roadways along the King's route. The Saudi royal standard, crossed swords and a palm tree on a field of green, would wave proudly above the Dhahran Main Gate. The royal car would whisk the Royal visitor through cheering crowds, accompanied by military jeeps, muscled bodyguards in leopard spotted robes. I would love to see the white hooded hawks chained to leather gauntlets. But, ladies did not participate in such events, especially when you lived one hundred kilometers from the center of excitement.

This fact had nagged me for a long time. How could anyone live in a foreign country, for as long as I had resided in the Kingdom of Saudi Arabia, and feel so distant from it. Given the diverse cultures, it was entirely possible.

Men and women of the Muslim world never engaged in mixed social activities. The men entertained their guests in the *mejlis*, a salon set apart for this purpose. The women remained in the privacy of the *hareem*. When invited to the home of a male friend, his hospitality was boundless. But, behind closed doors, the family women argued with their men that I be allowed to visit them.

To offset questionable situations, ARAMCO's unwritten policy warned that any social contact with Muslim women would result in deportation. Thus, we wives dutifully remained within our pleasant compounds. We enjoyed our morning "coffees", activated Scout Troops for our children, conducted Christian Sunday Schools, sponsored fashion shows, to revive our spirits whenever vacationers returned with the latest fashions from the States, pursued the tedious art of pot picking, and with ingenuity made a home for our families in a land so different from our own.

When Russ came home for lunch, he brought more tidbits of information. His Majesty intended to visit local townships and to participate in numerous festivities. Al Khobar, our native shopping center, Thugba, boasting the only gas pump (hand driven), Saihat and Umm Sahwich, in Qatif, and our own local Rahima were making preparations to receive him. ARAMCO officials would pay their own respects, and departmental personnel were expected to attend the Governor's reception at the Amirate. American Aramcons put their own title to the feast— the goat grab—for you sat on the ground, tore off hunks of whole roasted sheep (make that goat) and ate it with your fingers.

Since its nomination as provincial capitol of the Eastern Province, Dammam had exchanged its origins as a fishing hamlet for the promise of a bustling town. Its selection for seat of government, over the ancient trade center of Hufuf, served increasing economic changes, for it was closer to Dhahran, center of the expanding oil industry. The oil well on Jabal Dhahran, known as Dammam #7, first indicated oil in commercial quantities.

ARAMCO assisted in Dammam's development by constructing a deep water port and an eighteen-kilometer breakwater with railroad spur to facilitate the unloading of supplies imported from world countries. Dammam was also distinguished for its offshore Portuguese Fort, a booming camel market, and an assortment of scribes and money changers. One of the first shops advertising western merchandise, proudly fulfilled the needs of its American friends: a string of brassieres, all size forty, strung on a rope from corner to corner of the shop.

Dammam and neighboring Al Khobar—accessible by road, when sand drifts were cleared away—brought the first independent business enterprises to the Eastern Province. To divest itself of supply and service operations, necessary for the continuance of three complete American communities and a mammoth petroleum industry, ARAMCO offered guidance and "know how" to local entrepreneurs interested in founding small businesses. Out of this program emerged the Ashraf Paper Company, the Al Khobar Bottling Plant, the Dosiri Transportation Company and Al Gosaibi, Inc., import contractors, who stocked ARAMCO's food markets and warehouses.

Patience was the rule for American families during the learning process. Pepsi Cola came bottled with the local salty raw water and ill fitting caps, coarse paper towels stretched like rubber and refused to separate into sheets, toilet paper wound without rolls and squashed flat bumped erratically against bathroom walls. For weeks the commissary shelves were empty of staples, such as peanut butter and frozen milk because orders had not been refilled.

The Saudi Arab could not understand why once ordered,

provisions did not keep coming. If an order brought initial results, it should continue to do so—*inshallah*. Gradually the budding businessmen accepted responsibility for the needs of a generation they had not caught up with. They shared in the profits from chicken raising and started poultry farms. Without refrigeration, eggs feathered or putrefied in piles. For want of proper grain, chickens were fed dry fish, the same as horses during drought. Such economic advances were a far cry from earlier years, when a man earned a living by date growing, sheep raising, pearl diving or keeping a small shop. The ultimate success of the Saudi Arab attests to his mercantile shrewdness.

Expatriate women discovered that maintaining a home in a country of limited resources resulted in frustration and challenge. The least task needed to be accomplished the hard way. Raw salt water for bathing and cleaning, lack of materials and services, the ever present dust blown in off surrounding deserts required hiring a houseboy. Why—even the houseboys had houseboys.

Opportunities for employment developed, and Saudis working in American homes sought less degrading jobs with local contractors, or, after years of training school, ARAMCO hired them. Imports, such as our Ahmed from the Yemen, took over the household tasks.

I sensed something was amiss the minute I heard the back door slam, and Ahmed returned to begin his evening duties.

"Everything okay in Rahima?" I asked. It happened to be the wrong subject to bring up. He launched an attack on me.

"You see this thing that happened," he said. "You won't believe, *memsa'b*, but I swear on my God it is true."

"You didn't get into a fight," I said, fearful he might suffer deportation.

"Oh, no. I don't die in a Saudi jail!"

"You mean—about the King. . . ?" The question didn't require me to look up from the package of frozen meat I was defrosting for dinner.

"Very good, *memsa'b.*" A brief hesitation, as he walked to the sink and began scraping a scorched mess from the bottom of a pan.

"I expect you to come to work, Ahmed, even though we have a holiday.."

"Oh, yes, *memsa'b.* I don't want anything to do with these people—not like my country."

He often repeated the glories of the Yemen, that small, suffering kingdom at the southern tip of the Arabian Peninsula. After a visit to his homeland, he brought me a gift: a gleaming brass hubbly-bubbly water pipe with a bright red hose and decorated with Arabic engravings and hundreds of dangling charms. It was by far the most highly polished item in my house, and I often wondered if brass wore out.

"You see this thing, *memsa'b,* what happens now . . ." Ahmed said, turning to face me. "My roommate, Ali, tells me his cousin from Tarut would like to take a bath. So I agree he can use our shower. But when I go for lunch, Ali stands at the door and won't let me in. I say to Ali is he crazy or not. And then, Allah!—I hear such screaming you won't believe. My room is full of Bedu women! I am angry. I push Ali in the face."

Ahmed paused to catch his breath. His demeanor changed from anger to good humor, his words garbled by uncontrolled laughter.

"I think this thing is funny. I laugh and laugh! Ali asks if I've lost my mind. Can you imagine, *memsa'b,* maybe twelve Bedu women and all their children in my room! Allah! Such a thing never happens before!" Ahmed's laughter bordered on the fanatical, his eyes rolling from side to side.

"Ahmed!" I exclaimed, hoping my sharp tone would bring a measure of sanity.

"I think on these women," he continued. " . . . they take off their dirty clothes. They wash their hair, and paint their feet, and scrub their children in my room. Maybe all year they don't take a bath. Allah! How they stink!"

I couldn't accept his story as true.

"Ahmed, you know there are no women in your room," I said.

"You see, you don't believe." His tone was sharp. "I am a good man. Every Friday I go to the mosque. I honor my God, and I swear on my God it is true. Maybe twenty Bedu women. They scream. They laugh. They throw water all over. Such noise. I will never get it cleaned up!"

I tried to shake his story. "The Bedu never come to Rahima . . ." I said.

"Ah, *memsa'b*, you see—you don't know how it is. Now there are many Bedu. Thursday *wajjid* big tea party in Rahima. Maybe the King throws out the gold coins. The Bedu come from the desert. They show loyalty. There is much singing and dancing. So, all the women want to take a bath. *Memsa'b*, I think that is very funny!"

Funny? Exaggeration is characteristic of the Arab. The glint of truth in Ahmed's story was more than humorous. It was a wedge, an opening, an opportunity—in Rahima, only a stone's throw from Nejma—women milling about the tents—could it work to my advantage?

The Eastern Province was tribal territory for the Bani Khalid, Bani Hajar, Awazim and part of the Ajman tribes. They normally kept to the mainland, for Ras Tanura and neighboring Rahima were built on a narrow spit that curved out into the Persian Gulf, forming Tarut Bay on its southern side. There were no water wells, nor camel grass, and the area was surrounded by *subkhas*: a fusion of sand and water, creating salt flats that disguised treacherous quick sand.

Rahima became a settlement for local Oil Company employees. Families followed naturally with accompanying sheep,

VILLAGE WOMEN AND CHILDREN AWAIT THE
ARRIVAL OF THE KING

goats and a few camels. *Suqs*, coffee houses and small shops showed up between walls of palm matting and pounded out rusty oil drums. Over the years, sophistication set in. A clinic and training school were added, together with stone dormitories standing line on line, their sameness broken by garishly painted doors in offensive colors. A seat of government, a few enclosed shops and a mosque made the town complete.

The proximity of the refinery, the tank farm and terminal pier, as well as the American residential community of Nejma, gave Rahima meaning. They were all part of Ras Tanura, considered the core of oil operations. The refinery sweetened sour crude and made cracked aviation gasoline. It poured millions of barrels of oil daily into monster tankers berthed at terminal piers and into Tapline pipes that pumped oil over and under sand dunes, across *subkhas*, and up the wadis of Saudi Arabia, Syria and the Lebanon to the Mediterranean port of Sidon. Topping all this, Nejma possessed the world's most beautiful beach: clean white sand and exotic shells fringing the turquoise waters of the Persian Gulf.

Whatever political reason brought the Bedu to our area suited my germinating thoughts exactly. Could I make contact with the women?

"How many *bait ash sha'ar* are there?" I asked.

"Now, *memsa'b*, how is it you ask me these things?"

Knives and forks clattered into a drawer.

"Maybe you passed some on your bicycle."

"And why should I look at Bedu?" Ahmed turned and vigorously wiped the stovetop. The small brightly colored *qaffiyah* on his black hair bobbed in unison with the push of his shoulders. "I close my eyes. I don't see anything—*inshallah*."

Inshallah. The Arabic word that tried my patience. The constant reminder of Allah's participation in the daily life of the faithful. Readily defined as "if it is the will of God", only the true Muslim can experience its full depth and significance. A nonbeliever may easily become aggravated at its implication of lack of personal responsibility; yet, find himself mesmerized by the musical intonations of its syllables. In times past I had tried to counter it with "God helps those who help themselves", only to be rebuked with: "That's very good, *memsa'b*, I shall remember—*inshallah*." Since those early days of indoctrination into the Muslim way of life, I have learned to respect the word, to accept the spirit in which it is spoken, and as I would discover later, to obtain a glimpse of the depth and truth of its meaning.

For the moment, its use in this sequence neither aggravated nor impressed me. I simply ignored it.

Ahmed escaped to the dining room and began setting the table for dinner. The subject of Bedu women had been dismissed. I shrugged, realizing Allah would not protect me if dinner wasn't on the table by 5:15 PM, when Russ got home.

I hadn't thought about the new horse until Cyndy's arrival

home at 3:07 PM. The slip of paper announcing the holiday lay in my hand. I set it on the table. We would have all day tomorrow to decide what to do, for I knew Ranch members would spend the day grooming and riding their horses.

I reached for a saucepan and set out an egg, sugar, chocolate, tapioca and milk. No vanilla: it was on the government banned list because it contained alcohol. Keeping Saudi Arabia dry had infiltrated the kitchen. I would make chocolate pudding for dinner, Cyndy's favorite. It might brighten her spirits.

The front door opened. Linda and Monica Dowling, a classmate, bounced in. They were out of breath.

"Mom—there's a lot of stuff going on in Rahima. Ed's dad is going there and says we can ride with him, okay?"

Ahmed answered before I could. "You not go to Rahima, Linda. Too many crazy people."

I gave the pudding a stir.

"Please . . ."

"I'd rather you didn't . . ." I said.

Her eyes challenged. "Why?"

"Well, there'll be a lot of national feeling. It isn't a good time for American girls to be seen in a local town."

She turned and flounced off. "We won't get to see any of the celebration for the King."

The pudding bubbled, and I turned down the heat. "Don't be so sure about that," I said.

Linda glowed with anticipation. "What do you mean?"

"Daddy told me at lunch that the Dhahran Corral is organizing an Arabian Horse Day and putting on an exhibition gymkhana for the King."

" . . . and we can go?" Linda threw her arms about her friend. "Monica can come, too?"

"If she would like to. There are a few items I need from the commissary, if we are going to have a picnic . . ."

I left the stove, found a pad and jotted down a few notes.

Linda hurried to change into play clothes. The sniff of scorched chocolate nudged my reflexes, as Cyndy came into the kitchen.

"What'd you have to burn it for?"

The pudding was kind of stuck to the bottom of the pan.

"I'm sorry, sweetheart," I said. "But see—it's okay."

"If you like it that way." There was no denying the disgust in her tone. The lid clattered on the cookie jar. "I'm going to Tracy's house . . ."

"Five o'clock whistle, remember . . ."

"I know." Then a pair of braids disappeared behind a clump of flowering frangipanis fringing our *jareed* fence.

With an aesthetic shudder I poured the chocolate dessert into a blue bowl, finished the grocery list and sent Linda on her way. The excitement of the King's visit was catching up with me, not that I hadn't seen a King before.

In the early nineteen fifties I had sighted the tired face of Abdul Azziz, fondly known as Ibn Saud, the founder of modern Saudi Arabia. His desert kingdom had been new and strange to me then, and my prime concern had been for security in this foreign land. Three years later I waited under a blistering July sun to see the present King Saud and Crown Prince Faisal, shortly after Saud became Sheikh of Sheikhs on the death of his father. Neither event could have been as thrilling as the arrival of Abdul Azziz in Dhahran in nineteen thirty-nine with a retinue of two thousand. He set up a magnificent tent city to celebrate the discovery of oil in commercial quantities from Dammam well #7. Those were the pioneer days, and I belonged to the second phase of the oil venture, that of mass production and expansion.

It was not only oil that emerged out of the desert. Social change, business enterprise, improved health care and academic education developed hand in hand with the ever increasing flow of oil and profits. The fact of bringing a more comfortable life to eastern Saudi Arabia made American families pioneers at the social level, no different from the geologists and engineers who first explored the concession area.

To me, there remained another untouched field: the women of this land, who could teach me the restraint and courage that lay behind the veil. They were here now, the Bedu women Ahmed had described, and the ladies of the King's entourage. For Russ had mentioned, that with King Saud came the royal *hareem*, the first event of its kind, and one that would provoke endless problems for ARAMCO officials.

It seemed the opportunity of a lifetime. Nothing short of a miracle would bring me face to face with the women of the King's court. Yet—Saudi Arabia had produced one miracle, could it work another?

Chapter Eight

THE BEST OF PLANS

The circumstances of my arriving in Saudi Arabia were quite simple. I wanted to get married. My prospective groom had made the long trek some eight months before, as an employee of the Arabian American Oil Company. On arrival, he had been issued a number, 9747, his official I.D. He shared a frame *burasti* with eight other bachelors and received indoctrination into the dos and don'ts of a considerate guest toward his host. Besides the performance of his duties, Russ sat out the long months building up seniority points and awaiting the availability of family housing.

The arrival of a wife would effect some changes. The I.D. number would remain steadfast, a wife attached to it as a dependent. A family man, Russ could then expect to be assigned a home of his own, with privacy undreamed of, home cooked meals and the blessings of feminine companionship. The dos and don'ts would remain the same, though complicated by the additional requirement of being responsible for whatever a wife might take it into her head to do.

The long, lonely months on the desert worked wonders. Instead of two years, the usual waiting period, Russ acquired housing in a mere eight months. An executive on a year's leave to New York had asked Russ to care take his house. A temporary move it might be, but my arrival would put Russ at the top of the list for any vacancy.

"Can you meet me in Rome in two weeks," the cable read. I could and did.

Christian marriages were not permitted in Saudi Arabia, custodian of the sacred places of Islam. Russ and I were married at Michelangelo's Campodoglio in Rome.

Our flight from Rome to the Kingdom of Saudi Arabia revealed limitless expanses of unvarying sandscape. Monotonous, trackless desert emerged into murky yellowness and erased all other colors from the earth. Nor did it stop there, but swept into the sky, a billowing mass of glittering particles, screening the mystery of its mirages as effectively as though a handful of sand had been thrown into the eyes.

Finally, there it was far below me, the country where I would live for more than thirty years, and where we would rear two daughters. Our American heritage would be the same as in any small town in the United States; yet we belonged nowhere. Guests of a desert king.

The years challenged my ability to find a place for myself in this country of mystery. What lies in that foreboding emptiness? What are the people like who have survived such desolation? And, the women—my counterparts of a closed society— what about them? Small determinations to contact them had been growing over past months, that on this day, when a slip of paper had been pushed under my nose, an opportunity arose that must not be lost.

My resolve started with Terminal Road that led past the Ras Tanura Main Gate to the ever-expanding refinery, storage tank farm and port facilities for shipping oil.

The road lay on top of a man made spit about six miles long. Half way to the terminal on the Tarut side of the road stood a small white clubhouse and snack bar, slips for a dozen fiberglass boats and a bathing float. These comprised the Sandy

Hook Yacht Harbor, product of adventuresome American Persian Gulf sailors. Here Yacht Club members hosted barbecues, yacht races, campouts for Nejma residents and welcomed yachtsmen from neighboring Gulf countries. Captain Ed Wennesland, Norwegian master and pilot for tankers entering terminal berths, dedicated his free time to teaching every Nejma child to swim.

The tidal action on the open Gulf side of the spit ate at the shoreline, necessitating the deposit of tons of scrap metal and concrete blocks to hold the sand and to protect the road from erosion. Where the spit ejected from the land lay a broad stretch of beach, pinkly phosphorescent with powdered cowry shells. Hillocks of sand backed the beach, keeping the Gulf waters from dousing the flats beyond. Here in the early 1940's ARAMCO had constructed a camp to house Italian employees, former prisoners of war from Mussolini's campaign against Ethiopia in 1936. It became known as Italian Camp.

The venture of Italian labor was short lived. The volatile Italians longed for families and their own culture. Many shipped out to their native land, the remainder housed near Rahima. With them went delicious Italian dinners and our only place for "dining out". Italian Camp was demolished, save for the skeletal remains of the large former recreation hall, now home to the Ras Tanura Ranch Association.

Here a dozen horse loving residents of Nejma stabled their Arabian mares, purchased directly from Bedouins, picked up as discards from the Royal Stables at Al Karj, or through interchange with a similar group, the Corral, in Dhahran. Gone were the checkered cloths, the gleam of candles, the strains of a concertina. Yet, sometimes of an evening, if you listened to the off shore breeze, a long forgotten "O Sole Mio" returned to serenade the silent stalls.

Eager to assist self directed recreation groups, ARAMCO donated the dilapidated structure for stable use, piped in water and hooked up an emergency telephone line. They also provided a big red bus to take members and friends to the Ranch and to Sandy Hook. The rest of the operation was handled by family horse owners. Members became barn builders, painters, tree planters, groomers, farriers, diagnosticians and veterinarians. Since the facility was outside the Nejma perimeter fence, members hired Salim, a native of Rahima, as caretaker. Hassan Bin Khalifa, a farmer in the nearby village of Saihat in the Qatif Oasis, supplied alfalfa for the Ranch.

A Thursday morning delivery required many hands to offload, weigh and spread the green alfalfa for drying. All the Ranch children helped, including Hassan's eight sons and two daughters, who arrived sitting atop a load high above the truck bed. What a rousing, happy time!.

On the day before the King's Tea Party in Rahima, I told Russ we were out of dates for the horses. Local residents would be participating in activities for the King so tomorrow would be a good day to ride our mares to the date *suq* in Rahima to get some. The date *suq* was away from the center of town. Actually, we had a full supply. I hoped to get a glimpse of the festivities—even of the Bedu women Ahmed talked about.

Russ might question my motives, but I knew the needs of the horses were a priority with him. Shipping in grain from Basra in Iraq was costly and unreliable, so we added dates to their diet. The fruit filled a nutritional need. Besides, it was worth a laugh to watch Dee's stallion, Bedu, churn up a mouthful and one by one spit out the pits. He gave me a long look, then agreed. We would have to saddle up early and take the back road to avoid the entourage of the King.

Next morning, Cyndy was first to take her mare from the stall. Sharifa's black mane hung well below her withers, and her tail touched the ground. She was a hot blooded desert pony and allowed few people to ride her. Her maternal instincts toward Cyndy were a natural outgrowth of the desert mare being raised as a "daughter of the tent" in the *bait ash sha'ar* of the Bedu.

I would ride my own Murrawiyyah, a golden chestnut with an unusual gait. The way she arched her neck, and the graceful motion of her body was almost a dance.

Russ's mare was a discard from the King's stables. A spotted blue, we called her Zerqa.

It was a forty-minute ride to Rahima. We had to follow alongside the huge refinery. Its roaring and leaping flare created shadows that rolled above the flat in swirling black waves, as changing winds toyed with the spiral of thick smoke from waste oil dumped into the flare. Once past the refinery, the way was sandy fill and secure. We never questioned a horse's instinct to change direction in fear of the *subkhas*, where the land sucked up the sea.

We cantered across the long dry flat south of the refinery, ignoring a few camels chewing on clumps of salt grass, and pulled the horses in at Terminal Road. We waited for a tank truck to rumble past, then walked the horses over the blacktop and into sandy ground.

The outskirts of Rahima revealed preparations for the King's visit to be well under way. Saudi flags flew from rooftops, bringing a dimension of importance to this otherwise quiet town. A generator sputtered its indisposition, as men in holiday dress tested strings of colored lights, twisting them up a crude archway of palm logs erected across the main street near the mosque. Two four pole tents intertwined their ropes far into the street. Colorful *qatas*, tent dividers, hung from the roofs, and tribal banners streamed above the tent poles. Men gathered in opposing lines to perform the *Ardah,* and older boys built fires of dried palm fronds to heat the drums and tauten the skins. In time they would test their ripeness with the staccato rap of fingers.

Zerqa was in the lead, and Murrawiyyah's muscles rippled, anxious to keep moving. My last glimpse of the preparations included a woman and a girl grabbing a donkey by its ear and pulling it away from a tall gold and green velvet chair under a silken pavilion, where the King would sit to preside over the festivities.

Tea Party For a King, appropriate for this dry country. The traditional hospitality of the desert nomad extended into the towns and palaces with the serving of cardamom coffee and sweet mint tea. Three young camels stood in the slaughtering pen, awaiting their turn for the ritual killing. Large tufts of black hair blown up against the wire fence, attested to the fate of many sheep already roasting in huge pots for the banquet to follow. Amir Turki of Rahima would show his illustrious guest and relative a Royal welcome.

We skirted the rusty sheet metal structures of Contractor Camp, an area of makeshift dwellings for employees of contractors doing business with ARAMCO. Boys from the camp chased after the horses and began throwing stones. Russ had been holding Zerqa in. He signaled us to get away from camp and allowed his own mare to run. He would go ahead to the date *suq*, and we could follow at a walk, giving Murrawiyyah a chance to settle down before we started home.

Russ returned empty handed. The date shop was closed in honor of the King. The encounter with the boys had delayed our plans. We feared being caught near town should the festivities start earlier than expected. The roads would be blocked, and that meant picking our way through possible wet sand areas. We decided to return home the way we had come. We mounted and swung the horses back toward Contractor Camp. Murrawiyyah would not go forward. It meant facing a barrage of stones again. I couldn't blame her.

"We'll have to go around Rahima," Russ said, as he led the way. "See if Murrawiyyah will follow."

She did, and we started home the long way. This route would be exactly opposite to the one we had come. It would take us to a camel crossing with access over layers of pipelines that paralleled the main road from the Ras Tanura headland. With luck we would cross the road before the arrival of the King.

We made good time over dry, soft sand until a black tent came into view. There were three of them hugging the ground near some half buried palms. Bedouins riding camels, shouting children and black cloaked women fanning back and forth between the tents were too much for a nervous horse. We kept our distance from the encampment and moved on.

We were encouraged to reach our goal, until Cyndy thought she heard the distant sound of rifle shots and blaring horns. The cavalcade. We could not guess how far behind the entourage might be, so we urged the horses on through a stretch of firm ground. Murrawiyyah relaxed, and we made good time to the area of the camel crossing. If only we could gain the road before the King.

This was not to be.

Chapter Nine
MURRAWIYYAH GREETS THE KING

Triple rows of *bait ash sha'ar*, strung out on either side of the road, blocked our way. Multiple tribal flags and banners fluttered from tent poles. Men and children clambered over the pipelines for a better view of the King. Women flittered about at the rear, straining for a look at the approaching caravan. The first military jeeps appeared in the distance, welcomed by wild enthusiasm. Unrestrained, the Bedouins jammed the road until cleared away by soldiers riding the first vehicles.

We nudged the horses to the top of the camel crossing, making an attempt to reach the road, but were held back by the excited crowd. Russ settled down on Zerqa's back, realizing we would have to wait until the vehicles had passed. He signaled Cyndy to bring Sharifa closer for safety reasons in an unpredictable situation.

Military jeeps with mounted guns rolled past, followed by an endless stream of limousines flying the Royal Standard. We caught glimpses of Princes, government ministers, tribal leaders of the Eastern Province and Amirs of larger towns. Finally, the King himself appeared, riding in a black Cadillac bearing royal license plates and flying the flags of the House of Al Saud.

Military jeeps preceded and followed the royal vehicle, guns aimed on the King, himself. Bearded guardsmen in leopard spotted robes and bristling with knives and rifles, ran alongside the royal car. Who could doubt that the fanatic guardsmen would lash out with weapons should a spectator get out of line. The shouts of tribesmen, bawling of animals and staccato burst of rifle shots all added to the general noise and confusion.

The car ahead of the King's Cadillac slowed, and a man wearing the princely gold *egal* on his head, tossed small leather pouches to the crowd. Loosened coins rolled on edge along the road and into the sand and scrub brush. The shrill ululating of the women rose above the medley, as they rushed to get a share of the booty.

FORMER ITALIAN CAMP CONVERTED TO
STABLES FOR RAS TANURA RANCH ASSOCIA-
TION—1960s

The excitement was too much for Murrawiyyah. She re-acted to the flying black figures. Perhaps something in her past history brought on a fear of flapping robes. She began canter-ing in place. Her collected muscles swung into a high rocking motion, her own natural gait. It was graceful to see at any time, but activated under stress, she went backwards, tripping over tent lines, scattering people and bursting open goatskins of milk tied to wooden tripods. I tried to pull her up, but she rocked in a circle toward the face of a tent, and I ducked to avoid the worsted roof.

A woman's arm covered with gold bangles reached for her, but Murrawiyyah shied, never losing her rhythm. Other women cleared a path, and I urged her forward to a low dune just be-hind two tents. Breathing hard, she went up the soft sand at her rocking gait, as if to calm herself.

I slipped from the saddle, and with reassuring words ca-ressed her neck. The desert mare responds to the closeness of the human family. We walked back to join Cyndy and Russ. The noise had quieted down. The royal car had stopped, and an official stood alongside the open rear door talking to the pas-senger within. A respectful hush calmed the crowd, and Bedu cleared the way for a royal envoy who walked directly to Russ. Arabic greetings ensued, and Russ dismounted to return the courtesy.

The minister conveyed the King's desire to express his plea-sure at the interest Americans show in the Arab horse. His Maj-esty hoped to learn more of the training and performance of mares for purposes other than racing.

"He is looking forward to the gymkhana," the envoy said. "We are unfamiliar with such an event."

"We are honored to please His Majesty . . ." Russ replied.

" . . . and will your sorrel mare be taking part?"

" . . . *inshallah*."

"His Majesty requests that his favorite mare be trained to perform the unusual gait he has just witnessed."

Russ stepped forward in direct line with the royal car, Zerqa nuzzling his shoulder. He raised his Stetson in acknowledgment toward the royal visitor. Russ's fluency in Arabic knew no bounds, as he offered Murrawiyyah to His Majesty, that skilled trainers might learn the secret of her performance. Concerned with controlling the mare, I missed the significance of Russ's reply. The minister nodded in approval and reached to shake Russ's hand.

"Such generosity was not intended. The benefit of your skills is yours. I shall convey your wishes to His Majesty."

Within the car a regal hand gestured, and a smile split the heavy round face. Dark glasses screened the eyes. It was the man sitting beside the King I could not forget, the feared Saud Al Abdullah. Above the gold trim of his dark bisht projected a pointed red beard and whiskers bristling along the jaw line to the ears. His eyes held you spellbound. The straight tight lips would not hesitate to pronounce the death sentence where justified. The King was honored. The Governor was feared.

The procession moved on, rounded a curve, then continued along the Rahima road. Tribesmen on camelback beat on the necks of their mounts, and holding rifles aloft, raced after the entourage. Belching camels spat froth, tails carried disgustingly straight up. Men on small brown donkeys and boys on foot raced after, adding rifle shots and yells to the frenzy. The tents became deserted, except for an old man, several women and girls.

Young children still rummaged through the hillocks and brush seeking another coin. Women returned to the seclusion of their homes, chattering and rearranging headscarves that had become unbalanced during the excitement. Three ladies remained in front of a nearby tent. They seemed to be watching me, but made no gesture to come closer, as long as Russ was there. The personal encounter with the King left me breathless. I accepted the honor of the Royal acknowledgment, and with it—what Bedouin could refuse hospitality.

"What did that man want?" I asked Russ.

"Murrawiyyah! Yes, I offered your mare to the King."

"No! You didn't?"

"You know the rules . . ." he said. Then smiled. ". . . don't worry. At this minute she looks far to scrubby to be wanted by the Royal Stables."

"She does look pretty awful," I said. "Here, take her and Sharifa. See if the old man can get them some water." I tossed him the reins.

Russ eyed me with the conviction there was more behind my move than expressed. Collecting the three mares, he left Cyndy and me to the women and the tents. With Russ gone, two of the women came forward. The move was unexpected, but it encouraged me to speak to them.

I greeted them with traditional Arabic. They responded with an air of friendliness tempered by curiosity. One carried an infant in a sling under her voluminous robe. The second woman wore a silk *abbaya* trimmed with the common decoration of gold braid. She had pushed the hood from her forehead, revealing the top of her glossy black hair and a long chain with silver bells hooked to one side. The younger wife of a *sheikh*, I surmised, not missing the brightness of a smile lighting up her dark eyes. Timid, yet with assurance, she graced the weathered worsted and its scattered belongings with the beauty of an inner security that life on the desert had given her.

Tall tent poles flew tribal banners of brilliant hues. Rugs of vibrating green and orange, meticulously woven by the ladies in tribal designs, hung from the tent roof in decorative finery, to honor the King and to declare the tribe's loyalty. How could I let this moment pass? I sent Cyndy to get the camera in Russ's saddlebags. Who could refuse one acknowledged by the King? I acted on impulse, not with judgment.

I removed the Hasselblad from its case and slipped the cord about my neck. The women watched my every move. I decided to test the possibilities, feigning interest in the tent interior with

117

its embroidered *qatas* that divided the tent into two sections: one for men, the other for women and accessories. The ladies didn't seem to be disturbed. I photographed Cyndy near the frame of a large *maksar*, the protective saddle cover for women when riding camels on the march.

The Bedouin girl watched with interest and took a step forward, clutching her *abbaya* at the neck. She extended her hand, hennaed fingers tracing strands of Cyndy's honey colored hair. A smile blossomed behind the mask. I gestured for a picture of the two girls. She did not respond.

The oldest woman accosted me, not with anger but with business on her mind. Swathed in varying textures of black cloth, so that only her fingertips were visible, it was difficult to guess what her hierarchy might be. By all appearances, a woman's dress appeared to relate to her age. With a strident voice, she demanded that I pay thirty *riyals* for one picture. Bedu women love money, I knew, and the King's generosity had stirred their blood. But—thirty *riyals* for one picture! She, too, was taking advantage of the moment and capitalizing on my interest in her.

No, I would not give her what she asked, though I recognized this was a step forward to where I wanted to be. Would she show more friendliness, invite me into her home, if I complied?

"Ten *riyals*," I said, raising the camera.

"*La*. You must pay thirty." She rapped my hand with her rough skinned fingers.

"Ten—no more." I don't know why I said it. Perhaps my pride against hers. I could bargain as well as she.

The younger woman interrupted, but the matriarch held to her demands. She would have the full thirty for one picture. I had bargained for antique camel bells in the *suq*, but I felt unequal to her experience and lifelong skills. I must pay the amount she asked for, or forget about the pictures.

The roar of a fast approaching limousine startled me,

probably one in the wake of the King's cavalcade. I was fully visible from the road and decided to be cautious. I lowered the camera and pretended interest in the coffee fire and circle of broad beaked brass pots.

Cyndy heard the car, too. "It stopped," she said. "Looks like it's turning around."

The car pulled alongside the tents.

"Mom, a man just got out. He's walking toward us."

I felt a moment of concern.

"Let's get out of here," Cyndy said. "Dad's back of the tent with the horses."

She walked away, but I had no intention of retreating. Wasn't I just standing there? The well dressed man walked briskly toward me. I sensed a moment of panic. He spoke rapidly in Arabic to the women, then addressed me in flawless English.

"Did you take pictures of these women?"

My heart skipped several beats. I didn't want another encounter with the morals committee over the camera, especially at the Royal level. Without doubt, this man belonged to the King's party, an official perhaps, maybe even a Prince. The camera hung in full view. I could deny nothing.

"Did you take pictures of these women?" he repeated with some impatience. Obviously, he had been in a hurry to get somewhere.

I found courage to reply. "No . . ." It was the truth, although circumstances hardly backed me up.

"Why not?" he asked.

Now I was confused. What kind of question was that? A way out? Without thinking, I said, "They're asking too much money." A half admission was certainly the wrong thing to say.

"How much did they ask?" he wanted to know. His polite smile offered encouragement.

LINDA AND CYNDY TAKE THE MARES FOR A
RUN ALONG THE BEACH

"Thirty *riyals* for one picture." My every response seemed an admission of guilt.

"And you think that is too much?"

"I certainly do." I blurted. It was the only thing I was sure of at the moment. Was he trying to trap me? Why had he taken the trouble to turn around and stop at the tents?

"How much would you pay?"

What did that mean? I must tell the truth. "Well, perhaps ten *riyals*—if I could take all the pictures I wanted."

I waited for the axe to fall, but instead of a blistering reply, he reached in a pocket hidden deep in his long white *thaub* and extracted a thick wad of green Saudi *riyal* notes.

I had never seen such a bundle of money in my life—all stuffed into a pocket. He separated the bills and handed me two ten *riyal* notes.

"Here," he said. "I will pay twenty, if you will pay ten."

Was this offer the final trap? The women watched with interest. We spoke in English, but I'm sure they understood. I wilted under his offer, thinking the worst of his intentions. The wad of bills disappeared into his pocket.

"After you take the pictures," he said. "I would like to have some copies. Do you agree?"

"Why—yes," I stammered, the money in my hand clear evidence of my guilt.

He spoke rapidly to the women in Arabic, then walked quickly toward the car. I watched Russ and Cyndy bring the horses around to the front, interrupting the stranger's departure. The men engaged in a brief conversation before the Arab returned to the car and with a whine of tires, the limousine continued its race toward Ras Tanura.

An old man emerged from an adjacent tent, supported by a cane and with grey stubble sprouting along his chin. He spoke harshly to the women, shook his cane at them and returned inside. The women made no move to leave or a show of friendliness. This would be a business deal. I snapped a few pictures and gave the thirty *riyals* to the matriarch.

We mounted our horses and walked them past the tents and over the camel crossing. I was glad when we crossed the blacktop and headed the horses to the old Ras Tanura sand road that had long been abandoned in favor of the new and more direct route to Dhahran. The sand was still firmly packed, and other than a few drifts and potholes, the way uneventful. Cyndy loped Sharifa slightly ahead, so I sided up with Russ. He had just lit a cigarette and given Zerqa enough head to pick her own walking speed. The horses had a good coat of sweat, and we would walk them to the stables.

The man and his offer to pay for the pictures haunted me. I wondered about his purpose. I was in the wrong, and it took a lot of courage to address my failings to Russ.

"What do you suppose that man wanted?" I said.

"I don't know. What did he say?" Russ's expression didn't make it any easier.

"Nothing—really," I countered. Russ was giving me the opportunity to explain first. If there was to be trouble, he had to know.

"Do you think he was from the morals committee? He didn't look like a *mutaaw'ah* . . ." I said.

"I doubt it. Besides, why should that matter anyway?"

"He paid the women to let me take pictures, then said he wanted some prints. What if he uses them as proof I took pictures of Muslim women?"

Russ took a long drag on his cigarette. "You didn't agree?"

"Well—yes, I did."

Russ didn't answer.

"I couldn't very well not. He had seen me with the camera in front of those women. That was enough right there."

"You put proof like that in the hands of a government official, and there's nothing to do but sweat out the consequences." Russ wasn't helping my state of mind.

My involuntary tension reacted on Murrawiyyah. She collected herself and started jogging sideways. I swung her around in a circle and caught up with Russ. Zerqa was so even paced, she could walk all day in that odd little foxtrot of hers and beat every other horse to its destination. Did an animal take on the personality of its owner, I wondered?

"What government official?" I asked, reining alongside.

"The Minister of Protocol. The man you're going to give the pictures to." Russ's precise words left no area for doubt.

"How can you know that?"

"He told me. He's from Riyadh to talk with Mandeville about arrangements for a picnic on the beach for the Royal Hareem."

Paul Mandeville was head of Family Housing and had to be contacted regarding special activities that took place in Nejma. After all, supplies were limited, and he controlled how they would be used.

My mind switched gears. Russ's statement left me at once

indignant—and excited. Our own beautiful beach to be turned over to heaven knows how many royal women and children, to say nothing of servants and guards. They would be so close. What were pictures of Bedu compared to this!

"When is all this to take place?" I asked, hoping my voice didn't betray too much interest.

"I didn't ask. He took off in a hurry." Russ said.

Cyndy waited for us to catch up. We always kept the animals together passing the refinery and the bulk plant. Strange that the glare and the whirling of the flare never spooked the horses. We could see several camels lumbering toward the low beach dunes and the clumps of salt grass.

On the flat Sharifa jumped out ahead, and Murrawiyyah followed. As I kept my eyes looking at the ground for any possible soft spots—though we knew every inch of the way by heart—I thought again of the prints I had promised. But, how could I ever deliver them? He didn't know my name. And I didn't know his. What was there to worry about?

Chapter Ten
PICNIC FOR THE ROYAL HAREEM

The click of Mohammed's pruning shears attracted my attention, as I closed the screen door to the front porch and stepped
out into the garden. It was hot. Hotter than I remembered April
to be, and the humidity hung above the street like a cloud.
Even so, Mohammed's blue and gold *qaffiyah* bobbed up and
down on the far side of the jasmine hedge that enclosed our
garden. It was good to see him so industrious, as mid-morning
found most gardeners stretched out in the shade on the cool
dampness of watered lawns, sandals and lunch pails stashed
behind oleander bushes, wet *quttras* spread on mimosa branches
to dry.

Fluffy beds of pink periwinkles lined our front walk. Faith-
fully, though monotonously, these sturdy plants filled our homes
with color long after struggling annuals had failed.

I walked under our jasmine arch—the only one in R.T.—
and turned north along the sidewalk that bordered Persian Gulf
Boulevard. This broad avenue, the only through street in town,
had been constructed originally as an airstrip. With the coming
of additional houses, it was resurfaced but maintained its initial
purpose: to accommodate an airplane should emergency evacu-
ation plans ever need to be executed.

Old timers such as myself, lovingly referred to it as Persian Gulf Boulevard, its original name, refusing to acknowledge the less debatable title, Surf Drive, instated at the time the Persian Gulf was politically renamed the Arabian Gulf.

A narrow alley separated our garden from our neighbor's and led directly to the beach walk. As I approached the alley, Mohammed stopped his clipping and sopped the streaming perspiration from his face with his *quttra* that draped limply about his neck. His smile was as beautiful and open as the gardens he proudly tended.

"*Ya*, Mohammed," I greeted. "*Salaam*."

"Good morning, *memsa'b*," he panted, his tongue licking the salty sweat from his lips. Like most Arabs who worked in our town, Mohammed never used his native language, when the opportunity arose to improve his English.

"How is your family?" I asked.

"Very good—and today—very happy."

"*Alhamdulilah!*" I exclaimed. "But, it is too hot to work so hard."

"No—no! There is much to do."

"There's always tomorrow," I said.

A tight grin twinkled his eyes. "Tomorrow I not work. Tomorrow I take my wife to the hospital." Mohammed's time was pretty much his own.

I bore a close personal feeling for Mohammed and his family who lived in the small village of Safwa, some thirty kilometers distant on the fringe of the vast Qatif Oasis. Two years before I had rescued him from the distasteful estate of a houseboy and set him up in business as a gardener. He was grateful for having been returned to freedom and to the out-of-doors. Russ underwrote his power lawnmower, first one in town, donated a small shed for its storage and doctored its moments of indisposition. He also advanced Mohammed's wedding dowry. I guided him through early marriage days, when he tried to teach his girl bride some of the American ways he had learned as a

houseboy. Seema's childlike simplicity could not understand,
let alone achieve, her husband's goals she had neither experienced nor seen. I still shudder remembering the time she put
the baby in the refrigerator because it was a place that kept
things cool. (Even when they had no electricity.)

"Seema is not ill?" I asked.

KING SAUD ARRIVES FOR THE GYMKHANA

"No, *memsa'b*." Mohammed's face shone even in the shade
of the mimosa that branched out over the alley. "Tomorrow I
take her to get our son."

"Your son?" I could only stare at him. "You told me the
new baby was a girl . . ."

"That's right—a girl . . ." He laughed at my obvious confusion.

And I was confused. Surely he knew the sex of his own child, especially when sons meant so much to an Arab family. There could not have been a mistake. A rivulet of perspiration rolled under Mohammed's chin, down his neck and into the folds of his *quttra*. It was hot just standing there. We lived with heat and the shivering contrast of iced air buildings.

"*Memsa'b*, I didn't tell you . . ." He set the cutters on top of the hedge. "My wife have two babies. One boy. One girl."

"Twins!"

He nodded.

"Why, Mohammed."

"I didn't tell you about the boy," he said. "The doctor keep it at the hospital. I think it die. So we take the girl home." He paused to wipe swelling drops of moisture from along his hairline. There was no change of tone, as he continued. "Now the girl die, and the doctor say to take our son—he is well. And that is how now we have a boy!" He laughed at this joyous turn of fate—of Allah's generosity.

I felt a chill even in the heat. Would I ever understand this land I called home, or reach the families I wished to know? The facts were simple. A child had died. It was not unusual. And Allah had returned a son.

"*Alhamdulilah!*" I offered. "Take good care of him, Mohammed."

"*Inshallah*." He laughed.

This morning I had other things on my mind, as I continued down the alley that connected with the beach walk. Here I turned north for the few short blocks to the home of my friend Frances Richards. None of my neighbors were out, but white suited houseboys swept walks and hung up laundry. Endless sprays of sparkling water fountained over thick lawns from rotating and pulsing sprinklers. Tiny white blossoms peeped through the dense jasmine hedges, scenting the morning air with their sweet fragrance. Brilliant bougainvilleas crept up trellises or entwined their beauty around stark palm spines of *jareed* fences. Not a soul walked the wide white beach, but the sails of *dhows* capped the salty Gulf waters. Pearling season did not begin until late summer, but traders and fishermen plied the Gulf from Kuwait and Basra to Zanzibar and Bombay.

No wonder Ras Tanura was nicknamed "The Resort Town". The broad white beach was our bonus for living on a headland accessible to deep water. The third and last of the original Company towns had been built on a site to accommodate the needs of the refinery and the loading of tankers berthed at terminal piers.

The Persian Gulf coastline offered little difference between land and water. The meeting was a fusion. Shoals fingered through the shallows to form sandbars, as varied by the tides as the wind driven dunes, each a miracle of ever changing patterns in depth and color. The sky over the Gulf was clear, but the horizon above the land mass merged into distant billows of blown sand driven by spring *shamaals*. The headland protected us from the worst of inland dust and sand, but we suffered through unrelenting humidity.

About a mile to the south, the silver storage tanks of the oil Tank Farm reflected the morning glare, and white smoke emitting from tall refinery chimneys went straight up. About half a mile of sand hillocks and coastal dunes separated the oil activities from the residential area of Nejma. This had been designed in the early layout of Ras Tanura to distance residents from any possible fire or explosion at the refinery. At night, leaping flames from the Gas Separator Unit seemed to shut us all in with a wall of fire that spread an orange glow across the southern sky. To the north, tall dunes sitting on the curve of the coastline indicated North Beach, far beyond the confines of Nejma. Our town's northernmost boundary was marked by the Recreation Building, the Senior Staff School and a few *burastis* added as our population increased. A circulating bus traversed the rounds of the houses in less than ten minutes, and the high perimeter fence kept us neatly tucked in.

Between Persian Gulf Boulevard and the sea stretched ten blocks of Nejma's choicest houses with large gardens and direct access to the beach. They were four deep, and one needed seniority points and social standing to acquire one for your family. Most of the "upper crust" lived in this area from the District Manager on down. It was aptly known as the Gold Coast.

There was little friction between residents in general and the privileged few, though one was conscious of an envious social respect. In truth, these older homes were the first built in Nejma with appropriate concerns for the climate. They had overhanging roofs and screened porches plus good insulation. The rest of the town across Surf Drive expanded with comfortable, but lesser units, as oil activities warranted more families. We had "paid our dues" in a section of row houses, and now enjoyed living on the Gold Coast. To me it was a matter of added convenience to bus service, recreation areas, school and, of course, the beach. It also meant my friends were closer. Fran Richards was one of them.

After several years spent in Dhahran, Russ had been assigned to Personnel in Ras Tanura, making us one of the lucky families to escape moving to Abqaiq and the dry heat of the desert, or remaining in Dhahran where all the brass held out. Friendly rivalry grew up between our three communities. Each tried to out do the other in town activities and Company accomplishments. Yet, one community could not survive without the others. We were all part of the extensive operations that produced oil.

Three bulldozers worked along the south shore between Nejma and the refinery. Workmen unloaded trucks and carried rolls of wire and slat fencing onto the beach. "Operation Beach Party" for the royal women was underway. R.T. families had not accepted the event with enthusiasm, when announced by the District Manager. But at least it was a social coup and might be worth bragging about should anyone catch a glimpse of the King's family.

The home of Dick and Frances Richards bordered a few bachelorette apartments and the Executive Guest House that faced the beach. For several weeks, Fran and I had been formulating ideas for a Christmas pageant, which even in the early stages promised to be the most lavish ever attempted. Fran had come from Hollywood, California, the same as I, and we shared mutual friends in the motion picture colony, she in the field of music, and I in production. It was a natural that we combine our talents and produce a Christmas pageant with the school children each year, so that Christmas might be celebrated with some of the traditions we loved and missed.

Such projects had to be commenced months in advance with final execution dependent on concessions from Company officials and assistance of pressured husbands. This morning we planned to meet with Pat Johnston, "artiste", who shared her talents with the schoolroom. Pat had offered to design our set. As I entered Fran's living room, it appeared the morning coffee had deteriorated into areas of complaint and gossip. The subject: "The Royal Picnic".

Fran held the floor.

"Dick says the Company is going all out to make it a big success." Fran's husband was a golfer and picked up more information on "inside" trends on the sand links than the ladies did at their coffees.

"What else—for the King." I said, joining the group in the Chinese decor of Fran's living room.

"Eleanor! We've been waiting for you," Fran greeted. "What ideas have you come up with about how we can see some of the women?" Fran's eyes sparkled with the active roving of her mind.

"Wonder what part of the beach they'll be using," Pat said between nibbles on a slice of date bread.

I sank into Fran's upholstered rocker and took a cup of steaming coffee offered by the houseboy. Rashid knew I liked it hot.

"Bulldozers were working on the south beach as I walked up," I said.

DIGNITARIES ACCOMPANY THE KING TO THE
GYMKHANA

"Wouldn't you know. Just where there aren't any houses for us to get a peek."

"What's to prevent them from walking along the shore—or, for that matter, us?" I said.

"Knife totting guards!" Fran hated to be beaten at her own game. "Eleanor, why don't you ask Russ what's going on, when he comes home for lunch. I'll see what Dick knows. Maybe we can figure out something."

The doorbell rang, and Rashid hurried to answer. Virginia Larsen burst into the room with Helen Crawford close on her heels.

"Been to town yet?" she exploded. Virginia was doubly involved in Fran's and my personal affairs. The wife of the school principal was also a member of our circle of horse owners.

". . . no," I answered. "What's up? We're supposed to be working on the pageant."

"Then—you didn't get your mail?" Helen flushed with indignation. She was president of the Women's Group. Arab culture did not allow the use of the word club.

"Stateside mail so early?" Fran queried. We all knew the twice-weekly deliveries from the United States were not put up until five P.M.

"Local mail," Helen explained. She dropped a manila envelope on my TV tray. Fran picked it up and slipped out a sheet of paper. I leaned over her shoulder for a look at the contents, as Rashid returned with more coffee.

The communication was in the form of a memo addressed to: "All Employees And Their Dependents" over the signature of our District Manager. Along with the official confirmation of the royal event to take place the following day, there were listed a few courtesies we were reminded to observe, as hosts and hostesses of the royal guests. Fran began to read:

> "It is expected, in deference to the nature of our guests, that all American personnel, including the children, will refrain from using the beaches and will make no attempt to observe members of the royal party. The Main Gate will be closed to Americans, and you are asked to stay away from all roadways that give access to the Ras Tanura-Dhahran Road. Guards will be posted along these routes to insure the strictest privacy of the guests. It would be an added courtesy if those homes directly facing the Beach would draw their shutters during the entire day."

That last "request" did it. Frances flung the paper on the

table. "If I want to keep my shutters open, I shall. It's my house!"

"Just who do they think. . . !" Virginia was speechless. "They" always referred to the Company.

I picked up the memo. "Wait. There's more."

> "No houseboys or gardeners will be admitted into the District tomorrow as a precaution in keeping with Muslim tradition."

"Honestly!" Helen gasped.

"We haven't bowed to a king since George the Third!" declared Pat.

"Tomorrow's my big ironing day. I've got to have Ali!" Virginia sounded desperate.

"What's the matter with this Company," Fran said. "Are they Americans or aren't they! It's bad enough to know our husbands bow out backwards to the King. But this. . . !"

"Wait, here's the last line," I said.

> "If there are any questions as to the intent or content of this communication, please discuss the same with the employee member of your family who will then have it clarified by District Management."

"Great! Absolutely great!" Virginia said, her fragile Rosenthal cup teetering dangerously on its saucer.

"Well, after all it is their country," I said, returning the memo to Helen.

She took up the chant. " . . . and if we don't like it, we can . . ."

There was a moment of bristling silence. I broke it.

"Sometimes I think the Company is wholly responsible for acts like this. I can't believe such orders are the wishes of the women—even Muslim women."

"Women!" cried Pat. "Not much in the way of women if

you ask me!"

"Now, Pat, you know that isn't a fair statement," I said. "What would you do if you had to live in purdah?"

"Oh, you always take their side," she muttered.

"We're the ones who are locked up," Virginia said.

"One day things will be different . . ." I said, with optimism.

"And I'll be long gone . . ." Helen added

"Come on," Frances interrupted. "We all know what's expected of us, but sometimes . . ." She reached for a lemon tart and slapped it on her plate. "I can't see what it would hurt just to look at them." A sudden decision brought a gleam to her eyes, and she pushed her chair back to face the kitchen. "Rashid!"

He came in coffeepot in hand.

"Would your wife care if I came to visit her. . . ?"

"I no can say, memsa'b . . ."

Frances pursued. "My American friends come—would your wife come to see me?"

"She afraid. She not know." Then defensively, " . . . she not same as Americans."

"Bring some cream, please, will you, Rashid?" I asked, rescuing him from the barrage.

He escaped into the kitchen.

"Am I going to give Carlos a bad time," declared Pat. "Why don't we all? They're making us a laughing stock, and I resent it."

Yes. I intended to bring the subject up with Russ, but not in that vein. Memory flashed the image of a young Princess straining at the bonds of tradition. Did other Arab families feel the same way?

In the beginning, living in Saudi Arabia was an adventure, a movie in the making far from the back lot. The final "cut" left an emptiness and a gnawing need to share a relationship beyond perimeter fences and Islamic Law. Could Russ accept my viewpoint in wanting to catch even a glimpse of the Royal women? Not really, for he was bound to enforce the Company's position.

Could he recognize that the Princess in Hufuf was little different from his own daughters—a classmate—a budding friendship—the voice of youth asking to be heard above centuries of custom? And I wanted to respond.

"Look—I'm late for a committee meeting. Thanks for the coffee," Helen said, downing a final swallow. "Coming, Virginia?"

Things quieted down after they left, but I was in no mood to get back to the Christmas project. "Got to go, Fran," I said. "Need anything from the Commissary?" That was our one and only market, formerly known as the Family Issue Store. How we joked about that.

"No, thanks," Fran said. To the kitchen, "Rashid, call a taxi!"

I gathered up the few papers I had brought and waited until the sound of a horn announced the taxi's arrival. It was our one luxury. Immediate needs were satisfied by a local business enterprise, and taxis quickly transported us anywhere in camp we wanted to go for one *riyal*.

"Phone you later . . ." I said, as Rashid escorted me to the door.

Chapter Eleven

THE ELUSIVE VEIL

Shopping at the commissary was as much a social activity as attending morning coffees. Here the local news was gathered and spread, impending food controls and medical changes debated, and newly returned long vacationers caught up on activities missed during their absence. Here I received my Arabic lessons from Hassan, cashier on the No. 3 IBM. Not since celery shortages threatened the Christmas stuffing had the commissary been in the uproar that greeted me on this day.

The center of dissent seemed to be the refrigerator section against the north wall. Here a group of angry ladies demanded explanations of Paul Mandeville, the American supervisor of Housing and Personal Services.

"Why must you take all our supplies?" cried one of the women. "Why don't you get some from Dhahran and Abqaiq?"

"It'll take six months before any more frozen milk comes in . . ." declared another.

"Now, ladies," Mr. Mandaville began. "I assure you the commissary will be restocked as soon as possible." Paul had faced similar situations before and remained calm though unrelenting. His words were a stick in the hornet's nest.

"The next reefer isn't due for three months!" complained

my neighbor Sally Scheel. (We were well informed.)

"The Company has flown in shortages before," Paul faced his accusers unruffled.

And it was true. I well remembered the year Swissair dumped ARAMCO's shipment of chocolate eggs and marshmallow Easter bunnies in Jeddah. Families made such a fuss over no goodies for the children's Easter egg hunts, that ARAMCO sent a private plane to pick up the cargo and meet the deadline.

"What's all the fuss?" I asked Sally. She pointed to the freezer on the left.

I shoved my way to the frozen milk bin. It was empty. Above the bin and stuck to the shelf between the cheeses and the frozen vegetables was a sign: NO FROZEN MILK UNTIL FURTHER NOTICE. I stared at the empty bin. Frozen milk from Holland was an every day staple. My mind raced to review the number of cans I had stashed away in my own freezer—a two-week supply at the most. Why the sudden shortage? I noted that a similar sign was placed at the soft drink locker and another displayed above the shelf of boxed cookies.

"Why do we have to give all our supplies to the King's women?" an irate voice lamented. "The King brings everything else—why not food supplies?"

"Now, ladies," Mr. Mandaville said, trying to dampen the fury. "If you'll just quiet down and think this situation over, I'm sure you'll look at it differently."

We didn't have to think it over. We had faced the answer many times. ARAMCO was an oil company. Involvement in community affairs occurred only during times of emergency. Oil production came first. The King was oil. The King's interests came first. The picnic for the Royal Ladies demanded more of our small community than depriving us of our beach.

"So, the kids will drink orange juice and like it," I said, ignoring the fact we did have powdered milk though inhabited by weevils.

I picked up a few items and headed for No. 3. Here was

another test for the strength of the loom we were weaving on: a ragged hole to be fluffed over in time—nevertheless, a weakening flaw. Why did we have to give so much to the Company project? These Arab women were no more important to oil operations than we were. In fact, they were less! Weren't our husbands providing all the know how? You couldn't look at it that way. Those expatriates who did found no happiness in Arabia. They had to leave. I was not ready to do that.

"Very bad, *memsa'b*," Hassan said, as he checked my purchases.

"We've been without milk before," I replied.

"That's right! That's right!" Hassan agreed.

"Besides, who buys packaged cookies anyway? The kids fill up on homemade ones."

Hassan laughed. He didn't understand American women, but he was trying. He lapsed into Arabic. "*Memsa'b*, you need milk—you tell Hassan. I bring you much camel milk. Very good! Make children strong!" Hassan was small—a hunchback—but his heart beat as big as his grin.

I counted out the heavy silver *riyals* from a small leather pouch and gave them to him. Although Saudi Arabia's first soft bills were becoming increasingly available to ordinary citizens, I sometimes used up my store of hard *riyals* to buy groceries. Approximately the size of our U.S. silver dollar, the *riyal* exchanged to twenty-eight cents. We needed a leather pouch to carry them all.

The cash register belled open. Hassan handed me a few *quersh* pieces in change, and I dropped them into my purse.

"Thanks, Hassan," I said. "I'll let you know about the milk. *Shukran jazeelan (thank you)*."

"You just ask Hassan . . ."

"*Fiamanillah . . .*" I picked up the filled paper sack and headed for the exit door. From past experience, I supported the bottom of the sack with my hand, not wanting to chase after scattered groceries, if the glue pasting the sack together didn't hold.

One of the clerks from the main office waited for me by the exit door. "Hello, Ali," I said. "How's the new baby?"

"Oh—very good. Very good."

Ali wore western clothes and emulated American culture wherever possible. He had gone through the ARAMCO training program, and instructors considered him material for advancement. He spoke excellent English.

"Tell me, Mrs. Nicholson," he continued in his soft voice. "Would it be okay to feed the baby some of the foods in the commissary?"

"You mean the Gerber jars of fruits and vegetables?"

"Yes."

"Indeed, Ali. That would be fine." I said.

"Which should I try first?"

"The strained bananas or applesauce. Just a little at first. Ali," I cautioned. "And have patience. Some babies don't take to new foods right away."

"I understand," he assured me.

I felt warm personal concerns for friends such as Ali and his family. He could see the benefits and comforts in the way Americans lived and faced the gradual change in his own family life with courage and belief in the future. To these young Saudis, who worked in our town, we became mother and father figures and received the respect and duty Arab sons showed to their parents. A knock on my back door often came with a gift of live chickens, a brilliant scarf or some Gulf shrimp tied in a cloth.

"Mrs. Nicholson—you need some chocolate cookies? I have saved a box in my desk. I know Cyndy likes chocolate cookies . . ." Ali's face beamed.

"Thank you, Ali," I said "You take them home. Cyndy eats too many sweets."

He reached for my bag to carry it to the waiting taxi. "My

wife thanks you for the little shoes," he said, as he opened the door. "She keeps putting them on and taking them off the baby."

It had been a small gift from my supply on the bedroom shelf: a baby's first pair of shoes, coming of age at three months. Linda didn't have that, when we took her home to the States on our first long vacation. She had diapers from a friend who never became pregnant, a secondhand undershirt from a neighbor, and a pretty dress I'd sewn for her. But no shoes! How could she go home without shoes? She had her first pair in Istanbul, Turkey, our initial stop. They were soft white leather, ankle height and laced up the sides. How I loved to put them on her. Did Ali's wife have similar feelings?

I had never met her, just as I had never seen Seema. They were my friends, and I was beginning to know them—enough to want to know more, to feel I would be welcome in their society.

I blessed Ahmed, when I returned home just ahead of Russ and found lunch on the table. Linda was late from school as usual, too busy catching up on doings with her classmates. Cyndy was well into her sandwich and jiggling to get back for band practice. School children were involved in the first Tri-District-County-Fair, and Cyndy played the piccolo in the Ras Tanura Blue Devil Band.

When Russ came in, I brought up the subject of the commissary shelves depleted for the royal picnic. He already knew. He knew everything that went on inside our town. He offered little sympathy, other than to accept the situation as a fact of life and to quit chewing on it.

He spent that evening with the District Manager, safeguarding the Company's position with respect to the royal invasion, and drawing up directives for the morning. About eight PM Fran came over. Dick had gone to the meeting with Russ. We must have been on the same wavelength, for without preliminaries we began to formulate plans of our own. Virginia had been right. We were the ones locked in and needed to exercise a *soupcon* of defiance to protect our human rights.

Why couldn't we take just a peek at this royal family? I had seen the Queen of England ride to Parliament in her coach of gold, and watched the Queen of Greece ascend the stairs to the Four Seasons Hotel on her visit to Munich. We had been asked to give up our room at the hotel, that the Queen might enjoy the privacy of the entire floor. Muslim law allowed none of this. So it seemed. It shut out the world. Or, was it "they" who cast restrictions on us?

What Fran couldn't think of, I did.

My plans for the day included using the car, so the following morning I drove Russ to work. If he suspected anything, he didn't mention it. His look of warning should have been deterrent enough.

Actually, I couldn't go outside the Main Gate with the car. Women of Arabia did not drive automobiles. However, the Saudi government granted American women the right to drive the few confined blocks within District compounds. To make us all legal, we were granted a Saudi driver's license, provided we produced a valid Stateside license and passed the eye test.

Ras Tanura's very limited commercial area outside the Nejma boundary consisted of the impressive Administration Building for ARAMCO Senior Staff personnel, the maintenance and shops center, a combined laundry station, canteen and mailroom, an oil chemistry lab, transportation and reclamation yards, a fire station and the all important commissary. A long row of small bunk houses, known as the sheepsheds—former bachelor housing and clinic until new ones were built—now housed a hobby shop, women's exchange (clothes, not ladies), and at one end a prayer shelter for the many Muslim employees. I squeezed in a Christian Sunday School open to any Nejma child who wished to attend.

Between the Paint Shop and the Storehouse, a narrow receiving alley paralleled the Dhahran-Ras Tanura road just before the Main Gate. It could be reached by way of the commissary unloading zone. Sometimes it was possible to park a car there, though shoppers preferred to hire a taxi and have the Saudi driver load and unload the groceries.

As previously arranged, Fran came over about ten AM, and we drove to the Paint Shop—legitimately armed with an order for fencing paint. I had never filled it, but planned to do so now. The shops area was strangely quiet. All male employees had been given the day off, and the usual hubbub of men and machines was missing. The paint order served as an excuse for our presence should anyone be around. We were in the area for one thing: to watch the main road and the arrival of royal cars. I parked the Rover in front of the Paint Shop receiving door. The way seemed clear, so we got out. Behind the building, shadows of slowing black limousines flickered through the budding oleanders against the cyclone fence bordering the Dhahran-Ras Tanura road.

"They're here!" Fran cried. "I'm going ahead." She hurried toward the fence.

"Just a minute . . ." a male voice called, and John Cochran, one of the Personnel Department employees assigned to guard duty for the day, emerged from the storehouse inspection cubicle. "Sorry. You'll have to go back," he said, gesturing to Fran.

"I'd like to fill this paint order," I interjected. "Here's my chitty." A chitty being any scrap of paper with notations of information or clearance. I always wrote one for Ahmed to go to the clinic, or for Mohammed to take home items I gave him for his family. It took the place of a formal pass.

"There's no one here today. You'll have to come back tomorrow," John said. He took the piece of paper I offered him and put it in his pocket.

Fran made a move, itching for a better look at the cars as they trickled past. John blocked her way.

"I must ask you to leave," he said. Then, pointedly to me,

"You ladies know better than to come here today."

Fran retreated with a little waltz step, eyes suddenly damp with disappointment. "Can't we take just a little peek?" She could usually sweet talk her way into anything.

"Sorry . . ." He raised the walkie-talkie.

I knew who would be on the other end. "Come on, Fran," I said. "Let's go."

We drove to the front of the commissary. "Could you see anything?" I asked her.

"Not a thing—except the drivers—all soldiers. The windows were hung with black veils."

Russ would hear about this episode, I knew. Being a people person, he handled family problems. This meant wives, bachelorettes and children. I'd already stepped out of line, but I was determined not to retreat. It seemed such a little thing, and nobody would be compromised, least of all the ladies. Didn't we deserve a moment of excitement in all the sameness of our days?

Hastily erected wire and slat fences now bordered the road leading to the commercial area, which included the sheepsheds and the car roadway to the beach. Only the way to Nejma remained open. ARAMCO officials stood guard at the required access to the refinery and tank farm. We could see the limousines continuing toward the beach, but were too far away for an intimate look.

"They really meant to keep us out, didn't they?" Fran commented.

There it was, "they" again and enough of an irritant to spark retaliation. The sun glistening on the car windows, as they passed, dared us to penetrate the veils blocking even a silhouette of the occupants. It reminded me of a cortege of hearses, but was far from being a funeral procession. Arab soldiers riding dark green armored jeeps dashed up and down the route. Green flags bearing the Al Saud family crest fluttered from the front

THE NICHOLSON HOME, 2704 PERSIAN GULF
BOULEVARD, RAS TANURA

fenders. The rev of motors, the whine of tires making the turn
through the Main Gate, the blare of the intercom from the com-
munications center across the street flashed a warning and an
invitation.

"Look," I said to Fran, with sudden inspiration. "I've got
an idea. Are you game to walk a ways?"

"Anything. What've you got in mind?"

"You'll see . . ."

Even as I spoke, an official stationed in front of the commissary waved us back to Nejma. I drove the Rover to the open area that separated Nejma from the business district and refinery and turned down an abandoned dirt road that formerly gave access to the sheepsheds. I eased the car behind a clump of half buried palm trunks. To reach the beach we would have to scramble a quarter mile through low sand hills and dense patches of salt grass. It was familiar territory, since we rode the horses through on breakfast rides from Italian Camp to the Surf House Recreation Building.

"Oh, you . . ." Fran said, appreciating my intent. She started ahead, keeping a lookout for possible patrols and surveying the sand slopes and gulleys with the air of a conspirator. She seemed to interpret our actions as being ingenious and daring, though in truth they expressed motivation: the natural resistance to restraint, and the grasping of an opportunity—golden or not.

"Remember Murrawiyyah's saddle strap I lost last week? Well, I'm looking for it . . ." I said in answer to her concern about patrols.

We struggled up and down the sand hillocks, until sweaty and puffing we crawled atop the shore dunes. Success in our venture became the pure turquoise waters of the Gulf, slipping in to meet the wide sandy shore dotted with exotic shells we collected with pride. A few gulls strutted the beach, ignoring the picnic area some distance to our right. Careful to remain prone, we settled on this gallery view of the activities.

Soldiers stood guard along a hastily erected sand fence that enclosed the picnic area. Limousines appeared to be parked at all angles, blocking the forward maneuvering of late arriving vehicles. Impatient drivers leaned on car horns, adding ear-splitting noise to the tangle of servants and bodyguards trying to get through. Red ARAMCO service trucks loaded with provisions formed a barrier to the south. On the north stood a series of construction outhouses, discreetly veiled with black tenting. A portable boardwalk unrolled from the road to the water's edge provided easy access to the sea and to the silken pavilions flying Royal Banners of green and silver.

Curls of steam circled above huge cauldrons, testifying to the roasting of whole sheep since early morning. Much of the scene was not new to me. Russ and I had been invited to join a "first" in Arab hospitality. The Amir of Rahima had prepared an official banquet on the shore of nearby Tarut Bay for a few Nejma families. The women attending had been all Americans, yet it was an untraditional mixing of the sexes at a social function. Muslim women did not participate.

Now, distant female figures swarmed over the beach. There must have been two hundred of them. Children frolicked in the calm Gulf waters, while their older sisters struggled with sopping clothes and head coverings. What a treat from the desert locked city of Riyadh. Now and again we caught sight of brilliant color beneath black robes, as women visited between the pavilions. Some of the participants consisted of slaves and servants responding to the demands of a mistress or racing to collect small children.

A picture evolved from the scene, one my mind sought to develop ever since Linda emerged from the Palace in Hufuf. In the visual reality of her story, I wondered which of the figures along the water's edge might belong to the Al Abdullah branch of the Al Saud family.

It was not for me to know. At least, not this way. The dignity with which the young Amsha sought release from tradition, relegated my crouching on a sandhill to the antics of the ridiculous. Besides, Fran and I were pretty uncomfortable, knees scraping against sharp shell fragments and coarse sand, as we braced ourselves to keep from sliding down the slopes.

"Guess it wasn't such a great idea after all," I said, as we trudged back to the car.

The girls were waiting for lunch when I got home, their father due to arrive any minute.

"Linda, Ahmed's not here," I said, hurrying down the hall. "Get some peanut butter sandwiches going, will you?"

Our youngest followed after me, munching on a brownie. "Where ya been? The commissary? Any comics?" Lately, comic books had been included in the spasmodic arrival of Stateside magazines.

I dashed into the small bathroom, the warmest place in the house.

"Did you see any cars?" Cyndy called through the closed door.

"What cars?" I hoped I sounded disinterested.

"Jimmy Mulley said he went back of the Clinic and saw a whole lot of cars on the R.T. road—just like the King's entourage."

"Well, he shouldn't have done that," I said, shouting above the rush of water from the showerhead.

"I told him I had seen a Princess, but he didn't believe me."

"Can't hear you . . ." I sang through the rising steam.

There was a loud rap on the door. "Can I wash my hands?"

"Okay, come in . . ."

"How come you're taking a shower now?" Cyndy asked.

"Yes—how come?" echoed a male voice.

Russ! I had made it, but barely.

"How long are you going to be?" he asked.

"Maybe ten minutes."

"Then I'll go ahead and eat. Got to get right back."

"Anything wrong?"

"No . . ." he answered. " . . . but I'm the emergency clearing house."

There was a pause, and I thought he had gone until he added, "Be quick. I'd like to talk to you."

The soap slipped through my fingers and scooted toward the drain. I scooped it up and got a mouthful of hot salt water. Russ did not care to veer from Company instructions not to jury-rig sweet water—the supply was limited—into showers and washing machines.

What did he want to talk about, I wondered, my guilty conscience sopping up heat hotter than the bath? What did he know? Anyway, what could they do? Russ had finished making two sandwiches, and the girls were in the yard playing with the cat, when I sat down at the table.

"What ya been doing?" he asked, too casually.

"Not much." I hoped my voice sounded bored. "Went to the commissary with Fran. There was supposed to be fresh produce from Asmara today."

He looked up. "Today? Friday? The Asmara milkrun is always Sunday.."

"We heard a rumor about bringing in extra supplies because of the King's visit."

"You women get the darndest rumors." He pulled a slip of paper from his shirt pocket behind the clip of his gold pencil and handed it to me. "This belong to you?"

The folded paper was limp and damply grey. I knew what it was. John Cochran must have given it to him. I couldn't carry pretense any longer. Russ read people too well, and my silence said enough. The look in his eyes was firm, but his voice gentle.

"I'm warning you. Stay away from those women. We're not playing games."

And this I fully intended to do. Except—Fran phoned about two o'clock.

Chapter Twelve
THE VEIL EXPOSED

The girls were at school, and the house was quiet. I started to write a letter to my family in California, detailing a rundown of the day's happenings, adding a few embellishments of my own. The events appeared even better. The ringing phone startled me.

"Eleanor! Come on over—fast." Frances sounded excited.

"Well—I . . ."

"Quick! I can't tell you on the phone. Walk—don't call a taxi." She started to ring off, then added, " . . . and bring your camera."

Frances lived directly behind the Company Guest House, a beautifully decorated home reserved for "big-wig" visitors to our refinery town. Other than Dhahran's pretentious Guest House, the only local provincial hotel was a kind of fleabag at the airport. Foreign visitors came to Saudi Arabia's Eastern Province under the auspices of ARAMCO, or not at all.

I hurried along Persian Gulf Boulevard and saw Frances standing near her front door, garden hose in hand, watering an already soaked frangipani tree. She turned off the hose bib and dragged me inside. Her house was colder than mine, and I reached for an embroidered Indian shawl on the polished Kuwait chest in the hall. She led me across the living room, with its deep pile Chinese rug, to the dining room windows.

"Be quiet and keep down," Fran whispered.

Through the slats of the dropped Venetian blinds, I could see the ten foot high block wall that rimmed the gardens of the Guest House. The alley held several parked limousines, their window veils limp and partly drawn. The cars were empty, but drivers sat against the wall in the shade of overhanging eucalyptus branches. An armed guard stood on either side of a solid door that led to the garden. Curved knives at their belts formed threatening crescents from thigh to shoulder. Ceremonial weapons they might be, but fearsome enough to cast doubt in the bravest heart.

"Look . . ." Fran said, barely able to contain herself. "There are a lot of women and children in there."

She didn't need to tell me. The picture was quite clear, but I had given a silent promise to Russ—almost.

"Bet they'd invite us in, if we could get to them."

"Count me out, Fran," I said. "I'm not tangling with them." I nodded toward the guards.

"Oh, they're nothing!" Fran's tone was blithe. "We can get around them."

"How?"

"That's why I called you over. Think of something . . ."

I just stared at her. She rushed to rally my interest with fast words.

"I saw them get out of the cars. The children—so sweet— such beautiful dresses and gold bracelets—lovely smiles and expressive eyes. What an opportunity for a real photographer like you!"

ARAMCO's one and a half hour lunch periods produced beautiful babies, and there were no professional photographers to satisfy proud parents. Expanding my lighting skills, processing techniques and Hollywood showmanship brought every child in town to sit for my camera. I soon won acclaim as a portrait photographer, and parents brought their children for a sitting from Dhahran and Abqaiq. Frances knew this and played on my weakness.

"Imagine getting pictures of—them!" Fran added.

How could I drop her challenge? On occasion I took pictures of Arab children in Al Khobar, when we went to the *suq* for shopping. It was perfectly legal to do so. In fact, Muslim law spawned a strange philosophy, at least, strange to westerners. The crime was not committing an illegal act, but in getting caught.

"When will they ever be so close again." Fran pursued my indecision. "We're practically right on top of them."

The opportunity ranged beyond a rational decision. Could I give it up? I led the way to the kitchen. The shade was drawn, but potted plants on the windowsill above the sink presented protection enough. I had been here many times and knew her home, as I knew my own.

We went out the back door. A second alley on the far side of Fran's home, plus a high jasmine hedge and more trees, insured privacy from a row of bachelorette apartments. I ducked under the clothesline, side stepping a muddy pool near the trunks of young eucalyptus trees. Their branches dripped down over the Richard's patio roof. The dense foliage formed a natural screen between Fran's house and the Guest House.

Light laughter filtered over the wall from the garden on the other side. I passed Fran the Hasselblad, then gazed at the patio roof.

"Do you think it will hold me?" I asked.

"Oh, sure," she encouraged, eyes gleaming. " . . . but you know the local carpenters."

It was worth a chance. With an assist from the charcoal storage bin and a strategically placed branch, I made it on to the roof. The plastic sheets creaked but held.

"What can you see?" Fran asked, standing on tip toes to hand me the camera. I hesitated, torn between a stab of conscience and desire, then reached for it and hung it about my neck.

I worked my way through the branches to the edge of the roof. It almost abutted the Guest House wall. Dense clusters of leaves concealed my presence from anyone in the alley, but I felt close to suffocating from the thick dust, damp and clinging after the morning's humidity. The cadence of spirited voices became a temptation more tantalizing than forbidden fruit. I noticed the children first.

The face of a child, tightly framed in its sequined hood, diffused the mirage that had danced hauntingly beyond my grasp, the mystery of its ancestry exposed as humankind, no different from my own daughter.

The laws of isolation and tabu, the locked entryway through walls built of centuries of survival, the rush of desert *shamaals,* the flight of sound from the muezzin's minaret, the desert's loneliness were all there as I gazed into the forbidden garden. They cried out at my transgression of privacy, yet enhanced the call of human need for knowledge and for recognition of a relationship.

The children laughed and played among themselves, as do children everywhere. The girls' full-length cotton dresses in festive colors challenged the gardener's pride of blossoms, transferred to little hands for the joy of ownership. Older children, in laces and sashes, made a pretense of reaching the top of the wall facing the sea, to be shooed away by watchful guardians. Several ladies stood on the patio. They wore neither masks nor veils, their security in privacy expunging the frightened timidity of village women, seeking a shadow in which to hide. Scheherazade must have envisioned such a scene, delighting the Sultan, as well as me. I could not let the magic pass. It became a record of my camera—by whose hand is hard to say—perhaps, "*Qismat Allah!*"—the luck of God.

Temptation led me to lean farther out to catch the joy of a little girl laughing at a bed of pink periwinkles. She looked up, then ran to the women and pointed—at me. It was a mere second of exposure, one that the child alone could have seen, or sensed the movement of branches, as I retreated. But, it was enough to alert the servants. With shouts and high pitched cries, they herded everyone indoors. The leaves enveloped me, but I dared not move. A young girl ran to the wall directly below my perch and gazed at the eucalyptus screen.

"Hello!" she called.

I held my breath.

"Hello . . ." she called again. The inflection was English.

Two maids urged her to go inside. Then, hidden by the leaves, I crawled back the way I had come.

Fran jumped at me. "What happened?"

I scrambled to the ground, aware how my heart pounded. "They saw me."

We hurried into the house. I set the camera on the kitchen table and took a deep breath. From the dining room window we scanned the alley, expecting the worst. An African servant conversed excitedly with the guards. She pointed to the Richard's house. The guards moved out to search the area.

Fran followed their progress through the living room window. "They're standing staring at the house," she said. "One has moved on down the walk. Hopefully, they'll just go away." She came over to me. "What'd you get?"

"Some good ones, I think." I sank into my favorite chair, knowing the images on the film could never equal the moment of exposure. My concerns did not relate to stirring up a ruckus capable of involving the King, the Governor, the Company and, worst of all, our respective husbands. What did bother me was the slice of life I had stolen from a child in an embroidered hood.

"Looks like they mean business," Fran said.

She was right. The situation had become an urgency to be resolved, a line of dominoes to be stopped before the first one fell. I made a quick decision.

"Get me your camera, and hurry."

Fingers shaking, I removed the film from Fran's Rollei and set it on the table.

"Hey, I want that," Fran said with some surprise. She picked up the roll and dropped it into her camera bag.

"Got a new one?" I asked.

"Well . . . maybe. Why?"

"You'll see—and hurry."

I inserted the new roll in her Rollei, quickly brushed the worst of the dust from my clothes and hair and motioned Fran to follow me out the front door. I posed her for a picture in front of the frangipani and against the trellis of scarlet bougainvillea. She managed a forced smile, aware of the guards watching. I felt secure in the knowledge they would not accost an American woman. The husband was the responsible party. They had no authority within our compounds. But they could stir up a lot of trouble.

Fran was not sure of my actions, but went along with the assumption we would soon be relieved of our guilt. "Let me take one of you," she said.

"Don't press the release," I cautioned, passing her the Rollei. I beamed a big smile into the lens, right in front of the guard.

My Arabic greeting elicited no response—at least, not vocal. He took a step forward, extending a broad calloused hand, long scar slicing the palm. Ominous, but the reaction I had expected. With unwilling compliance, I wound off the roll and handed it to him.

"Why?" I asked.

"*Laaszim!*" (it is ordered) he said.

Somehow, I knew he wouldn't buy this masquerade. I didn't wait to find out, but hurried back into the house.

"What did you do that for?" Fran said. "Now he'll know we are the guilty ones."

"He knew," I said. "That's pretty obvious. Don't underestimate the Saudis."

"You practically told him we're guilty," Fran chided.

"No. I just let him think so. Anyway, we are, aren't we? I wanted him to think he had caught the culprit by giving him the film he asked for. He hasn't lost face by failing to protect the *hareem*, because he's got the evidence."

"Say—you're pretty slick."

"I'm not proud of my stupidity. I hope he's satisfied, and to save himself, won't spread the word any further. But, don't count on it."

"We can deny everything!" Fran said, thereby solving all our problems.

"No more tricks, Fran," I said. "Whatever happens, we've got to play it straight."

The blow fell that evening. Russ returned from work late. His walk, and the set of his head announced trouble. The District Manager had summoned him to run a spool of film delivered to the Government Relations people by a royal guard, and suspect of containing shots of the Royal H*areem*. The lab was shut down for the day. In any event, Saudi employees would be out-of-bounds, should Muslim women be involved. Russ had been asked to run the film. It turned out to be blank.

"That ought to prove something," I said, feeling relieved that my strategy had worked.

"Not exactly," Russ explained. "Why give an empty spool to a guard, unless there's something to hide?"

The District Manager would not risk the existence of a roll of film that might come to the attention of the Governor and the King. He assigned Russ to quietly investigate and to come up with an answer before midnight. He would not be home all evening. He was not interested in the identity of the offender, and no questions would be asked, provided the film showed up on his front porch by midnight. Otherwise. . . !

"What do you know about it?" His direct gaze bored through me. I needed time to think—to come up with a way to protect Fran, myself, Russ's integrity and the ladies of the Royal *Hareem*.

"Look," I said. " . . . nobody's eaten. Let's discuss it after dinner." There would be plenty of time to meet the deadline after the girls went to bed.

"Haven't got time," he said, as he hurried to the bedroom. "Pour me a glass of milk. I've got to start the ball rolling in the right places."

The stroganoff steamed under its lid, and the rice had been warming for a long time. I served two plates for the girls, then set some cookies out with a glass of milk.

"You could finish dinner in the time it takes to eat these," I said, as Russ returned and downed half the milk.

"By the way," he said. "Doesn't your friend Frances live next door to the Guest House?"

He knew she did. He and Dick not only worked together but were great friends.

"Phone her. See what she knows . . ." He opened the front door. "I'll be back in an hour with this thing all wrapped up—I hope."

So—he was going to leave it up to me.

Frances rang my phone before I could call her. "Did you hear?"

"Fran, hold on . . ." I said. There was no need to get the girls involved, so I took Russ's emergency phone in the bedroom. "I'm going to turn my roll in," I said.

"No! Don't be foolish. Nobody can pin it on us."

"You—don't know—Russ." I tried to sound emphatic.

Fran answered with a moment of silence.

"Look . . ." I addressed the phone. "I'm not going to tangle with Al Abdullah. Russ's job and his reputation are worth a lot more than how I feel."

"Is Russ there?"

"No . . ."

"I'm coming over. Don't do anything until I get there."

"You're not going to make me change my mind, Fran," I said.

THE U.S.S. LAFFEY TIES UP AT TERMINAL PIER,
RASTANURA

"Promise?" She hung up.

I opened the front door to her knock a few minutes later. She had a roll of Kodak film in her hand. It was to be a substitute for mine.

"You can't fool anyone with that," I said. "It's got to be my roll. I took the pictures."

"Not all of them," Fran said. "There's some on here of the cars driving up the alley, and a couple of some girls, as they got out. I snapped them before you came."

"It won't work."

"Why not? The pictures won't be any good, but women in *abbayas* might show up."

I hesitated enough for her to pursue.

"You've got to keep yours. There'll never be another chance."

I set my roll on the table next to hers. They were identical, except for a slight difference in the size of the spool.

"You swear this is the roll?" I asked.

"I swear it!"

"And there could be women on it?"

"Yes, but kinda blurry. I did it in a hurry through the window."

"Well—maybe . . ."

"Of course it's okay." Fran urged me on, overjoyed at my show of capitulation. "Who's going to know what pictures we took?"

I went to the bedroom closet and removed a pair of Italian sandals from a plain white box and set them on the storage shelf. They were labeled to be worn next summer. We always bought personal supplies two years in advance, not knowing what our circumstances might be. I returned to the living room with the box and some cotton wool and wrapped the padding around a roll of film—my roll. I didn't think Fran was that much of a technician to notice the difference. There wasn't enough cotton batting to fill the box and keep the contents from rattling when set on the manager's porch—in case anyone should be home. I returned to the bedroom and searched through my sewing drawer for scraps of fabric from a skirt I had just finished.

"Don't use those," Fran said, as I stuffed the scraps into the shoebox. "They'll be traced to you."

"Well—it's not all that important."

Fran didn't agree. "A lot of people respect you and Russ. That's what makes him so effective. I got you into this, and I'm going to take the responsibility." She went into the bathroom and came back giggling, some thick white pads in her hand. "Here!"

"Fran! Not—that!"

"Why not? They're female." She pulled out the scraps of cloth, stuffed the pads around to fill the box and put on the lid. "That'll do it. Imagine the manager's face, when he opens it."

We had a good laugh and agreed Russ should deliver the package. He asked no questions, when we gave it to him, and Fran waited until he returned after the delivery.

"Well—so much for that," he said.

"Thanks, Russ," Fran said, giving him a hug. "I'm sorry for all the trouble. Well—no, I'm not. I wanted those pictures, even if they're not any good." She laughed that little nervous laugh of hers, and I walked her as far as our jasmine arch.

"I'm glad that's over with," I said.

She agreed, then: "Except for this . . ." She held out a roll of film—my roll.

"Fran!"

"I can switch as well as you," she said, enjoying her contra coup. "Hang on to it. You owe me prints." The night flare cast an orange glow on her back, as she walked home along Persian Gulf Boulevard.

Russ called from the front porch. "Let's eat. I'm famished."

I had barely cleared the dinner dishes, when the phone rang. It was exactly twelve midnight. Russ answered, then dashed out of the house, saying he'd be back shortly and not to wait up. I waited. There was nothing reassuring about his entrance, when he returned and set up trays in the trunk room, once converted into a nursery Cyndy had outgrown and now the darkroom.

"Get some ice for these trays, will you?" He thrust a Nikor tank at me.

"Now?"

"I have to process this roll by morning."

"Tonight?" I was stunned.

" . . . one print of each negative by seven AM."

I went into the kitchen and returned with the ice. The District Manager was taking no chances about having the correct film.

"Let me help," I said, fearful of what, if anything, might be on Fran's roll.

"No sense you staying up, too. It won't make it go any faster."

He was right. Running the film was a one-man job. He shut the darkroom door.

" . . . light, you know." I stood in the hall listening to the rattle of spool and reel, as he loaded the tank in the dark.

"Russ—what if Fran really didn't get anything?"

"Will you go to bed, and let me do this?" I heard a clatter of metal objects, and something fell to the floor. "Damn!"

"What's the matter?"

"Where did you put the thermometer?"

"It's in the pencil jar beside the enlarger. Sure I can't help?"

"I'm sure. Go to bed."

Sounds from the darkroom kept me awake for a long time— along with my conscience. The Company really meant business. They always did in matters involving our host country. It wasn't easy for American businessmen to maintain an unpredictable balance between the needs of American and Arab employees. Restraint was the key to good relations, and the Company's own survival. Employees, dependents, as well as children, were expected to follow all directives from the president.

Somewhere in the confusion of guilt, anxiety and the realization of the utter harmlessness of the episode, I fell asleep. My dreams were accompanied by the ululations of Arab women, their innocence done in by my Hasselblad.

The sun streamed in through the kitchen window, even though the alarm had gone off a few minutes before five AM. Small photographic prints swam face down in a tray of water. I set the tray under the tap and let the sweet water run. Our principal water source was too salty for photographic purposes. The prints turned in the agitation. One by one I picked them up: a blurred shot of moving cars, a guard bent over opening a door, a fuzz of black robes through a gate, two young girls, veils half lifted, facing the camera with an out-of-focus smile. The rest consisted of kids and horses at the Ranch. All twenty-four exposures were accounted for.

I set breakfast on the table and awakened Russ. When I returned, Linda was at the sink bending over the tray.

"Hey, that's neat," she exclaimed. "Old Bedawaiyyah is sure running." Bedawaiyyah was Fran's white mare.

"Sit down and eat your breakfast," I said. "The eggs will be cold."

"Mom, who's this?"

"Can't look now—one of the horses . . ."

"No, I mean this one—the Arab girls." Linda lifted a print from the tray for a closer view. She turned toward me, her excitement causing the print to drip water on the kitchen floor. "Mom! It's Fahada! Sure it is. Where'd you get it?"

"Put those down. They belong to your father. And eat your breakfast." There was no reason to snap—just tired, I guessed.

I poured myself a cup of coffee. Fahada . . . The Princess from Hufuf. How could Linda be so sure? Did she call "hello" as I scrambled back off Fran's roof? Russ would turn the picture in, and if the Amir learned of it, Fahada would be clamped in an ever-tightening security.

"Do you think she might visit us?" Linda said. "I asked her to."

"No—no, I don't think so," I answered, realizing my foolishness, my over eager act of trying to penetrate Muslim tradition, had served only to draw the veil closer. "The Prince would never allow it now . . ."

Chapter Thirteen
THE LETTER

Two days following the picnic on the Ras Tanura beach, the Royal Hareem returned to Riyadh. The King remained another few days with the Governor in Dammam. He continued his open *mejlis* for tribal *sheikhs* of the Eastern Province and hosted Oil Company executives, who in turn honored the King with the promised horse show at the Dhahran Corral.

Russ delivered the prints and negatives from Fran's camera, and nothing more was heard of them. They had been spirited away by *jinns* to take their place in Time among other secrets of the desert. The only aftermath came the day Russ said to me: "Somehow I felt you had to be involved—except, the pictures were so lousy, and there were no notches on the film." A Hasselblad imparts its insignia on every exposed negative.

The ruckus over Fran's pictures had died on the District Manager's front porch, exonerating the integrity of the *hareem* guards, supporting the honor of the women, satisfying the non-intervention policy of the Company, and withholding knowledge of the episode from Saudi dignitaries. With Nejma families once again in full possession of their beach, and the commissary shelves in time restocked of all short items, morning coffees sprouted new topics for discussion. The episode of the royal visit became an affair of the past.

Except for one thing. I could not forget the deep toned voice of the young girl who had called "Hello" from the Guest House garden. The saucy periwinkles taunted me each time I stepped out my front door. Had I dropped her challenge with my trumpeting to shout down tradition, my thoughtlessness in lunging at the tabus? Capturing a woman in my camera that day in Hufuf had been an accident. Approaching the Bedu women on the Ras Tanura road had been an impulsive act. Breaching the privacy of the Royal Hareem was audacious and no way to be accepted by this Muslim culture I lived with.

That roll of film shot from the Richard's patio roof, summarized my mistakes. I could not blot them out by hiding the spool in an empty lamp box under the enlarger table in the darkroom. Breaches of tradition are not that easily healed. My desire for understanding, withheld by the fluff of a black veil, would not go away, but yearned for proper channels of pursuit. Humans being what they are, the way must come one day.

I didn't see much of Fran during the next few weeks. She and Dick took a trip to the island of Cyprus. June found the four Nicholsons on their way to Switzerland to visit the school Linda would attend in September and to complete her required shopping. Although our Senior Staff schools (make that American) were excellent and conformed to New York standards, they did not go beyond ninth grade. Students continued High School in the Lebanon, Europe or the States.

All too soon September came. Linda, Diana Rader, a classmate, and I waited at the makeshift Dhahran airport for the Middle East flight to Beirut. The quonset hut, that had served as an air terminal in the fifties, was being replaced by a magnificent marble structure of high Arab arches, stained glass windows and vast hallways. *Iffrits* exercised their magic through oil.

We stayed at the luxurious new Phoenicia Hotel in Beirut,

and next morning were at the airport by six AM: two tickets to
Zurich and one (mine) back to Dhahran the following day. The
girls were continuing to Lugano, Switzerland, alone.

"Linda, look . . ." I said. "I've brought my heavy coat, and
I can quickly exchange my ticket for Zurich—if you'd like me
to come with you . . ." A mother's fears for the imminent departure of a child lent urgency to my words. Linda accepted
that, but she looked at me with the confidence of youth.

"What could you do that I can't do?" she said.

I had no answer. The loud speaker announced the Swissair
flight. I took a diamond and sapphire ring from my purse. It
had been her grandmother's and promised to Linda on her sixteenth birthday, as I had received it on mine. That maturity she
had reached today—at thirteen.

"You'll never be closer to sixteen, than you are today," I
said and slipped the ring on her finger.

"Oh, Mom—are you sure?"

"I'm sure. Take care of it—and yourself."

The black contrails scarred the sky, as Swissair Flight 605
dipped toward the west and Zurich.

* * * * *

August and September are the months the Bedu dread most.
The long days of wet south winds bring one hundred twenty
degrees temperature and suffocating humidity. Hundreds of
men, women, children and animals share one shallow well. We
of the ARAMCO communities could not begin to understand
their suffering, human beings like ourselves. It was enough to
see our horses endure the terrible heat. We went to the Ranch
every day to brush them and squirt them with water from the
water tank. And every day women from small villages walked
miles to bring their children to our wash rack for a few moments of relief.

With the singing days of October, we lived at the Ranch,

throwing sleeping bags on the beach and riding the mares along the pink shore to the Surf House in Nejma for breakfast. Daily workouts became routine for the horses. The cooler temperatures aroused their fire, and wasted muscles quivered to be tried. Russ, Cyndy and I shared picnic barbecues with Fran and Dick, sometimes joined by George and Virginia Larsen. We were bereaved parents with children away at school. I basked in the sunshine of Cyndy's presence, and in her skill at handling Sharifa.

On this particular weekend, Russ lunged Zerqa in circles on the long line, while Cyndy finished polishing Sharifa's coat before saddling up. I watched Murrawiyyah running free in the corral. Fran hosed down her Samur at the wash rack. She tied the gelding to the rail to drip and joined me where I leaned against the corral fence.

"How are you doing with the tryouts?" Fran asked.

I had begun an elimination schedule to give every child a chance at the plum roles in the Christmas pageant. "The kids are great," I said. "They even like the idea of understudies."

"What about wardrobe?"

"It'll take a lot of help. We'd better get going on it soon."

Fran rubbed her boot with her crop. "Pete Garner's the one. I'll get after her tomorrow."

I watched Murrawiyyah roll, then flail on all fours, sand showering about her. I called out, but she was not finished playing and leapt on flying heels to the far end of the corral. Two dark shapes hurried away, village women keeping to the outskirts, while their men and children roamed about the Ranch. Only when the men weren't present, did the women venture to enjoy the horses, as did we all. At such times, I had a chance to pass a few words with them.

Fran and I walked back to the stalls. I stopped to watch several small boys darting behind Zerqa on their way to the hay shed. Russ strained to hold the mare in check. No one wanted to be held responsible for an injury or slight to a Saudi Arab. It could result in deportation in lieu of a Sharia'h Court.

Sharifa was a particular concern. Hot-blooded, she spooked easily, and the presence of an Arab excited her to the point of being dangerous. That moment was now, for a man sat on the bench next to our tack box. He had been there a long time and neither spoke nor moved, just observed. Why was he watching us so closely? I wished he would move away.

Fran paused in front of Samur's stall. "When am I going to see the pictures?"

"Pictures? What pictures?" My attention was focused on the Arab. What did she refer to?

"The Royal Hareem—what else?"

"Oh—those . . . Well, I haven't got them." I don't know why I said it. The words just came out.

"Haven't got them. . . ?"

"Ummm . . ."

"You must! You didn't give them to Pat Johnston—I hope."

Our local artist longed to deliver Arab women from her canvas, except she had no samples to copy.

"I haven't printed them," I said.

I knew my words sounded like an excuse. I just couldn't bring myself to process the film.

Fran swung in front of me, blocking the man from view.

"You didn't lose the roll, did you?" Fran's gasp of apprehension could be heard around the stall.

I tried to smooth things over. " . . . it's not in the camera case. I just don't know where it is."

"Do you suppose Russ found it?"

Loyal Frances. I hated to deceive her. Could she understand my feelings about the whole affair? To print the pictures would mean the acceptance of an act I wasn't proud of, even the closing of a door I wished to open. Would non-performance expunge an error of judgment?

"I didn't want to tell you," I said. "They weren't any good. Not worth the trouble they caused."

My best friend stood there looking at me. Fran rarely remained speechless.

"Come on—forget it, Fran," I said. "Be glad we didn't get caught."

"You're a fine one . . ."—was all she said.

I started to respond, but a scuffle of hooves drew our attention. Sharifa scraped the brick floor, as she tugged at her tie and swung wide.

"Sharifa!" Cyndy shouted, pausing in her task of painting the hooves with oil. The mare had knocked the can over, and a dark stain spread along the ground. "You stop that, girl! I'm not finished."

The man was standing, still watching us. He started to move away, his robe flapping with every step. The mare's rear legs swung wide, locking her head close to the pole.

Cyndy stroked Sharifa's neck. "It's all right, girl," she soothed.

"Well—I better go and take care of Samur," Fran said. She picked up a soft brush from her tack box and headed for the wash rack.

Sharifa calmed down after the man walked away. I saw him stop and talk to Russ. Curious, I walked past them on my way to get Murrawiyyah.

"El . . . ," Russ called after me. "This man is from Riyadh."

I paused to look at him.

"He's come for the pictures you promised the King's Minister."

It took a moment to switch gears—the Bedu women. Had someone finally come for them? Perhaps our conversation about pictures confirmed his suspicions. Could I brush him off as easily as I had Fran? Uncertain of the outcome, I looked to Russ for a clue. He wasn't any help.

AL KHOBAR, SAUDI ARABIA, 1962

"This man wants to know if he can pick them up."

I hesitated, not knowing how to answer.

"Well—are they ready?" Russ said.

The printed pictures had been sitting in the darkroom for a long time. "Yes." I finally admitted.

The men's conversation continued in Arabic. The visitor would pick the prints up *bukra*, tomorrow. He gathered his cloak about him and headed for the outer gates, not pausing to shake out the loose sand that flowed through his sandals.

How had he found us? Desert trackers are known for their

ability to identify camel tracks as to tribal affiliation, male or female and the load carried. They could certainly trace me.

Late the following afternoon a taxi stopped in front of our house, and shortly after the doorbell rang. Ahmed was preparing dinner, so I let the man in myself. He slipped his sandals off at the front door and stepped politely into the room. I did not recognize him as being the same person I had met the day before. He asked for the pictures, and I gave them to him. He smiled broadly without opening the envelope.

"You like the Bedu?" he asked.

Caught off guard, my heart jumped. I wanted him to leave and get it over with. What was he leading up to?

"Yes . . . ," I mustered. "But I have never met any."

"You will. You will," he assured with enthusiasm. "I shall arrange it." He moved toward the door. "Then, you can take more pictures." He laughed.

What did that mean? I had to find out.

"Why do you want pictures?"

"*Laaszim* . . . (it must be)," he chuckled. "The ladies . . ." Then, seriously, he stuffed the envelope in the pocket of his *thaub*. "Too many Bedu are gone. We must remember our history."

The man really wanted them and not to trap me. Puzzled by this unexpected outcome, I watched him leave, as mysteriously as he had arrived. How much I had to learn.

The Bedouins of the desert, not a mirage but real people. Was I to visit them at last? The man had become a benefactor—the door to the real Arabia and its families. Had I been implying something that wasn't, that the real barrier lay in custom, not the people? Why didn't I recognize this before?

I couldn't wait to tell Russ. The light was on in the darkroom. I'd forgotten to turn it off when I picked up the photos. A print lay half curled on the shelf—a duplicate of one I'd given the man. She was just a Bedouin girl in long black robe and mask standing in front of her tent, but her eyes saw beyond my narrow world.

I leaned under the shelf that served as a working counter and felt for the empty lamp box. The spool of film rattled, as the box tilted. It took only a minute to extract the roll and slit the gummed seal with my fingernail. The red paper covering popped open. I pulled it with my left hand, right holding the spool, exposing the dull grey film to the glaring light bulb. The emulsion blackened—the silver shadows of the Royal Hareem gone for all time. I cringed at this betrayal of my friend, but the act cleared my conscience of guilt.

As is often the case, the unexpected turns up in more than one place. No sooner had the possibility of visiting the Bedu arisen, than a second veil lifted. Again, a man proved to be the intermediary. This time someone I knew casually, a Saudi employee of the Government Relations Department. Adnan Assad presented himself at my door after working hours, with the kind of smile that bespeaks knowledge of subversive activity.

"I have a letter," Mrs. Nicholson," he said. "It is from Hufuf."

"Why, Adnan, thank you. But you could have saved yourself some trouble and given it to Mr. Nicholson."

"Actually, it is for your daughter, Linda. To be delivered in person."

I held out my hand. "Linda is away at school. It is all right to give it to me."

Did I take the letter too hastily?

"If I can be of further help . . ."

"Thank you."

He drove off.

I turned the plain white envelope in my hand. It was limp and soiled from much handling. Mail delivery outside ARAMCO was spasmodic at best, but an improvement over delivery by camelback, village by village.

The address in Arabic was repeated in English across the top, perhaps translated by Adnan himself. I opened the envelope. The single sheet of paper bore a brief message in finely written Arabic characters. I sounded out the signature: Amsha Bint Al Abdullah. I had never told anyone, not even Frances, of the encounter in Hufuf. Now I wanted the whole town to know we had received a letter from the Amir of Hufuf's daughter. Later, Russ confirmed my deduction that the communication was the forerunner of more to come. The Princess intended to visit Linda. Her father had granted permission. She would come some Friday in the near future.

How does one entertain a Princess? What protocol should be followed? Linda had said the Princess wanted to know about Americans. I decided to receive her within the precepts of my own culture. She would see family life as we lived it. Cokes and cookies—dainty sandwiches—maybe even a chocolate cake—would be kept in the freezer against the day she might arrive. There would be one exception. The language barrier required I seek assistance from someone more fluent in Arabic than myself. That person would be Sara Nashibi.

Sara was a recent acquisition of our community, hired by ARAMCO to teach Arabic in the Senior Staff School. She was unlike anyone I had ever met. Eyebrows arched in disbelief when our town learned that the carelessly groomed and eager to please new arrival intended to teach Arabic to the primary grades.

Russ had told me of her arrival, since he briefed new hires on the "dos" and "don'ts". I was more than anxious to meet this western-easterner, whose presence threatened to disrupt our passive routine. Circumstances arranged such an opportunity within the week.

In addition to my portrait studio, I served our community needs by providing photographs for the Al Rasool, the school yearbook. Thus Sara came into my lens on the day scheduled for faculty sittings. Evelin Alarie, the French teacher, had just finished her stint before the camera, when Sara burst into the vacant half of the second grade portable, temporarily set up as a photographic studio.

She spotted the large mirror, borrowed from Housing, and began combing out her long dark hair. I had been concerned about effecting rapport, but it was quite clear that Sara meant to be in complete control. Deft fingers wound spit curls about forehead and ears, then daubed so much *kohl* around her eyes that the pupils blazed like glowing coals. Sara slinked her way to the camera area, draping her body across the stool with the grace of a panther and appearing equally dangerous. This was not the photographic style traditional for yearbooks. I snapped all the poses out of sheer enjoyment. A repeat session for the yearbook would be a must.

"That's all, Sara," I said, turning off the strobe light. "And thank you for coming." Bob Klein, the music teacher, was due any minute.

She jumped up. "But—I haven't finished!" Her hands yanked at the lace trim of her dress to create a plunging neckline. The curves of her shapely bosom rolled pleasantly above the black bodice. Almost in tears, she raced to the mirror, rearranged her hairdo and added a heavy necklace to her costume. The gold chains dripped pendants and pearls to her waist. She returned to face the camera, dark hair hanging in streaks down her face, and teeth set in the snarl of a tiger, reminiscent of the early days of the silver screen.

I couldn't resist taking a few shots and promised Sara to complete her sitting the next day. It took four sittings to get one pose acceptable for the purpose. Even at that, it out-glamorized the delicate beauty of Emily Antanossi, our Grecian third grade teacher.

Sara's pictures made her a celebrity. She showed them to anyone who would stop for a look. She resided in the bachelorette dorm near Fran's house, and more than one American school teacher threatened to quit rather than put up with Sara's incessant overtures of hospitality. When Emily and I offered our friendship, she forgot her posing, eyes misting with gratitude.

Some days she visited me after school. I learned much about her unusual life. Her country was Jordan where her family lived. The Nashibis, relatives of Jordan's former rulers, claimed a long history of nobility. A changing government deposed her father from his ministerial post, but this did not alter the nobility of the Nashibi name. Sara was a Princess in her own land. She abhorred eastern traditions for women and refused to lead a life of idle subsistence. Fighting for the right to make her own living, resulted in alienating herself from her family. She left Jordan. To return would bring dishonor to those she loved.

Sara went to the Hadramout in South Arabia. The ruling *sheikh* gave her permission to open a school for girls. She would walk miles to a distant tent just to encourage one Bedouin family to send their daughters to her school. It required long hours of hard work, but Sara had the satisfaction of knowing she set the foundation for women's education in South Arabia. She accepted employment with ARAMCO to further her experience in teaching and to pursue personal western advancement. Her anxiety to please, to be accepted by the west, smothered the sincerity of her Arab warmth and charm.

Sara was more than willing to help entertain my expected guests. As the weeks passed and nothing more was heard from Hufuf, I began to doubt the Princess would come at all. The sandwiches and chocolate cake in the freezer had been eaten and replenished twice by the time Jassim Said, chief security officer on the Main Gate, picked up his telephone one Friday in February and dialed my number.

"Mrs. Nicholson," he said, when I answered the ring. " . . . are you expecting Saudi visitors? A car is on its way to your home."

Chapter Fourteen

THE LAVENDER CADILLAC

It was quite in order for Jassim to call. Dhahran, Ras Tanura and Abqaiq were closed communities, and the local population required a pass to enter. Such a policy minimized the Company's involvement with villagers and nomads who might wander in. It also allowed ARAMCO to maintain some control over its own security system in order to prevent the American compounds from coming under the jurisdiction of the local police. The royal insignia on the car's license plate was pass enough for Jassim.

For a moment I panicked. My mind raced to organize first things first. With the arrival of Muslim women, all males must be out of the house. Unlike Arab homes, that provided separate salons for men and women to entertain guests in strictest privacy, our houses were constructed in western style.

Ahmed! I could hear him cleaning the girls' room. He insisted on finishing, until I convinced him that Muslim ladies were on their way for a visit. He looked up in shock, tossed the feather duster on to a bed and raced off on his bicycle without looking back. Sara! Thank goodness she was at home and would come right over. Russ! He had gone to the Ranch. I tried to phone and warn him not to come home. As usual, the humidity had created a short, and the number didn't ring. I'd have to take my chances about him showing up.

There was barely time to tell Cyndy to change into a dress and to comb my own hair, before a lavender Cadillac drove to a stop in front of our jasmine arch. The car seemed to pause, to take a deep breath, even as I needed to absorb the reality of its arrival.

"Is this okay?" Cyndy asked. She had slipped into a native cotton dress of brightly printed flowers, purchased in Rahima for a school festival honoring Arab custom. Wearing it changed her manner to the charm of a first performance. She loved to sing the songs from "Gigi", "The King And I", and "My Fair Lady".

"You're fine," I said.

The driver appeared on our front walk. His dignified stride created an air of expectancy, not associated with trainee servicemen who on occasion answered a call from my home to repair a leaky faucet.

"What if I don't remember her?" Cyndy said.

"I'm sure she will remember you."

I met the driver at the front door.

"Mrs. Nicholson?" he asked.

"Yes . . ."

"The Al Abdullah family of Hufuf." In keeping with strict decorum, he lowered his head to avoid looking at me.

"Please . . . tell them to come in."

With polite compliance, the driver returned to the car and opened the curbside front door.

I was unprepared for the emergence of a man; his layers of clothes and erect demeanor gave warning of a princely presence. He glanced at the house, adjusted his *quttra* and waited while the driver offered assistance to the occupants of the back seat. I had not counted on the presence of a man. But, of course, a male family member would be in attendance. Women never went out without one.

Two slight figures enveloped in black cloaks emerged, their heads concealed by layers of veils. Unlike the cars that had brought the Royal Hareem to the Ras Tanura beach, the lavender Cadillac had no black curtains covering its windows. Occupants seated inside were clearly visible, also allowing them to see out. Without surveying their surroundings, the figures drew their cloaks closer and hurried under the jasmine arch. The man remained behind to speak to the driver, then followed his companions to the front door.

"*Ahlan...Ahlan...*" I said, inviting our guests to enter, as the lavender Cadillac pulled away from in front of the house. "*Ahlan.* You are welcome. Please come in." I led the way into the living room.

Why didn't Sara hurry? She would know the proper etiquette to follow. Should I ask to take their cloaks, or would they prefer to remain covered up in the presence of strangers?

An awkward pause, perhaps unnoticed by our guests. They seemed intent on absorbing the contents of the room, even the locomotive whirr of the air conditioning machine that pumped life's blood into every room from a monstrous contraption in a closet at the rear of the house.

The taller of the two girls turned to face me.

"I am Mrs. Nicholson," I said. "Please—*tafadhalu*—make yourselves comfortable." I indicated the cushioned sofa, Company issue of Swedish origin. Without hesitating, she loosened the gold cord fastening the *abbaya* at the neck. The man, who had followed the girls inside, caught the garment as it slipped from her shoulders. He handed it to me, and I had the opportunity of observing him more closely.

He wore a carefully groomed reddish stubble of a beard, and the humor of it matched a spark of merriment in his deep grey eyes. Here was no subordinate, but a man of influence whose present role portrayed one of deference to his companions.

"*Ahlan . . .*" I repeated, taking the black silk to set it aside.

"My home is yours . . ."

The release of the cloak unfolded an Arabia I had hitherto only imagined. Its clinging texture across my arm seemed less ominous than the custom it represented. I could readily associate myself with Queen Elizabeth, Sophia Loren or Mamie Eisenhower through a familiarity of culture. But to reach the Princess Amsha, one faced a void that filled ever so slowly with bits and pieces of comprehension, until finally she came alive out of the isolation and antiquity of her land.

Proud, unafraid, positive, she had come in open friendship, not wearing the faded sack-like dress of village and desert, but a French creation designed in the Arab style. The gown was of palest blue Swiss embroidery, bodice minutely tucked to the high neckline and skirt layered with lace to the floor. Of accessories, a plain gold watchband showed through a frill of lace edging the sleeve at the wrist. Was I not to see her face, or that of her friend who remained darkly intact?

"May I introduce myself," the man said in excellent English. "I am Amir Khalid Al Abdullah, uncle to the Princess Amsha." He indicated the taller girl. "My brother, the Amir Mishari Al Abdullah of Hufuf, sends his warmest greetings."

I felt quite at ease with Arab men, whose homes Russ and I had visited many times. Prince Khalid was easier to accept than his niece. But I could not forget he was brother to the Governor, Saud Al Abdullah. Cruel, relentless, swift in meeting out punishment, he was judged to be fair to the offender and helpful to the ARAMCO communities in his province. There appeared no such awesomeness in the brother, who brought his two young nieces on a social visit to my home. Incidents of stonings, lashings, public beatings and severed hands on the Dhahran Gate had no place in this meeting.

" . . . and her aunt, the Princess Hussa of Buraida," Prince Khalid continued.

Princess Hussa swung off her cape in one wide gesture, and the light bubbling of a laugh made me eager to view the face behind the veil. A flying gold tassel snagged the sheer head covering and threatened to dislodge it. With automatic dexterity two slender hands reached upwards to keep the piece of fluff engaged. I could not imagine myself struggling with all that "cover-up", nor tolerating the apparently humiliating *abbayas*. Women's hands were forever on the move to hold down a mask, adjust a veil or to clutch the necks of their billowing unbalanced robes. The resistance of such garments to stay in place seemed a caricature of their intent.

I came to another conclusion. The moment I had awaited so long was here, and I did not know what to do with it. It was a far simpler thing to entertain the Anglican Archbishop Campbell of Jerusalem on his visits to our town, than to know what to do with these two young Saudi Arab girls. They appeared to be completely at ease, while I wavered with uncertainty in their presence.

"Please, sit down . . ." I said, as I set the cloaks on a large Kuwait chest near the hall.

Prince Khalid took a chair at the far end of the room. Princess Amsha sat on the long sofa, joined by Princess Hussa with a minimum of fluttery gestures.

"We have not come at a bad time?" Amsha said. Her self-assurance, second only to the vibrant alto of her voice, reflected what Linda had related of the Princess.

"No—no." I hastened to reply. "I have been expecting you."

She could not know for how long. Not merely since the arrival of her letter, but rather since the day I first set foot in her Kingdom—almost from the day she was born. My desire feasted on her presence, this young Arab girl who brought the essence of Muslim women into my home: a presence that promised association with others, hitherto obscured by isolation and tradition. How long it had taken. How smooth the crossing from the unknown to the known.

I rushed through the obvious preliminaries.

OUR JASMINE ARCH—"THE ONLY ONE IN R.T."

"Was the drive long to get here?"
"I hope it wasn't too hot."
"Did you stop to rest in Abqaiq?"

As we talked, Amsha removed the outer veil from her head and draped it across the back of the sofa. A wisp of chiffon remained, dimming the ebullient independence that glistened in the depth of her eyes. Bangs of dark hair overhung the brows, and the full lips seemed too sensuous for her years. She sat as one schooled in the grace of movement, though the simple gesture of lifting her skirt to sit reflected the innate quality of her ancestry. The fire, the flowing oneness of a desert mare are

179

its living heritage. The unadorned grace of this girl was hers. I dismissed as irrelevant the debacle of the Richard's patio roof.

Hussa's fascination centered on Cyndy. With joy of recognition she exclaimed, "Cyndy—Cyndy—come here. How pretty you are in your long dress."

"I like to wear them." Cyndy said, awed by Hussa's spontaneity.

"Then, you are Arab, too." Hussa threatened to pull up her own skirt, as she added. "And I shall wear your short dress and be from America." She laughed at her boldness.

"I am glad Amsha came. I wanted to thank her for the sandals," Cyndy said.

"It is nothing. You like them?"

"Oh, yes. See, I am wearing them."

That unforgettable day in Hufuf began to weave itself into my world: a thread of remembrance, a strand of recognition. Today held reality, and I asked our guests if they were tired after the long journey, reminded Cyndy to serve sweet cakes and juice, and introduced Sara when she finally arrived. Sara, who wore her hair pulled back and an Arab style dress to the floor with long sleeves. Before I knew it, Sara had Arab coffee frothing in the broad beaked pot, and thimble sized cups—souvenirs from the *suq*—filled with fragrant brew.

You are most welcome—make my house your own—the depth of desert hospitality expressed in the serving of cardamom coffee. Before every business deal, every social occasion, the assurance of pleasure in your presence. Three times the little cups are filled, then, with a shake of the wrist, a guest expresses his sufficiency, and the host is served. It was not the American way, but a social grace any hostess would savor.

A second round refilled the cups.

"How is Linda?" Amsha asked. "My cousin Princess Fahada would like to see her when she returns from Riyadh."

I explained that Linda was at school in Switzerland.

"Swit-er-land . . ." The Princess struggled with the English pronunciation.

"Yes. It is closer than Arabia to the United States, and Linda wanted to come home on vacations."

Amsha reverted to Arabic. "When I learn English, I will go to New York. Is it good for school?"

How does one compare this most exciting and turbulent of cities with the untouched wilderness of the Arabian desert? How do you convert the madness of vehicles and the crush of pedestrians into the lull of blowing sand and palms?

"Well, it is big . . ." I began. "So many people—cars—tall buildings . . ."

She leaned forward, brushing aside the final sheer covering to reveal a flush of excitement rising beneath the olive smooth skin. "Yes! All those cars! You hear this, Hussa? Isn't that what I told you?"

Her hands reached out, as if to scoop up the whole of Fifth Avenue. What did she envision, I wondered, this eager girl in her concept of a metropolis built on conversations with Royal relatives who had visited there? Hussa still clung to the anonymity of her veil, as though that estate excused her failure to respond promptly.

Then, she said, "That's all you ever talk about. And you know you will never go."

"How can you be so sure?" I said. "I never thought I would come to Arabia—but, here I am."

Prince Khalid listened without interruption, being an escort and not a participant. He extended his cup to Sara for a third round. How grateful I was to Sara for this contribution to the occasion, for I had not acquired perfection in brewing cardamom coffee. The beans must be roasted to the precise degree, the cardamom pods lovingly crushed, and the brew allowed to froth up three times into the upper belly of the pot before it may be served.

"I see you understand us, Mrs. Nicholson," the Prince said. "For you are right. We are all in the hands of Allah."

"And do you like it—Arabia?" Hussa asked, alert to a challenge. " . . . isn't it too hot and too many *shamaals?*"

A test. A challenge to the austerity of her country. Not many American families had stayed as long as we had. Certainly the heat was a trial, even with air-conditioned homes, and the flies were impossible to deal with. The violent sandstorms that could last as long as forty consecutive days drove you slowly up the wall.

"You see—I have stayed." I said. "And I have been wanting to meet you."

Princess Amsha leaned forward, hands clasped, eyes alight with excitement. "That's why I came," she said. "I want to meet Americans. I want to know everything about them."

"Even American husbands?" Hussa nudged her niece and giggled at her own daring.

For the aunt, the talk was just that—a dare. Not so the determination of Amsha. The chiffon revealed Hussa's hair piled loosely with flyaway strands on top of her head, while Amsha's luxurious mass hung neatly down her back. Perhaps Hussa felt confused by my attentive look, for she flipped the square of gossamer from side to side, baring half her face at a time, her gestures accompanied by self-conscious laughter.

On impulse, I sat on the far end of the sofa. She stiffened, eyes flashing glints of emotion that matched the iridescence of her green gown. Agile fingers flipped the veil to conceal the cheek nearest me. It was a game she continued to play with each movement of her head. Although introduced as the aunt, she appeared to be the same age as her companion. In the complex intermarriage of Arab families, any relationship is possible.

I became aware of Sara standing in front of me, her eyes dark orbs of torment signaling quiet disapproval. Without a word she poured a third round of coffee for the girls. Seconds later I caught her waving frantically above the Dutch door to the kitchen.

Prince Khalid noticed their car had returned and excused himself to speak to the driver. I suggested our guests might like to freshen up after their long trip, and Cyndy accompanied them to her room, promising to play the latest records from the States.

Then Sara jumped me.

"Mrs. Nicholson! You didn't tell me the truth."

"What do you mean?"

"These girls. They are cousins of the King. And here I am an Arab, and I must entertain them generously." Then, in accusative tones, ". . . and no one sits next to a Princess!" Her look of complete disapproval ignited the fire of decorum burning into my conscience.

"Sara, I think they came because they wanted to see an American home. I meant no disrespect, only to assure them of my pleasure in their visit, and to make them feel at home."

"Well, it's not customary. It's just not acceptable. I must treat them in Arab style."

Her distraught state showed Sara to be more Arab than she thought. Her roots were deep in the Middle East, no matter her desire to pretend otherwise.

She hurried off toward the kitchen, rolling up the sleeves of her dress. Pushing open the Dutch door, she turned back to challenge me in no uncertain tones:

"Now—we must prepare dinner!"

Chapter Fifteen
DINNER IN THREE LANGUAGES

Dinner! This unexpected declaration came as a shock. That was more than I had bargained for. Besides, it was already the middle of the afternoon.

"I have plenty of sandwiches—cake—ice cream," I said. "That should do."

"No! No! That is not enough! It must be dinner—Arab style. It is my duty!" Sara cried.

"Sara, everything is ready to do it my way. The sandwiches are in the freezer. We just have to get them out."

She burst into tears. Her voice rose to a high pitch. "No! No! I am Arab. I must follow the custom! It is my duty!"

And so I agreed. Sara went into action, at least verbally.

"We must have chicken—lots of it—lamb for *kibbee* and stew—rice with saffron and pignolas—tomatoes for slicing and cooking—*aubergines* with onions and mint—watermelon—*hubbuz*—*baba ganouch*—*hummus fi tahini* . . ."

"Sara! There isn't time for all that cooking."

She shrugged off my concern with a philosophical answer. "Time is not the issue."

I started digging into my stores. The freezer contained items we could use, but not nearly enough. Each time I set out a package, Sara would say: "Is that all? We must have more."

I wondered how many people she expected to feed. Finally, from the depths, I dragged out a whole leg of lamb.

"There's this," I said. " . . . but we could never get it defrosted." The frost on the foil wrapped package burned my hands. I quickly set it back in the freezer.

"No—wait . . ." she said. "We must have it."

She reached in and picked up the lamb, as if to test my assessment of the situation. Her expression told me she had come to the same conclusion, but Sara was not about to give up.

"We've got to have it," she repeated. "A man could handle it . . ." Then with scheming excitement, " . . . where's Mr. Nicholson?"

"Nowhere in sight—I hope."

"We've got to have a man with a strong arm."

I did not wait to hear the rest. Sara's ideas under pressure bordered on the outlandish. The ARAMCO facilities were closed for the day, so I dashed out the back door to scour the neighborhood and to beg favors from my friends. The contributions consisted of more frozen chicken, packages of lamb stew that could be spiced with peppers and tomatoes, boxes of French fries, and a gallon of frozen spaghetti offered by Lindy Dowling. The mother of six children, Lindy always kept something extra in the freezer for emergencies.

"Where are the *aubergines*, tomatoes, spinach," Sara demanded when I returned. "And—look—this onion's moldy."

"Sorry . . ." I said, making haste to unwrap the spaghetti and to separate the chicken pieces. "We had no produce this week."

Fresh vegetables in Arabia irritated a sore spot that never healed. ARAMCO produce was flown in from Beirut in the Lebanon or from Asmara in Ethiopia. It was left to wilt and mold in the sun, until Customs agents got around to issuing clearances.

"Well, I have some," Sara said.

She shopped at the native *suq* in Rahima, something I had not geared my sensitivities to do. Though I had to admit that produce trucked down in gaudily painted lorries from Iraq was often more appetizing than items for sale in the commissary— if you disregarded their dubious beginnings. One never knew if farmers used night soil, nor what hands had been doing before the vegetables were picked and packed. If necessary, a bottle of Clorox would take care of such problems. Many times I had washed a head of lettuce, leaf by leaf, in a solution of bleach.

Sara wiped her hands from trying to defrost the leg of lamb under the faucet. "I'll be back," she said. She dug in her pocket for the keys to her apartment. "Now, Mrs. Nicholson, you chop the onion, slice the two tomatoes and defrost the rest of the chicken."

I set the spaghetti in the oven to start the defrosting process.

"No!" Sara cried. "We can't serve that."

"Oh, yes, we can. . . !" I insisted. "It'll be something different." I intended to have my way on this. I was a hostess, too, even if relegated to the station of pantry boy for chopping onions. Sara soon returned with three plump eggplants, six flat rounds of Arab bread, a jar of *hummus* and—Chico!

I couldn't believe my eyes. Sara had brought a man into the kitchen. She, who insisted on Muslim protocol. My startled expression prompted a cursory explanation. Chico was a new friend, a Chilean who spoke only Spanish. He had been among those recruited by Bechtel International to construct the new five hundred thousand barrel oil storage tank at the Ras Tanura terminal. It would be the largest tank of its kind in the world. Chico guaranteed to barbecue chicken fit for a king. More importantly, he had been a champion skier at the Olympics in

Santiago two years before, and an athletic champion could certainly cleave a frozen leg of lamb down to size.

Between gestures and a jumbled jargon of Spanish and Arabic, Sara and Chico had the kitchen in organized disorder. I couldn't bear to see my hoarded leg of lamb reduced to pulp under the cleaver. I went into the dining room to set the table and to check on our guests.

Music and voices from the bedroom indicated the girls were taking care of themselves. I turned toward the front window to see what had become of the uncle. The lavender Cadillac was nowhere in sight—but the Land Rover was, even as Russ and the uncle approached the front door.

VILLAGE GIRLS AWAIT THE KING'S ARRIVAL

Animated conversation about Arab horses overruled my attempt to high sign Russ. He strode into the living room sweaty, dirty and smelling of horseflesh, just as Princess Amsha, Princess Hussa and Cyndy entered from the hall. An impact of silence against rent cultures stunned me speechless. A moment ago the walls of my modest home seemed bright with promise. Now, they resounded with foreboding horror. In one second the sudden appearance of a man threatened to terminate hopes for recognition and friendship. To my mind, the embarrassment and confusion of my young guests must be the ultimate indiscretion against Muslim tradition.

Hussa went into action first. She snatched the wisp of black hanging over one shoulder, whipped it across her face and raced a retreat toward the bedroom. She was halfway down the hall, when a quick check on her niece revealed the Princess facing her uncle with statuesque dignity. Unflustered, she graciously acknowledged Prince Khalid's introduction of Russ.

Poor Russ! Pale fury roiled beneath a cool exterior, I knew, as he found Arabic pleasantries suitable for the occasion. Excusing himself to clean up, he threw a look at me that said: "I want to talk to you!"

I tried to regain my composure by checking on the progress in the kitchen and asking Cyndy to serve the hot, sweet tea Sara had made. Our guests were engaged in a conversation of their own that seemed not to include an immediate departure. With a sigh of relief, I followed Russ down the hall.

"Why didn't you warn me?" he said.

"I tried to. The phone was out . . ."

"How much longer are they going to stay?"

I hedged. "Well—Sara is fixing a meal. It's about ready." Nothing could bring me to tell him about Chico.

"I've got to get back," Russ said. "Sharifa cut her frog. Where's the antibiotic ointment of Dr. Liggett's?" Then, with emphasis: " . . . and do something. I'm not going through that again!" He nodded toward the living room.

"Such timing," I said. "It couldn't have been worse. Frankly, I think the Princess enjoyed it."

"Yeah. I'm probably the first male stranger she's been exposed to without her veil."

A thought crossed my mind. "Prince Khalid knew the girls were here. How'd you meet up with him, anyway?"

"At the Ranch. He came to see the horses—said he was killing time, so I invited him over . . ."

"And he never mentioned our visitors?"

"No. Why should he? There was no connection."

I could not erase this embarrassment to our guests, but the incident seemed to be of little impact to them. Prince Khalid insisted that Russ stay and join him. He was interested in furthering their discussion on the heritage of the purebred desert mare.

Princess Hussa flirted with her veil, uncertain what to do with it, finally resorting to tying it around her hair. Even then, it failed to enfold escaping strands. Princess Amsha paid no attention to the nudges of her aunt, but rather brushed her off, and taking advantage of the moment, eagerly asked Russ his opinion of American cars. She was tired of the Cadillac. It was too large and didn't go fast enough. What make of car did he prefer?

"It must go very fast," she told him. "I love to drive fast cars."

Of course, she didn't drive. Perhaps that was a teenage fantasy. Hussa showed no interest in the conversation. She finally relaxed in our ladder-back rocking chair, lifting her feet with every backward tilt.

I could hear Sara laughing in the kitchen, though the Dutch door was closed, and wondered if anyone noticed how the voice changed from time to time. Every so often she peeked out to say dinner was almost ready. Obviously, the girls were, too. Princess Amsha slipped her hand into a concealed pocket in her gown and showed me a small square of paper. It was a photograph of Linda.

"May I keep this?" she asked. "It was in the bedroom."

"You are welcome," I said. "I wish she was here to greet you."

"I like Linda very much," Amsha said. "You will visit me in Hufuf and bring her?"

"Oh, yes . . ."

"You must meet my mother and sisters, and all my family. They want very much to see you." Then without hesitation. "Mr. Nicholson must come, too. My brother will show him the royal stables."

How different our first encounter with this girl. I was glad she didn't know. Speculation due to lack of association breeds distortion. Already, I sensed our guests to be little different from ourselves. Responsive and fluid they rounded the day with comprehension and enjoyment.

In the matter of a meal, custom posed a problem. The dining room of our Company assigned home was an offshoot of the parlor area. Small but adequate, the sexes would have to share the meal at one sitting. I could probably dismiss Russ, but how to deal with Prince Khalid. Arab protocol set the pattern of men eating first, the family women to follow, seated on cushions on the floor.

Sara signaled Cyndy to help prepare the dining table, and in short order it abounded with platters, practically every dish I had in the house, including the green and gold dragon that wound around a bowl decorating the lamp table. The steaming food wafted a tantalizing mixture of cardamom, nutmeg and mint with an overtone of spicy barbecue sauce. Sara had wrought a miracle.

The chicken, piled high in golden splendor on my best Rosenthal platter, was a tribute to Chico's deftness in the kitchen. The lowly spaghetti in its rich sauce overflowed the bounds of a Chinese porcelain tureen. My once hoarded leg of lamb bristled with pignolas and mint in finger size portions of *kibbee*, bowls of lamb stew with *aubergines* and kebabs with peppers and onions. Sara was proud, I could tell. Her damp, high colored cheeks said it all.

My fears were soon put to rest, for Prince Khalid insisted

we all sit together in intimate family style, the American way. Princess Hussa scrunched close to Amsha, eyeing Russ across the table with concern. She unwound the veil from her hair and tossed it over half her face, allowing room for fingers to pass food to her mouth. Spontaneous laughter broke the tension when the Prince exclaimed: "He won't bite you!" Sara refused to join us. She insisted on carrying out her duty to see the guests' plates were never empty.

"You have no servants?" Hussa asked, as Sara stood by to answer every need.

"Our servant is dismissed for the day," I said. "We are pleased to serve you ourselves."

Sara passed a tray of folded napkins, moist with lemon water for wiping fingers before eating. It fulfilled the requirement of washing hands before meals, where fingers are favored over knives and forks. Many a slip occurred between fork and mouth, until Cyndy and Hussa resorted to the best way to eat chicken in any culture: fingers. Our guests piled their plates from every dish, even expounding their pleasure over the lowly spaghetti. Dinner was indeed the menu called for. Our guests were hungry, no doubt about that. Sara kept pushing food onto their plates, and I realized how chagrined I would have been with anything less.

Finally, the cake, rich with chocolate icing, made its appearance. Impishly, Hussa snatched a fingertip of icing, as slices were cut and served. Amsha studied it with interest.

"I have never had this before," she said. "It is sweet and light. What is its name?"

"It is called a cake, Princess," I said. "Most countries serve a torte or pastry. We celebrate a special occasion with a cake. Do you like it?"

"Very much. What is a special oc-cas-sion?"

"Like a birthday, or a graduation—or today, because you came to visit. This is a very special occasion."

"We must leave now," the Princess said shortly after the meal was finished.

KHALIFA'S TRUCK ARRIVES WITH ALFALFA FOR
THE HORSES

"So soon?" I pleaded, following Arab etiquette. It was late in the day, and they had a long way to go. "You have only just arrived."

"I am so glad we came," she said, offering an infectious smile. "I like Americans. Do not forget your promise to visit us in Hufuf." She hesitated, as if wanting to impart a gesture she was not sure of, the Arab expression of affection.

We set the visit for December, when Linda would be home from school. All of us must come: Cynthia, Sara, Russ. Amsha would send a letter setting the day.

Abbayas soon concealed feminine charm, and the girls turned toward the front door. I had been aware of Sara frantically emptying leftover food into plastic bowls and sacks.

"You must not be hungry on your way home," she said, passing the sacks to Amsha.

I walked our guests to the car. The lavender Cadillac seemed to have returned at exactly the correct time. Last goodbyes were said, and the driver opened the rear door.

"What a lovely color, the car . . ." I said. "Is it yours?"

"Yes." The Princess smiled, as she arranged a veil over her hair. "It is what I wanted for my sixteenth birthday. Lavender is my favorite color."

"It's Linda's, too."

Later I would recall her words, but now I stood and watched as the lavender Cadillac headed for the Main Gate. I wondered how many of my neighbors might have noticed my distinguished visitors, but everybody was out of sight. I remarked about this to Russ.

"They wouldn't have noticed anything unusual because Prince Khalid kept the car moving about town," he said. "Thus their presence at our house was not obvious."

The visit was a concession to the Princess and not to be publicized.

Russ and I walked toward the house. "You know," I said. "I keep wondering how the girls were allowed to visit. After all, we are complete strangers to the Al Abdullah family."

Russ took my arm and squeezed it. "I'm sure they knew we were okay," he said. "Probably thoroughly investigated. Whether that's an honor or not you'll have to decide. Don't forget I've had numerous contacts with Amir Turki of Rahima on Company business—and he's an Al Abdullah."

"Maybe we've got an 'in' now." I said, recalling my dubious attempts at contacting local ladies. "I can't wait for that trip to Hufuf. Imagine meeting the Governor's wife."

"If that letter ever comes."

I ignored his attempt to discredit the idea.

"I was horrified when you walked in—so humiliating for the Princesses."

"Not that bad . . ." Russ said. " . . . though I was enraged at the time."

"What do you mean? It couldn't have been worse!"

"Oh, yes it could. Fortunately, I'm not a Muslim. That makes a difference in Islam's rules of order."

"You mean—that makes you a non-man?"

He laughed and kissed my cheek. "Not exactly. Being a non-Muslim eased the situation." Then he added with humor: " . . . the Prince confided that I have a good heart. In other words, I was not a threat to their chastity."

It took a while to ingest this male and female relationship. Maybe one day it would clarify itself. Meanwhile, Cyndy had changed her clothes and was ready to take off with Russ to doctor Sharifa's hoof. I was glad for a few minutes to catch my breath. As I entered the house, Sara challenged me.

"You see, Mrs. Nicholson," she said. "How they expected to have dinner?"

"You were exactly right," I said. "But, all that food you gave them. Weren't they embarrassed?"

"Oh, no. It was expected. The driver needed something to eat, and they will, too, before they get home. Then what is left they will share with the family and servants—especially the cake."

Arab generosity: to give the best, the last that one has, as well as of one's self.

I dropped into my favorite rocker. "Sara . . ." I said. " . . . what we need now is a cup of coffee—real coffee."

"Sen-or! Chi-ee-co!" she called.

A male head popped above the kitchen half door.

"*Ghawa! Minfudlak . . . ,*" she said with deliberation. Chico responded with a blank stare.

"*Ghawa . . .* coffee . . . cafe!"

With a grin of understanding he disappeared, soon to reappear with large cups and a pot of hot coffee straight from the stove.

"He's smart. He'll learn fast," Sara said. She patted his head, as she might a trained puppy.

And I'll learn, too, I thought, for the invitation to visit a family was more than I had hoped for.

Chapter Sixteen
THE LION GATE

After long months of waiting December came, and we were a family of four again. What an exciting moment, when the British Overseas Air Corporation 707 from Rome touched down at the Dhahran airport. Linda, along with several other returning students from schools in Italy, Switzerland and England, deplaned laden with holiday packages, hand luggage, winter coats and, miracle of miracles, shouldering real live Christmas trees. The woodsy fragrance of living fir added to the joyous spirit of Christmas, far and beyond artificial trees, too tattered after years of use to support tinsel decorations and twinkling lights.

Nothing was more important than giving her a big hug and listening to her lively chatter of school experiences all the long drive home to Ras Tanura. It took several days to get caught up. Yes, the horses were fine—Cyndy still played the piccolo in the Blue Devil Band—and I was busy rehearsing the Christmas pageant. Fran Richards invited her to join the chorus, if she wanted to. And—oh, yes—we had heard from the Princess in Hufuf and were awaiting another letter with details about visiting her.

That letter arrived sooner than expected, hand carried from

Hufuf by local government officials. The graceful Arabic lettering was in a fine hand. I tore the envelope open.

"Dear Friends . . ." it began in studied English. The message followed in Arabic script, and the signature was clearly legible: Fahada Bint Mohammed Al Abdullah. Russ wouldn't be home for a couple of hours, so I phoned Sara to come right over.

"It's from Princess Fahada," she said with great excitement.

"Yes, I know," I retorted, impatient to learn the contents and unskilled in reading Arabic. "What does she say?"

The impossible gutturals scraping easily from her throat, the flying eyebrows, the unrestrained gestures conveyed the delight and interest of the reader.

"Sara. . . ?" My patience was wearing thin.

"Oh . . . yes . . ." She suddenly remembered I was there. "Well, we are all invited to Hufuf! Princess Fahada expects us to come. Of course we must go. She is expecting us. Mr. Nicholson can drive us to Hufuf."

"Sara!" I tried to restrain her enthusiasm and to get to the root of the invitation. "Just read what she says."

"But, I did!" Her astonishment was genuine. "We must go. It is an invitation from the Princess."

"Of course we shall accept. What day are we invited?"

"She doesn't say. She will let us know."

Two hours later, Russ confirmed the contents. "You'll have to wait," he said. " . . . until you hear from her again."

When Linda came in from an afternoon at the pool, I showed her the letter.

"Say, that'll be great!" she said. "Boarding school and Switzerland are so different, I'd almost forgotten about the Princess."

An expanding interest in her own culture would one day leave the desert behind. Childhood would slip away, leaving memories of a land that would always be home.

She must have been thinking along those same lines, for

she added, "I wonder if she will remember me."

Cynthia's reaction was not immediately favorable. She declared all her weekends to be committed to the swimming pool.

"You may bring a friend," I said. "Perhaps Margaret would like to come."

"Say, I'll go ask her. She's never visited any Arabs."

"Tell Mrs. Davis I'll phone and explain later," I said, as the back door banged, and the fence jasmine wafted her off in a sweet farewell.

The second communication from the Palace in Hufuf was not long in following the first. This time the Mayor of Rahima, Amir Turki himself, delivered the letter in person. If he wondered about its contents, he gave no indication that this was an unusual procedure. He was well acquainted with Russ, who often represented the Company on business with the Amir. As in situations involving Muslim women, male attitudes considered the incident not to have taken place.

Our lack of contact with Muslim women provided little understanding of this point of view and furthered the concept of purdah, or isolation of the family. Doubtless Amir Turki had knowledge of our impending visit, but delivering the letter did not invite conversation with outsiders relative to family women. A knowing smile and friendly greeting disclosed more than words, and I knew the letter contained the long awaited invitation from the Al Abdullah family.

"Come and spend the whole day with us," the letter read.

"We must leave early," Sara translated. "They will be expecting us at eight o'clock."

"Sara!"

"But it is Arab custom." She had a way of looking at you, as if the world was falling apart.

"That's just not reasonable," I said. Hufuf was at best a three hour drive from Ras Tanura.

"We must be early. Saudis are up by sun time for the first

prayer of the day, and they will be expecting us soon after," Sara insisted.

"We'll get there in good time—and without rushing," Russ declared, taking control of the matter. "U.S. style . . ." By choice, he was not an early riser.

"Mr. Nicholson," Sara wailed. " . . . they'll be expecting us—they'll be looking for us, I know."

I sometimes suspected Sara's idea of Arab custom coincided with her own wishes. Nevertheless, Russ made a concession. We would drive to Abqaiq Wednesday evening, spend the night there and drive on to Hufuf next morning—at whose convenience might be the most persuasive.

THE LION GATE ENTRANCE TO THE BAIT AMIR,
HUFUF, 1964

We were up early and left Abqaiq just as the morning shadows on the wrinkled face of the Shedgum escarpment receded with the rising sun, imparting a smoothness to the pale pink limestone that belied its age. The great Al Hasa Oasis lay quiet and dusty, disturbed only by jingling bells on busy little don-keys, and the grind of cartwheels jogging in and out of oasis gardens. The brassy horizon took form, and the light glare gath-ered density to reveal the still standing ancient walls and for-tress towers of Hufuf. A blast of horns came out of the silent distance, and soon several limousines screeched in madness about us.

"That's Princess Amsha's car," exclaimed Cyndy, recog-nizing the lead car as the lavender Cadillac.

There were no black veils, only red checked *quttras* and broad grins of several men, who leaned out the windows to indicate we should follow them.

"Do you think the one in front is Amsha's brother?" Linda nudged her sister.

"Don't ask me. They all look alike."

"Are we going with them?" asked Cyndy's friend Marga-ret, who had decided to join us. "Aren't you afraid?"

"You'll find out." Cynthia sometimes enjoyed being non-committal.

"I told you they'd be waiting," Sara said, barely able to contain her excitement, yet horrified at having committed a breach of etiquette.

The cars raced ahead, but Russ maintained his eighty kilos, the speed he adhered to on desert roads. They waited for us at the Al Khamis Gate, main entrance into town. The great green doors had only just opened, and guards surveyed pedestrians anxious to shop at the famous Thursday Market. Our escort paused long enough for us to catch up, then turned right and followed the old wall to the Bab Al Khail, horse entrance to the inner courtyard of the Al Kut.

A broad open area spread before us, intruded upon by low stone buildings, the casement of a large well and barracks for the horse guard, now empty. A stable hand, walking two of the Amir's personal mares, was the only pedestrian in sight. The cars moved on and stopped near an entryway in the low stonewall that surrounded the Palace grounds. I tried to relate Linda's earlier encounter with the Princess to this section of the Al Kut, but the small garden I had seen after the passage through the wall was nowhere visible, nor were the few shops I remembered. Entering from a different point of view revised any recollections I might have had.

A few steps to the entryway, and the full beauty of the graceful Bait Amir appeared before us, its white plaster stories rising to a cupola tower, mindful of elaborate layers of a wedding cake. Each story diminished in size as the building gained in height, its scalloped arches topped with a plaster border as delicate as fine lace on a bride's gown. Decorative pillars, taller than the wall, stood on either side of the entryway. The gate itself, designed in fanciful open ironwork, seemed small, but wrought iron rods intermittently fanned out from the gate frame to become anchored in the tall columns on either side. The lacey effect stood out in deep contrast to the overwhelming might of the Al Kut wall.

Carved into the pillars on either side, sculptured lions with curly manes faced each other from scalloped niches. Above them in large proportions, a palm tree set between two crossed swords in high relief announced the entrance into the home of the Al Abdullah family. The plaster lacework that edged the Palace layers carried over to decorate the top of the archway.

To me, who anticipated entrance, the tall iron and gold guardians of Versailles, the silver standards of Buckingham, the broad boxed hedged gardens of Schonbrunn—even the primitive Al Kut wall with its remnants of a moat—could not infringe on the historical significance of the grace and simplicity of the Lion Gate. We, who would pass through its portals, entered into the storied past of this desert Kingdom that told of family strength and faith, of future global supremacy, and to me, an acceptance by a closed society.

We left the cars in the courtyard and followed our escorts through the Lion Gate and along a tiled walkway. Just getting out of the car was a welcome relief from the spewing engine temperatures collected by the Rover's rubber matting and transferred to our vinyl soled shoes.

The warm fragrance of the hardy bush jasmine seemed a gesture of welcome, even before their dark green leaves became visible where the bushes fronted tall arched windows with deep overhanging casements and slatted wooden shutters, designed to catch the breeze. Hand scrolled and brass studded doors opened into a hallway with hanging filigree brass oil lamps.

Surrounded by our retinue, we entered the large *mejlis*, salon for men. We were not permitted to remove our shoes, although sandals were arranged in neat rows by the door, indicative of those who had. Deep box shaped chairs upholstered in worn velvet lined the walls, and we found ourselves sinking to our shoulders.

A faded reproduction of King Abdul Azziz, founder and first ruler of the Kingdom of Saudi Arabia, was the only decoration on the walls, save for tall wooden shutters covering window archways. Stripped palm logs painted in geometric design of high color interspersed the length of the ceiling. An unskillfully installed air-conditioning unit labored noisily, foretelling its inefficiency. The high ceiling, thick walls and window design, that captured and dispersed the slightest breeze, did more to effect coolness than this product of twentieth century America. It was a strange gathering: the predominately female guests and the all male hosts, increasing in number to extend hospitality and to participate in the unusual assemblage within the normally all male salon.

A distinguished looking gentleman in sheer woolen robe approached Russ and extended his hand in greeting. The male attire of long white *thaub* was quite familiar to us, but on this man his elegant cloak was an enhancement for any male.

"*Ahlan wa sahlan . . .*" he greeted. "Your presence does us honor."

"Allah's goodness has directed us to your door," Russ replied. "May his generosity be never failing."

The proud man scrutinized the speaker and smiled in appreciation of the compliment. "The Amir regrets not welcoming you himself, but he has accompanied the Governor to Riyadh. I, Sultan Al Abdullah, am here to serve you."

"We thank you for your hospitality and shall welcome the opportunity to convey such to His Highness the Amir," Russ said.

"May I introduce Prince Naiyf, the Amir's son," our host continued.

But the interest of the young Prince was elsewhere, as he surveyed the line of faces sunk in the deep chairs and stared unrestrainedly at Linda, whose blushing cheeks fired brilliants in her eyes.

"Don't think I didn't see," whispered Cynthia, as the Prince turned away to acknowledge the introduction.

"What. . . ?"

"The way he stared at you."

"Don't be silly . . ." Linda's glance took refuge in the blue depths of a turquoise ring on her left hand.

"Who's silly. . . ?" Cynthia pursued her conviction.

The entrance of coffee bearers covered Linda's embarrassment. Three times the tiny cups went the rounds, and the amber liquid flowed in an arc from the long beaked pot, while servants watched attentively to fulfill their customary obligations of hospitality. A shake of the wrist, to indicate sufficiency, sent the watchful bearers on to other guests and hosts. We sat in silence, savoring the pungent cardamom lingering on our palates, together with an air of expectancy for the overly sweet tea we knew would follow.

Several men near the open doorway stepped aside, and servants hurried off with their trays. In single elegance the Princess Amsha entered the room. With grace and assurance she faced her guests and her relatives with a freedom of spirit impervious to challenge. This young daughter of a Saudi Prince

VILLA OF PRINCESS FAHADA, HUFUF, 1960s

was no longer the teenager who had laughed uproariously at the antics of my platform rocker. Today she upheld the honor and prestige of her family, the courage and pride of ancestors. It showed in her unwavering inspection of the room, eyes barely discernible through a sheer face covering. She glided across the floor, her white dress of draped silk exploding with fiery circles that flamed from neck to hemline, much as a high priestess of antiquity braved baptism by fire to uphold her sovereignty. With an imperceptible dip of her shoulders, the Princess Amsha turned on her scarlet shoe and extended a hand to me. It was our custom, and she accepted it.

"We welcome you to our home," she said, the light touch of fingers unfamiliar with western formalities.

She moved on down the line of visitors, not waiting for a reply, gave a nod to the girls, spoke to Sara in her own tongue, addressed her uncle briefly, then left the room.

Was this all, I wondered? Were we not to see her again? Had we offended by being late? I caught Sara's glance, but her thoughts were far away on some cloud of yesterday, reminder of youthful days when the Nashibi family maintained influence in the State of Jordan. I admired Sara's adaptability and transformation from Arab restraint to western permissiveness. That she sometimes got tangled up in her own confusion, didn't hinder her from leading a double life.

Wondering what next, I watched our host approach Russ in open friendliness, engage him in conversation at some length, join several young men at the door and leave the room.

"What did he say?" I asked Russ, as I tried to lean around the high arms of the deep chair. "What's going on?"

"They're taking us to the Amir's summer residence. Prince Sultan is leaving Prince Naïyf in charge."

I passed the word along to the girls, and surrounded by our escort, we left the Rover behind and drove off in limousines. We women were all in one car. Russ rode with the young Prince and his numerous bodyguards. From the outskirts of town, we headed for the palm gardens, where drooping fronds rippled in a blue haze above the tortured ground. The powerful American cars, built for the States's super highways, took to the rough desert with barely a jostle.

The cars entered the shaded oasis and followed a hard packed road that meandered through the gardens. After the open glare of the sun, the depth of the trees was cool and inviting. We hadn't gone far, when an entranceway appeared in a high plaster wall built to keep the desert and intruders from encroaching on the privacy of a rustic garden. The roadway wound through the palms and underbrush, over gurgling irrigation ditches and came upon a pathway where the cars slowed to a stop. Our escort indicated we should take the path ahead, while all the men remained behind. Undaunted by fear of intruding upon a society I knew little about, we started walking up the path.

Cyndy and Margaret hurried alongside. "I don't see anybody," Cyndy said, and Margaret reached for my arm.

Sara pushed ahead to lead the way, as Linda remarked, "Do we know what we are doing?"

Between overhanging branches of mimosas dotted with yellow buds and the dense leaves of the loquat, I caught glimpses of tall light standards with oversized globes that rimmed a swimming pool. White wicker tables and chairs were set on a terrace, reached by ascending a few steps at the end of the path. I felt encouraged by this sign of human habitation, but somewhat disturbed by the sound of an engine starting up. I looked back in time to see Russ spirited away in the lavender Cadillac.

Beyond the swimming pool stood a pink stucco house, easily recognizable as an ARAMCO *burasti*, here renovated and redecorated for the pleasure of the Prince. It seemed out of place in this setting, where time had collected its years, but brought a suggestion of change and added comfort into the lives of the Amir's family.

One by one, several servants appeared on the terrace to plump cushions on the wicker chairs and to set up small tables for service. More than one eyed us at their work, especially the younger ones, eager to see the girls in our group. An assortment of family members arrived on the terrace and came forward to meet us. It seemed strange to be walking into their lives along a pathway where even the scarlet bougainvillea peeked from under ground brush for a stolen glimpse at strangers. We had barely reached the steps to the terrace, when the Princess Fahada appeared through the family group and came forward to meet us. The formality of honor and hospitality we had witnessed a short time ago, now gave way to open charm and a freedom of spirit typical of youth's eagerness for contact and knowledge. Her every gesture expressed sincere pleasure at our arrival.

"He will join us later," she said, quick to observe my concern over Russ's departure. "Please, you will find it cooler and more comfortable here in the garden." She invited us to have a seat on the terrace. Her smile was welcome enough, even if her eyes hadn't glowed with pleasure. How attractive she was without the black film that stagnated her charm. Her long and very thick hair was pulled on top from the sides of her head and held in place by a red bow, allowing the bulk of her shining femininity to tumble freely below her waist. The dark eyes, heavily rimmed with *kohl*, might have stood out harshly against a paler skin, but the warm tones of the desert gathered around their depths, as camels might about a life giving well.

She surveyed our little group and recognizing Linda, took a step forward to greet her.

"Linda . . . I wanted to see you again. I must know everything about Swit-zer-land."

I watched them walk away and sit on a low stone wall at the end of the pool. Soon they removed shoes and dabbled their feet in the water, Fahada's silk gown up to her knees, matching Linda's short skirt. Their laughter aroused Sara's curiosity, and not wanting to be left out, she skipped off to join them.

I recognized Hussa immediately, as she came to welcome me, secure in her own element, delightfully uninhibited, returning the favor of having visited my home. "And so, here we are . . ." her smile seemed to say of the several ladies who discreetly followed after her. "You are welcome. May our hospitality be as great as our delight in your presence."

One by one Hussa introduced her relatives: a cousin from Dammam, a sister from Qassim, more cousins, an aunt newly arrived from Buraida, all wanting to meet the Al Abdullah's

American friends, and perhaps to challenge disturbing questions our presence might arouse. Open minded, interested, these ladies of the Eastern Province did not adhere to the lavish life style of their sophisticated and money conscious relatives filling the marble palaces of Riyadh, their traditions fighting for continuance against the new wealth. Nor did they appear to embody the bored and pampered ladies I had imagined they might be.

I could never forget their friendly faces, but would I remember all the names? Alia—Muna—Nejela—Hessa—Misha'al—another Muna—Fatma—words not a part of my vocabulary. Yet, it didn't really matter, for interest was beyond remembering names. Their display of solidarity, pride and desire to please displaced any feelings of uncertainty. Perhaps our differences of culture would never blend, but today we would · enjoy just being women.

Gone was my sense of being a stranger, to whom the desert nomad gives refuge for three days. Rather I relished my position of being a friend, one bringing visions of desired change—even western complications from unknown relationships—here to sit alongside security and strength of family, the knowing who you are and how far you may go. In no way would this day be shared with automatons of tradition, but with guardians of a lifestyle women alone held in their hands.

With the ever ready "Ahlan", Hussa pointed out the white wicker chairs, their bright cushions bursting with welcome. I was glad to sit down instead of feeling awkward standing. Hussa encouraged two shy little girls, snuggling against the security of their mothers' skirts, to invite Margaret and Cyndy to join them in an area of piled cushions under the shade of a betel nut tree. Margaret held back but brightened when the portable red phonograph appeared and Stateside rock and roll rhythms became a universal method of communication. Any doubt about Cyndy's story of Elvis was gone now. A dark skinned child wriggled her way through the group of ladies, eyes wide, as she offered an assortment of syrupy sweets from a large tray. A woman followed with the ever-present coffee service, intent on seeing the child perform her duties without disaster.

Were they slaves, these black servants, known to exist in some families? Saudi society followed the custom of acquiring a black child to be the lifelong companion of one of its own—not a form of servitude, but of belonging. I watched this child through concerned eyes—her tousled hair, pert grin and hands too small to hold the oversized tray that dipped, leaking sugary drips on her cotton skirt. Where would she go, this child and her family, if they were free, as King Faisal would do? Exclude them from their only home and lifelong family ties, reminiscent of our own history?

Several women had gathered beyond the terrace. They seemed to be watching the road. With some urgency, one of them sent a curly headed child hurrying toward the pool, her gaudy yellow dress flashing progress through the undergrowth. She stepped wide of Linda to deliver a message to Fahada, then rushed off. Immediately, the Princess slipped into her shoes, and taking Linda by the hand, hurried to stand at the top of the terrace steps. Hussa and other ladies joined her, their interest centered on the road at the foot of the pathway that had brought us to the Amir's summer residence.

Someone was expected. Who?

Chapter Seventeen
THE WELCOME CAKE

A car could be heard rounding the curve of the driveway. Several ladies moved closer to the terrace steps in anticipation of the arrival of other guests. I watched with interest, as a black Mercedes limousine emerged through the trees and stopped at the foot of the garden path. The driver swung out, walked briskly around the back of the car, came to the front and opened the rear door. He averted his gaze as a woman emerged.

For a brief moment she stood erect, harvesting the attention her presence aroused. I sensed the power and dignity of her every step up the garden path that could belong only to one of noble birth. Her long red velvet gown appeared to gather the vivid blossoms on either side, forming a scarlet carpet worthy of royalty. A dramatic entrance, equal to a queen without courtiers in this simple garden setting.

I leaned forward in my chair for a better view of this newcomer, as she walked up the steps to the terrace. The glow in her almond shaped eyes, accentuated by a heavy application of *kohl*, her ripe apricot skin and lips that spread into an open smile were decoration enough for her demeanor that carried assurance of who she was.

She approached the Princess Amsha, gracefully lifted the

tip of a light veil and draped it over her hair that fell freely to her waist. She offered a warm greeting to the young Princess, kissed her several times on each cheek, then surveyed the scene to accept adulations from those present. Who is this elegant lady, I thought, so richly endowed with her own personal gifts she wears no more than a few gold bangles and earrings to enhance her appearance? Someone deeply respected honored us with her presence.

She engaged the Princess in quiet conversation. Then, Amsha turned to address me. So much had happened since the arrival of her letter, that I prepared myself for most anything. This moment could be the ultimate of events.

"Mrs. Nicholson . . ." Amsha said. "*Ummi*—my mother, Amira Azziza Bint Rashida."

That moment became the culmination of all my hopes. It was one thing to meet the daughter, but the gracious welcome by the mother erased all concerns for the differences I represented. True, her studied gaze appeared to access my credentials, and her dark eyes expressed an interest in the strangers who had set down roots in her country.

"I am honored to meet you," I said, realizing I was in the presence of the Amir's wife.

She acknowledged with a nod, then turned to fulfill other obligations. She walked toward the house, and several children ran after her, tugging at her skirts and raising their up-turned faces for a kiss. After a few embraces, Amsha sent the children away, but not before the Amira had cuddled a dark skinned boy. Perhaps the son of a slave, sharing the love she gave all children. The Princess accompanied her mother to the house, where servants whisked her inside.

"Who was that?" Linda asked.

"Amsha's mother. You told me you saw her."

"Yes, I did. But she looked different. She's pretty when she smiles."

"We all are," I commented. "If we'd only remember that."

We accepted a glass of mint tea. Its relaxing sweetness re-wound a replay of the scene I had just witnessed, for my interest was again drawn to the roadway where a second limousine had just driven up and stopped. Again, the driver circled the car to open the rear door.

Was there a significance to these arrivals I wondered, as a tall gaunt woman stepped out and with long strides made her way up the garden path. She, too, wore a red velvet dress, but unlike the first, hers was trimmed with black lace at neck and sleeves. A white cotton scarf, folded tight across her forehead and the line of her ears, presented a rather stern visage. This image soon disappeared, for she tossed her long black plaits over her shoulders and with open arms and deep laughter allowed the children to jump into her embrace and to press their lips against her cheeks. Her rather angular frame lacked the grace of Amira Azziza, but when she turned in recognition of Linda and me, her manner was sincere and carefree with no concern for who we might be, other than guests of the family.

The young woman, Lulu, whom I had met as Azziza's sister, hastened to join us for introductions. "Umm Naiyf . . ." she said, and the inflection of her voice revealed pride that Umm Naiyf had borne a son.

"Praise be to Allah for the gift of a son," I said.

The woman's eyes sparkled with pride, softening the lines in her face. She may have lacked elegance, but a glow from within made her quite handsome.

"*Fi welad?* (Do you have a son?)" She asked.

"I have not been so blessed, but I have two daughters. This is Linda."

"*Jamila!* Beautiful . . ." she crooned. "What age is she?"

"Fifteen . . ." Linda contributed, wanting to appear older..

"Oh! It is the same with my son. *Alhamdulilah!*"

Already we had something in common.

"Later—God willing—you will have sons." And on that fruitful wish Umm Naiyf retired to the house.

I watched Fahada embrace her, before returning to join Linda and me.

"*Ya, Sara . . .*" the Princess called.

"Yes—I am coming." Sara dragged herself away from some ladies who had engaged her in conversation.

I reached for Sara's hand as she passed by. "Do you know who she was—the second woman in red?" I asked.

"Where? I don't see anyone."

"She went into the house."

"Oh, well—I don't know."

"Ask someone . . ." I said, but Sara had already drifted away.

Again wheels on gravel, and a third limousine came to a stop. With much squirming and pushing an obese woman worked her way out of the car door. Her shoes became ensnared in her long robe, as she clutched a tiny girl against her bounty. The child tugged at her pale pink dress, French and chic, as she struggled to be set down. She brushed a fluff of curls from her forehead and urged her toddler legs up the path to the terrace. Princess Amsha hurried forward and gathered the child into her arms.

"Aysha . . ." she whispered, smothering the pretty face with kisses. She swung her toward me. "My sister . . ." she said, presenting the child and her guardian, Reema.

Aysha shied. Her face clouded, as a flower in fading sunlight. Hussa carried her off to listen to the music, Reema following with a watchful eye. Aysha stamped her foot to escape the well meaning hands, but she could never flee from the love nurtured in the depths of a Muslim family.

"I found out what you want to know," Sara whispered, hurrying over. "Umm Naiyf is the mother of Prince Naiyf."

"Well, I figured that out myself," I said, knowing that the mother always carries the name of her first born son. "But how does that make Amsha and Naiyf brother and sister?"

"They are both children of the Amir—but with different mothers . . ." Sara explained.

"You mean . . ." Somehow I could not speak the words, the revelation too startling. "I have just met two wives of the same man?"

"Of course."

" . . . living and talking together? Even wearing the same dress?"

Sara shrugged. "Why not? It is Arab custom. But of course, each has her own villa."

"How can they. . . ?"

"The husband is good to both. They are happy. He treats them equally."

A thought struck me. "Does Amira Azziza have a son?"

"No. Amsha told me Naiyf is her only brother."

The only son of the Amir. No wonder his mother was proud. She had an edge on everyone. Her place in the family would always be secure.

Sara didn't linger but joined Fahada where she was introducing Linda to relatives. I looked for the two wives, but they did not return to the terrace. Custom allowed a man to have four wives. He must treat them equally—sharing his days and nights with each—even to the red dress? It was one thing to be aware of this, quite something else to see it.

A moment of privacy gave me time to dwell on the events of the morning, on the attitudes and sincerity of the women I had met. Such an opportunity might never come again. Now and then I glanced toward the summerhouse, hoping the Amir's wives might return.

Engrossed in my own thoughts, I failed to notice the arrival of a fourth limousine, until the occupant was half way up the walk. In trying to accept Arab customs, I was unprepared for the appearance of a completely western young woman, even to the four-inch heels. She came up the steps and approached me directly, a radiant smile, eager and delightful, spreading happiness across her face. There was no one to introduce her, so for a second we stood completely aware of each other. If she had worn a veil, it was not visible, and her loose hair curled softly about her shoulders. The short skirt and jewel neckline of her lavender dress seemed in defiance of the formal cavalcade of distinguished Arab women. Voices on the terrace reduced to a murmur. The children paused in their play.

"How nice of you to come," she said in a soft sibilant, her smile completely disarming, her easy English lightly decorated with a foreign lilt. It was not the English of a Middle Easterner, but of a European. My expression must have amused her, for she continued, "You are surprised that I speak English? Well, of course, I am not Saudi—although my father is Jordanian."

I listened, entranced, the unexpected more difficult to accept than the anticipated. There was something about this girl that made me want to take her hand and never let her go. She might have been Linda forced into an unfamiliar environment. How could I explain the sensation that I had been waiting for her to come into my life?

My first words blurted from a depth of feeling without justification or understanding. "What are you doing here?"

She laughed. "I live here." She started to move on, then paused. "My name is Latifa. I must go now, but I shall see you again."

Her tender glance warmed my disturbed emotions. It seemed to say, "It's okay." Her presence appeared to be as unrealistic as my own. I hoped she might stay, but she followed protocol, as if a member of the group. My longings to meet Saudi families seemed directed toward this moment, when Latifa came into my life. The fact needed no explanation. It was just there. Reluctantly, I watched her pay respects to the other women who received her kindly, if coolly, then continued on into the house.

Latifa. She was not one of them. Then, who was she? And why did she arrive in that cavalcade of cars? I looked for Hussa. Perhaps her good humor would excuse the gross error I was about to make. After all, with a language barrier, mistakes could be more readily forgiven.

AMSHA AND FAHADA PRESENT US WTH A
WELCOME CAKE

"Latifa . . . is she a European?" I asked.

Hussa was not so easily entrapped. She evaded the question, as if aware of my purpose. "She speaks English very well. One day I will, too," she answered.

"Is she your teacher?"

"No. But now I do have a teacher, but she is not the one." Then, overwhelmed with a sudden idea, "You must meet my teacher. It must be arranged."

"Then—Latifa is a visitor?"

"Latifa is Amira. You know what is Amira?"

"Why, yes—I do." I answered. Hussa seemed reluctant to

explain any further. An Amira is the wife of an Amir, I thought. But there are so many Amirs—princes, elders, and village authorities. Somehow I must find out.

The chattering on the terrace gradually eased, the children's voices the last to be heard. I escaped from my thoughts to discover another limousine parked at the bottom of the garden path. The formality was endless, and my curiosity waited to review this latest arrival.

Dressed completely in black robes and heavily veiled, the lady who started up the path appeared to be quite old, her uncertain steps indicative of tiredness and poor health. Refusing assistance, she raised her veil as she ascended the stairs. A slave woman, equally old, gathered her skirts and hurried to lead her mistress to a chair in the shade. She squatted at the old lady's feet to be close to the woman she must have grown up with and guarded all her life. How difficult for the companion to be separated from her mistress, even for the brief time the woman arrived alone. Who was this gentle lady who had made a supreme effort to favor us with her presence? Or, not so much us, as to uphold the honor of the family and its hospitality toward guests. She must be the Great Aunt. Linda had called her Nura.

Family members gathered around the distinguished lady, bending to embrace her and calling to the children, one by one, to do likewise. Aysha scampered in and out of turn, begging to be allowed to sit on the old lady's lap.

Studying Nura's face, I determined that her lack of a smile was not ill humor but a tiredness resulting from early hardships among the nomad tent dwellers of the desert—long before oil promised comfort and ease of living, bringing with it concern for the future of the family.

It was a difficult life, a dedicated life, one that required strength, self-sacrifice and loyalty. Now, there were new elements to tempt the Muslim woman. Her very presence portrayed an understanding that these things must be seen and dealt with, not by seclusion, but by exposure, as not being relevant to the *hareem* . The young Fahada had forward ways, not suitable for a Princess of the royal House of Al Saud. Exposure—not retreat—was the way to handle it.

How many American families would hold the aged in such respect. Here, young and old, everyone belonged. Even I, a complete stranger, felt enveloped in that warmth and was beginning to sense a relationship with them.

Lulu beckoned me to come. "You must meet our Great Aunt. She is asking to see you."

Why, without reason, did I recall my days of Hollywood— the premiere of an important movie—the lights, the cars, the actresses vying for supremacy in that thin world of chance and fleeting success? Here the scene was different, but the old lady who faced me commanded awe of her presence—not for any glamour or ostentation, but for what she held in her hands: the honor and survival of a family.

The pride that kept her head erect questioned previous concepts that came rushing back to me: the words of scholars on a printed page, a pink satin dress against a fortress wall, a stolen moment from a patio roof, all superficial glimpses of Saudi family life. In the Great Aunt I found new depths for discovery and truth.

The dark shadows beneath her eyes, more deeply drawn than *kohl*, the lines engraved about her narrow lips were not merely the product of age, but rather a fulfillment of destiny. The light of life feebly flickering told of a woman's surrender to tradition: to the comfort and prestige of a man, to the laws for survival of the group, to the designation of the unseen: "*ily wu raq*" (those who are behind you). The truth was there in the coarse veil she dropped that covered her head and neck, reminder of the value of a virgin daughter, a treasure to be guarded at puberty from the eyes of males. I sensed that the rough skinned and knobby fingers, reposing quietly on her lap, could now lay aside the burden they had carried over the years, guardian of family honor, as though it were a fragile flower, never in her lifetime allowing it to wither and die, for the indiscretions of a woman are the family's fatal flaw.

I didn't understand all I thought I knew, except that Nura was the distillation of family behavior, the desert flower that blooms unseen, the streambed that passes greatness to the young Fahada: pride in unbroken tradition.

We Americans were a challenge to all she stood for. Why had she come? Those narrow-drawn fading eyes carried no fear, no weakness, no capitulation, but rather a challenge and concern for an intrusion of inevitable forces that presented a threat to her way of life. She knew the decadence of character that oil, wealth and western permissiveness had brought to the sons, who could not rise above their weaknesses. Would these influences undermine the daughters? Could the women of the family stand the test? I stepped forward, careful to avoid the companion. There was no hostility or lack of interest in Nura's expressionless face. She had seen, she had evaluated, and in time she would react.

"*Marhubba . . .*" I said to break the silence. "I did not expect to be so honored."

There was no audible response, but the depth of her eyes flared feverishly. Then, they looked beyond me to Fahada and Linda, laughing and enjoying each other by the edge of the pool. Except for the dress and skin tones, the girls could have been relatives.

"Are you not tired after your long journey?" she said.

"Oh, no, indeed," I answered, glad for a sign of recognition.

"Your daughter?" A quick movement of the eyes indicated the pool.

So, she had noticed Linda. "Yes, I have two."

A quietness descended upon her face. Had her limited experience understood a basic similarity common to all peoples? Only through contacts can we know each other. She seemed to accept what she could not change. Quietly, and without further questioning, she slipped into the private retreat of age. I felt dismissed. At least she had come, knowing Americans would be there.

"Come! Hurry! We are leaving!" Hussa's cry carried across the terrace, as she snatched a scarf from a servant and flipped it on her head.

The cars had returned. I didn't want to leave without seeing Latifa again, but she was nowhere on the terrace.

"Mom, come on . . ." Linda said. She headed for the cars along with Fahada, Sara and Hussa.

"Have you seen Cyndy and Margaret?"

My question was answered by the appearance of Reema, who it seemed had extended her largess to include the American girls. She bustled them, Aysha and herself into a car. The rest of us followed suit.

"Where are we going?" I asked.

What else would this day bring forth? I was anxious to open a conversation that might lead to Latifa.

"It's a surprise," Hussa said. "Something special." She smoothed the folds of her long gown and pulled a veil over her face, as the car rounded the garden gate and headed for Hufuf.

"I wonder how Mr. Nicholson will know where to find us," I questioned.

"He is with the Prince and will be back soon."

The cars headed for the Bait Amir, then drove down a side street that ended in a grove of ragged palms buttressed by a crumbling wall. A grey bearded shepherd herded his goats, squatting against the wall in a thin line of shade. The hard packed ground held nothing for them to eat, but the goats kept up their incessant nibbling. The cars whirled around and came to an abrupt stop in front of a high wall with a sheet metal gate. The flat roof of a house showed above the wall, along with a few branches from a mimosa tree. Fortress towers of the Al Kut loomed behind, their heroic proportions standing in the pathway of change.

The gate opened, and Hussa played hide-and-seek with her veil as we emerged. Several women waited on the porch. Some we had seen before. Amira Azziza and Umm Naiyf had arrived already and sat in deep chairs that lined the salon walls. I had not been aware of their departure. Perhaps while I was preoccupied with the Great Aunt. I looked for her, but she was not there. Neither was Latifa.

"Please, make yourself comfortable," Princess Amsha urged her guests. She quickly slipped from the room, followed by her mother.

"Is this where you came before?" I asked Cyndy.

"No. We were in the Palace. The room was much larger—and different."

A dark skinned child struggled to control a large box of chocolates. Her fingers barely reached the edges. The chocolates were in danger of spilling, and Cyndy gasped, as the box tipped dangerously in front of her.

"Gosh!" she exclaimed. "I've never seen one so big."

Neither had I. Christmas candies sold in the ARAMCO canteen never came packaged in such huge boxes. Nor did they have bright red ribbons tied around each gold papered sweet.

Glasses of pomegranate tea followed close behind. Additional girls entered the room. Their cheerful faces expressed pleasure at our visit, although none were bold enough to come forward. A maze of color permeated cotton dresses and embroidered gowns. With inquisitive and staring eyes, eagerness and restraint, they leaned around each other, shyly peering for a view of unfamiliar guests. Some hurried to fill empty chairs, while others sat on the floor, competing for a place near the visitors—near, but not too close. The youngest ones gathered around Umm Naiyf. Their long dresses, lace frilled and embroidered, simple jewelry of gold bangles and rings, and a lump of turquoise to discourage the evil eye, decorated the simplicity of the room's furnishings. Hair, brushed and plaited fell over their shoulders, strands escaping in ringlets about ears and forehead.

An undercurrent of excitement aroused gestures and whispers, not to betray a confidence. Even the youngest held tight lips to refrain from spilling a secret. What do you say, when they are all looking at you, eager faces wondering what you are like, how you are different. How do you bridge the centuries in a single room?

"Linda," I said. "Speak to the children. They want to look at you."

"What shall I say?"

"Anything. Arabic or English—and take Cyndy and Margaret with you."

It was then I became aware of additional women stealthily drifting into the room. Heavily veiled and completely covered by their *abbayas*, they hugged the rear wall. Servants passed them by, and no one acknowledged their presence. They stood there motionless without speaking a word.

Who were these silent specters and what part did they play in this event? I looked to Umm Naiyf for an answer, but she was busy attending to the children, completely ignoring the invisible observers. I felt some discomfiture at their presence and wondered what else I might discover about these families I wanted to meet.

Amira Azziza returned. She had changed her dress and appeared less formal in a frothy violet gown. Activity ripened as the Amira proceeded with introductions: cousins, aunts, sisters—all relatives of the Amir. The Hufuf branch of the Al Abdullah family was extensive. I kept returning to the silent ones dressed in black, motionless and ignored, a strange accompaniment to a festive gathering.

Princess Amsha appeared, having changed into a lemon silk dress stitched with gold thread in intricate designs. She called excitedly to the servants, signaled everyone to sit down, then herself dropped into a chair next to Linda. Reema hurried in from a back room, Aysha toddling after. The little girl ran from all the outstretched hands, dodging and laughing, until she wound up with her sister. Evidence of anticipation prepared the way for something special to take place. The family knew a secret I didn't. Aysha could not keep from whispering to her sister, a little finger singling us out, one by one. What fun getting acquainted! How could it be a forbidden thing?

Servants entered carrying large pitchers of orange juice. Behind them, two men wheeled a table into the center of the room. It was laden with trays of honey cakes, pistachio rolls, stuffed dates and other delectable pastries. On a lace cloth in the center of this array stood a tall pedestal bearing a square shaped, four tiered cake iced in white. All four sides of the bottom and topmost layers were decorated with English block letters in red, white and blue icing that read: "WELCOME!" Any doubt of sincerity disappeared in this revelation of declared friendship. Never had the colors of our flag meant so much. I could only marvel at the depth of ingenuity and determination that produced this evidence of good will.

Linda jumped up. "Oh,—it is beautiful! Thank you— thank you."

"Is it for us?" Cyndy gasped.

Princess Fahada's eyes glowed. "I hope it pleases you. It is but a small thing."

Amsha turned to me. " . . . for a special oc-ca-sion."

"Sara!" I looked around for her. "Please express our sincere thanks to everybody for their kindness."

Sara did and repeated Fahada's reply.

"We are happy that you came. We wish this will not be the last visit."

Reema took possession of a large knife, ready to plunge it into the cake.

"Please," Linda cried. "Let me cut it. We always do when it's special."

Sara translated, and Amsha agreed. If this was not customary for the *hareem*, no one disapproved but accepted the situation, because it was our way.

Reema relinquished the knife, and Linda made the first cut. Alia joined Cyndy to assist in serving the slices. Aysha squirmed on her sister's lap and tugged at her shoulder to whisper in her ear. She jumped down and with caution approached the table. Linda cut the next piece and gave it to Aysha to serve the person of her choice—Amsha. The children selected their own sweets, and when they were finished eating, Reema tucked a small drum under her arm and chanted a rhythm so they could dance.

"Whose home is this?" I asked the Princess Amsha. "I would like to thank her, too."

"I live here now," she said. "Before it was the Palace."

"Do you like it better?"

"The Palace is very old." She used the term Bait Amir— home of the Amir. "The floors creak and the walls fall down. Now they try to fix it, so we live here."

"Does Hussa live with you?"

"No. Just my mother and sisters. But there are always other people, too. Fahada lives here when she visits from Riyadh."

"Won't you miss living in the Palace?"

Fahada shrugged. She called for Sara to help with ideas she wished to express. " . . . I want to see the changes to my city—to go outside the gate."

"Linda told me how she met you."

"That was the first time I dared to do it. I was upset when my uncle came in. I knew my mother would not give me away."

"I am glad you did it—because otherwise we would never have met."

"I like Americans. I want to know more about them. I want to speak English and go to school in America. Is it true boys and girls go to classes together? It is in my mind all the time."

"Yes, Princess," I said. "Our system is different, but we are still people the same as you."

"When I live here, maybe I can learn other things, too."

"*Inshallah*." I said. If it is the will of God. "First you must have an English teacher."

"Oh, I do," she sighed. "But it takes too long. She is from Jordan and comes here, but we do not learn very much, because there is no one to speak to."

At last the opportunity to mention a subject I felt uncomfortable about pursuing. "There is Latifa. I met her . . ."

"She is different . . ." Fahada hesitated, as if unwilling to say more.

It was clearly a moment of impasse. I let the subject drop.

Hussa had overheard our conversation and interrupted. "I promised you would meet our teacher. Now we must go to her place."

A bell rang to summon a car. Fahada's manner changed. "We must show you our city," she said. "We will drive around and you shall see the change that is going on."

I wondered at her pride in municipal improvement, not realizing at the time her passion for fast cars. Here was an opportunity for another spree in the lavender Cadillac.

"I love to drive," she said. "Visiting my relatives in Dammam gives me a chance to do that."

Linda, Sara, Hussa and I joined her in the car. I wouldn't leave without Cyndy and Margaret, so Reema ordered another car, and she, Aysha and the girls followed close behind.

"I told my uncle he could give Naiyf all the jewelry. I wanted a fast car for my birthday," the Princess said.

"You are lucky," I said, accepting her fantasy of being in control.

She signaled the driver to start the car, and once again the lavender Cadillac sped through the town.

Chapter Eighteen
LATIFA

We drove along the line of the old battlements, where the inner walls of the Al Kut joined the exterior fortifications. The driver pounded on the horn and shouted at pedestrians, as he maneuvered the car through partially blocked roads. Progress was slower heading out of town. A section of the old wall with its bastion was being demolished to make way for city improvements. Bulldozers piled heaps of rubble and raised clouds of dust, as the old stones and dried mud crumbled to the ground. We jostled over debris and potholes, where a bulldozer ripped at the road. Curious bystanders watched, fascinated—not so much at the destruction, as at the mechanical monsters that accomplished it.

The driver shouted, shook his fist and blew the horn, but such efforts were less effective than the fall of ancient marl and rock. An endless chain of men and boys scooped up the debris with their hands, tossed it into leather buckets and dumped their contents into a tangle of donkey carts waiting to carry the refuse to swampy areas outside the city. A rhythmic chant accompanied the workers, bringing unison to each pair of hands, and the men labored en masse, as if manipulated by unseen strings: the verse and chant of the Koran.

Older men squatted amongst the rubble, reluctant to give up the force that had protected their city from invaders. This was not the enemy of battle being destroyed, but another danger unseen and unrecognized: disease, illiteracy, malnutrition.

Unheedful of pedestrians and onlookers, the car backed up to negotiate a detour through a maze of citizens, sheep and peddlers. The driver wormed the car down a narrow alley between rough walls and stopped near a low building. He got out and went in search of the English teacher. People stared and frowned, compelled to squeeze past the parked lavender Cadillac, a familiar sight to the residents of Hufuf.

Hind, the English teacher, arrived. We made room for her on a jump seat. She immediately engaged us in conversation, and I was only half aware of the driver shouting his way down the alley. Sudden stops to avoid hazards distracted our interest in the teacher, until we picked up a smooth trail that led away from the city.

I asked after the aptness of her pupils and was told that they didn't work hard enough. Hussa ignored the comment with a shrug and said we were all out to enjoy the day and not to be reprimanded for shortcomings.

We first visited one of the fresh water springs that abound in the Al Hasa Oasis. Under natural pressure, the fresh water rose through saline soil from table rock deep below the surface and emerged as clear wells and pools amid the palm gardens. Hufuf was renowned for these wells, the only natural source of sweet water, together with similar wells found in the Qatif Oasis that bordered our coastal community of Ras Tanura.

In one of the larger pools, a man gave his hennaed donkey a bath, and separated by a fence of palm matting, fully dressed women enjoyed an afternoon of frolicking in the water. An irrigation system under construction projected through the trees. In time, clay ditches would carry water to any part of the Oasis gardens.

Princess Fahada directed the driver to stop at a nearby field where men were herding cattle into a low building. She leaned close and grabbed my hand to make sure I understood the significance of this experimental dairy. Many breeds of cattle were being raised and tested to develop a milk producing animal with stamina to withstand the intense heat of summer. The Brahma cattle had the edge.

"See how much we are doing to improve our city," she said. "Soon we will have everything."

Laid out beyond the dairy were rows of surveyor markers, indicating future wider streets, new enclosed shops and permanent more comfortable homes. It was all a miracle and the expertise of Americans who made the means possible.

"That is why I want to go to school in America," Fahada said. "We must be ready for tomorrow."

"Soon all girls will have the chance to go to school," Hind said. "Now, I have private classes, but we are working on a system to build and equip schools for girls in the Al Hasa Oasis.

"In Safwa near where I live," Linda said, " . . . there is a building, but there are no books and no teachers."

"It cannot be achieved all at once," I explained.

"I shall be a teacher," Fahada said. "I want to teach at the new schools."

Hussa poked her with an elbow. "A teacher. And what will your husband say to that?"

Fahada frowned, not appreciating the comment. "I do not intend to get married. I shall never marry a man who already has a wife." Her words took on a serious tone. "Our country needs many things. I see the differences with Americans, and I want to help."

"We shall need teachers, Princess," Hind said. "It will take many of them to staff the schools."

"I shall be one of the first." Fahada's determination brought color to her cheeks.

"Leave that to others," Hussa said with a sense of the re-

alistic. "You cannot be anything but a wife like the rest of us—
even when you marry the King's brother." Then, further baiting
her niece, "Of course, when you get tired of that, you can refuse
to have sons and be divorced."

Fortunately, our tour continued without further contention.
We drove back from the Caves of Garrah, where skilled potters
produced the famous Al Hasa pottery. Ahead lay a broad stretch
of open desert. Fahada spoke to the driver, and the car took off at
a reckless speed. We all lurched and hung onto each other with
each swerve of the lavender Cadillac.

A car speeding off the road headed toward us from the opposite direction. A rifle shot rang out. Before anyone could deter-
mine where it came from, the approaching car caught up with us
and raced wildly past, male voices yelling and *quttras* flying.

"*Ya,* Naiyf!" Hussa cried, squirming in her seat to keep the car
in sight.

"Daddy was in that car!" Linda exclaimed with excitement.

"How could that be?" I said, hanging onto seats and straps.

Hussa instructed the driver to catch up with the speeding vehicle. The Princess chased her cousin to within a short distance
from the Oasis gardens. Prince Naiyf's car came to a stop. We
pulled alongside. I was relieved to see that Reema and the girls
remained some distance behind, with no hint of racing like a madman. I felt sure that whatever Hussa and Naiyf were up to, Reema
would take her charges safely back to the summerhouse.

"*Ya,* Naiyf," Hussa cried again, wildly waving her arms out
the window and hanging on to her veil.

The young Prince swung outside the car and aimed a long
barrelled rifle at the branches of a *sidr* tree. A sharp retort rang
out, followed by shouts of approval, and a bodyguard hastened to
retrieve a small fallen bird. Naiyf examined where the shot had
struck. With pride of accomplishment, he squared his shoulders
and prepared to take aim again.

"*Mabruk!*" (congratulations) Hussa shouted.

"The marksmanship of a *sheikh*," Fahada said. She turned her head to adjust the veil she had allowed to slip from her face while driving across the open country. .

The Prince acknowledged the compliments, as he studied the occupants of the Cadillac. He tossed the tiny victim to a guardsman and raised his rifle. Linda hid her face against my shoulder, not wanting to witness the slaughter. Naiyf took aim, and a second grey body fell from the trees.

"*Alhamdulillah!*" the shouts went up.

I was startled to see Russ come forward, his face clouded with concern over the Prince's demonstration of accomplishments for the pleasure of his sister's guests. Once again the Prince examined the bird, nodded his approval, and handed it to a guardsman. The man smoothed the torn feathers and approached our car.

"The Prince offers a token of his skill," Hind explained, having accepted the bird from the driver. " . . . for you..," she concluded, extending the shattered feathers to Linda. She shuddered with horror, much to Hussa's amusement.

"Sweetheart," I prompted. "You may not refuse the Prince's gift."

"I can't possibly touch it! Poor little thing," Linda cried, pushing away the hand that held the victim. I looked for assistance from someone—Sara—Hind—but none was forthcoming.

Aware of our predicament, but not wanting to interfere, Russ walked over to the Prince. If anyone knew the Arab psyche, the intent of a proud young man, and the appropriate classical Arab phrases, he did. Prince Naiyf seemed momentarily offended. He rubbed his hand over the gunstock, turned to Russ with a nod of approval, then ordered the guardsman to collect the bird from the driver and to remove it from our sight.

The chase continued, cars twisting over the rough terrain. The sudden claw of brakes threw us against the seats each time the Prince jumped out, aimed his rifle and ordered the car to take off again. Hussa and Sara rocked with laughter. Fahada kept urging the driver to go faster, but never out running the Prince.

CYNTHIA AND MARGARET ENJOY LUNCH IN
THE GARDENS OF HUFUF

"Why does he do it?" Linda said, her voice tight with stress.

"Never mind," I said. "It can't last much longer. See, here are the gates to the garden."

We entered the driveway. Reema's car was parked at the pathway, all passengers discharged. The summerhouse shone as a pink pearl glimmering in the fading sunlight through the trees, and the shadowed pathway offered relief from the glare of the open desert. It had been quite an episode, and I was glad to be back. Not until the girls ran chattering up the garden path, did the Prince's escort emerge and remain at a discreet distance. I waited behind to talk to Russ, aware that Naiyf had moved off in search of other targets, and that the Cadillac had turned around to return Hind to her home.

"How have you been making out?" I asked Russ.

"Okay," he said. "How about you?"

"Wait 'till I tell you. You won't believe it. Where did they take you?"

"Oh—with the Prince most of the time."

"What a chase!—Keystone cops," I said.

"He's not that bad. Just a young man with a chance to show off."

"Well—he made the most of it"

Another shot shook the leaves, and a shout went up. Linda came hurrying toward us.

"Does he have to?" she cried. "I can't stand it."

"In a way, yes," said her father. "I've been to the stables to watch him ride. Excellent, too."

"Hey—can we see the horses," Cyndy asked. She ran from the house to join us.

"Yes. Why not?" Linda brightened up.

"I'm afraid not," Russ said. "Don't forget, young lady, today you are one of the *hareem*."

Linda's retort splintered the air like a rifle. "I am not!

Never!"

"Well, let's say today you must follow the customs of your hostess—and—look—she's waiting for you."

Sara and Hussa glanced around the terrace, as they accepted cologne from a servant who doused it over their hands.

"Linda! Linda!" Sara called.

Hussa started down the steps to get her, then remembering men were near, she changed her mind. Another shot rang out accompanied by the crunch of feet over dry leaves. Linda headed toward Hussa.

"I'm going before he brings it back."

"You've forgotten the Prince is merely exercising the qualifications for a *sheikh*: horsemanship, marksmanship, and luck," Russ reminded.

"And how is he going to demonstrate his luck?" Linda asked, her words touched with sarcasm.

Russ knew his daughter well and responded to the challenge. "Could be in the choice of—a wife . . . ," he teased.

"Humph!" she scoffed and stomped off, Cyndy following.

"Looks like you better join them," he said to me. "See, they're preparing dinner."

Tantalizing fragrances drifted through the gardens.

"What about you?" I asked. "Where will you eat?"

"Don't worry. I'm sure the Prince has it all arranged."

I joined the group on the terrace. A flurry of hand washing was in progress over a large tub set against some trees. A black child offered a cake of soap. An ample bosomed woman, enveloped in an overlarge apron, poured rinse water from a slender ewer. A towel was instantly available, then hands were doused in generous portions of rose scented cologne.

Bright colored rugs and straw matting displayed a sumptuous dinner set on the cool side of the terrace. Several servants stood over the many small dishes of sliced tomatoes and cucumbers, hot lamb stew, finger *kibbee* and fruit being arranged by the family cook. Their sole function was to wave fans of woven palm fronds or to snap towels to chase off the flies. Meanwhile, as preparations continued, we enjoyed more hot sweet tea served in tiny glasses with gilt edges and bearing the crest of the House of Al Saud.

The family women returned to the terrace, refreshed from an afternoon nap. The children soon had the record player pounding out the exotic half tones and rhythm of Arab music. The Great Aunt was nowhere to be seen. Her presence earlier, even for a brief time, was significant enough.

I signaled Sara. "Have you seen Latifa?"

"Who?"

"The girl who speaks English."

"Oh—Latifa . . ."

"Have you seen her? Is she here?"

"I don't know. But I found out who she is."

"Yes. . . ?" Was I too eager?

" . . . the wife of the Amir."

Sara's words were so casual, I accepted them as insignificant. Then, a quick reaction, " . . . which Amir?"

"Mishari Al Abdullah—Amsha's father."

I felt stunned without reason and struggled with thoughts that would not stay in place. "But—I thought Amira Azziza was Amsha's mother—the distinguished lady in the red velvet dress."

"She is," Sara confirmed. "And Umm Naiyf is the mother of the Prince."

There was only one answer to this unexpected confusion I had difficulty accepting as true. " . . . then, Latifa is . . ." I could not say the words.

" . . . the third wife," Sara completed my sentence with no concern at all. "They are waiting for you to wash your hands— dinner is ready."

LUNCH IS SET UP ON THE TERRACE

Amira Azziza and Umm Naiyf were seated on the rug next to each other and facing the extensive spread of food. Amsha squeezed into a place near Cynthia and Margaret. Reema settled Aysha on the far side of the circle with Alia and Muna, another sister, then helped all the children pile their plates with lamb stew, roasted chicken, rice and other goodies.

I rubbed the last of the cologne into my wrists and throat. It felt refreshing after the afternoon's activities. My skin dried quickly in the warm air, and the lingering perfume blended with the smell of savory lamb and spiced rice. I was hungry, even after the cake and all the coffee and tea.

"Did you enjoy the ride?"

How welcome—the sound of her voice.

"Latifa . . ."

She smiled with controlled gentleness. "I'm afraid you'll be tired before you get back to Ras Tanura," she said, adjusting the embroidered shawl draped on her shoulder, perhaps a concession to Muslim custom of covering the arms.

"I was afraid I wouldn't see you again," I said, my words too bold, considering we had just met. Yet, it seemed I had always known her.

She laughed, amused at my concern. "I knew you would be back for dinner, and so I stayed." She brushed aside the wispy hair that fell in a swirl about her face and shoulders. The musical accent and rising inflections of her speech revealed a remnant of her native tongue, but I couldn't place it. I could only wonder at her presence in these surroundings.

"It is good to hear someone speak your own language," I said, rather thoughtlessly.

"Yes—I know. You see, I have lived mostly in Europe, and I don't speak Arabic very well."

Perhaps that explained the clear green eyes with the crispness of the north.

"Your English is perfect. You must have studied a long time."

"Since I was a child. My father is Jordanian. He attended an English school in Amman and wanted me to do the same."

I sensed a delicate balance between outward self-assurance and a yearning for the western world she had left behind. My eagerness to learn more of Latifa must not upset that stability.

"Will you join me," I said. "There is room for two." Linda had saved space for me on the rug where she sat enjoying expert guidance from Sara and Fahada.

"Thank you. You are so kind."

It was difficult to sit gracefully, and far from comfortably, with legs tucked under. To show the soles of the feet would be an offensive gesture. There was something to be said for long skirts, only I was not wearing one.

"It is difficult for me, too," Latifa said, amused at her

efforts to achieve the Arab custom of sitting on the ground.

Balanced on a brass pedestal at the center of the circular array of food lay an immense tray with high fluted edges. A mountain of saffron rice, glistening with meat juices and rendered fat, formed the bed for a mountain of roasted chickens. The bloated eyes stared, and distorted beaks took on a grimace of terror. The heads nodded, then slumped grotesquely as hands reached out for a share of the succulent meat. A hand with red velvet sleeve and hennaed fingers reached for a fistful of rice, juices and gee dripping down the wrist. An involuntary shudder for this lack of social graces—my code of manners—quietly slipped into an acceptance of the custom of my hostess. After all, I had a lot to learn.

"Look, Mom," Linda said, " . . . watch me." She tore off a piece of flat bread, folded it into a scoop and pinched up rich juices and meat.

Nearby, Hussa ripped off a wedge from a chicken breast the carver had set on her plate at knife point, then rolled a cluster of rice into a ball and popped it into her mouth. In spite of using fingers, she never once brought them to her mouth for a lick.

Forks were set intermittently on the cloth, but I hesitated to reach for one, observing that everyone else was eating Arab style. I had to smile at Cynthia's pained expression, as she gave up making rice balls, brought the plate to her lips and sucked up the rice Chinese style, without benefit of chopsticks. Reema helped Margaret compress the sticky rice into a ball, but it showered into a thousand grains all over her lap.

Latifa enjoyed watching. Perhaps recalling her own experiences. "The three American girls are your daughters?" she asked.

"Two of them," I acknowledged. "The blonde one is Cynthia's friend."

A momentary silence ensued before Latifa spoke again.

"I, too, have a daughter . . ." she said with a sadness in her voice I didn't immediately recognize.

"How nice. Is she here?"

"No. She is in Dammam." A sidewise glance controlled loneliness into joy of remembrance. "She is very little—just three years old."

"Did you drive all the way from Dammam? I'm sorry you did not bring her," I said.

"I live here in Hufuf. My daughter lives with her grandfather."

I heard the words as a statement of fact without full understanding. What longings lay behind them? It disturbed me that a child so young was not living with her mother. I knew only hearsay of intimate family relations. Expressed feelings might cause embarrassment or hurt, for I knew nothing of this girl or her circumstances. I turned to my plate and picked up a chicken leg for ease of eating.

"Her name is Haifa . . ." Latifa said. She selected an orange and began to peel it. There was no other food on her plate. "Haifa . . ." she said again, as though the name aroused a conflict between desire and submission.

A fleeting piece of history crossed my mind. Abdullah Al Abdullah, father of Amir Mishari and warrior at arms alongside Ibn Saud, had been dead for more than twenty years. His feats of honor were well known throughout Saudi Arabia, for his skill with the lance had more than once saved the life of his royal cousin. It was not for me to question a relationship unknown in my world.

"I don't enjoy family parties, so I seldom come . . ." Latifa said. Had she changed the subject to conceal her emotions—closed a door she had partly opened?

" . . . and today?" I asked.

"My husband insisted. He is the Amir of Hufuf. And I wanted to meet Americans."

"Are you disappointed?"

"I am so glad I came . . . you can't imagine."

There was so much I wanted to know of this girl—western in every sense, yet a member of this Muslim family. How had it happened? Had she chosen marriage of her own free will? Was she somehow a prisoner of circumstances? How could I ask, when we had only just met?

"Latifa . . . I feel as though I had known you all my life—and yet—may I ask you something?"

"Please, do."

"What brought you to Arabia?"

"Oh, I guess I hated the cold," she said, amused but in complete control. "Europe can be very cold in the winter. Sometimes, even in summer, you must wear a coat. I longed for warmth and sunshine I knew in Jordan as a child."

It sounded like a half-truth, so I answered in kind. "Well, there is plenty of it here." What answer had I expected? That she'd been carried off by a desert *sheikh*? That was Hollywood. Latifa was real.

Cyndy had finished eating and came bouncing over. "Reema's going to show us a baby camel—okay?"

"Where?"

"Over there—in the garden. Aysha wants to come, too."

"She'll be perfectly all right," Latifa said. "Reema is a devoted companion to all the children."

"Very well, but don't stay too long. It's getting late, and Daddy should be back soon."

She ran off to join Reema, Aysha, Margaret and Alia. Several women were getting to their feet to allow others to take their turn for dinner. Along with the ensuing chatter erupted loud belches from over laden stomachs, a sign of enjoyment and customary compliment to the hostess.

I couldn't help it. I blurted: "Latifa, how do you stand it?"

Without a moment's hesitation she answered, "I am married to the most wonderful man in the world."

Her head held high, a flush of remembrance coloring her cheeks told of a man who enlightened her whole being with an inner glow of happiness. I felt humbled and ashamed. It had never occurred to me that a deep and consuming love could be possible under the circumstances. The idea nagged at my soul. Yet, there in front of me stood proof of the sincerity—the beauty of one's faith.

Just because I, brought up under Christianity and western culture, couldn't accept it for myself, didn't mean there wasn't something rich and satisfying about the tenets of Islam, to which one fifth of the world's population subscribed. I needed to search my own soul, to find tolerance within myself and not to dismiss the questionable because it was different.

Again, we followed the formalities of hand washing. This time they really needed it. The second round already filled the dining area. After that would be the female slaves, servants, and retainers. The drivers, cooks and guardsmen would receive their share somewhere in the garden behind the pink house. Final leavings would be distributed among the poor and the beggars of the town. Nothing would be wasted.

A handsome servant woman, tall and trimly dressed approached us with a large brazier of burning incense. We wafted the spiraling fumes from glowing sandalwood toward our faces and arms, breathing in the intoxicating fragrance. It was relaxing, satisfying, heady like an aperitif— and the ultimate gesture of friendship. It also suggested time for departure.

I felt like walking in the enveloping warmth of late afternoon that augmented the sensation of well being. Since there was no sign of Russ, I suggested the idea to Latifa.

"I, too, would like that," she said. "Come—let me show you our garden pool."

Through the trees we came upon a natural spring, one of many found in the Al Hasa Oasis. Clear, vibrantly blue in its depths, the sweet water pulsed into a shallow dugout pool edged with palm trunks for steps and used as seats for bathers.

It was peaceful there by the spring with the bubbling water, the scurrying of small creatures through dried grasses, and the diminishing light of afternoon reflecting its golden streaks across the shadowed pool. It was, I realized, the first moment of privacy I had experienced all day. How could one ever be alone with so many people—all female—all day long? Again I felt the need for answers.

"Look, Latifa," I began, stumbling over words, the tranquility of this girl refuting my concern. "I have to ask you something—I have to know . . ."

She laughed at my awkwardness. "Please do."

I hesitated.

"Don't be afraid to ask."

I bungled into her serenity with my foreigner's lack of finesse. "How can you live this way?"

If she had not been so polite, so completely at peace with herself, she might have been embarrassed. As it was, I detected a slight smile of amusement.

"I am not familiar with all the customs of this country. I stay pretty much to myself. And, then, I am always busy . . ." She paused, as if to withdraw a truth that was hardly whole. "Of course, at first I was very frightened. I used to hear strange sounds at night, and I thought all kinds of horrible creatures would come crawling out of the old walls. And the screams were terrible. They came from the jail where prisoners never left alive—but I didn't know it then. Now the jail has been torn down, and I don't hear them any more."

"But, you weren't brought up to live in such seclusion," I began, then desperately, " . . . there must be times when you long to get away."

She didn't answer, just looked at me without a waiver.

"Please . . ." I said. " . . . will you come and visit me? My home is on the beach. It is small but comfortable."

A blend of desire and reality crept across her face. I rushed on before she could refuse .

"Mr. Nicholson is gone all day—the girls are in school, and I am the only one at home."

The moment of indecision became positive.

"You are very kind," she said, and the music of her voice sang with the flow of the spring.

"Please—I mean it sincerely . . ."

"You see, I would like that very much, but—it is impossible." Then, opening herself to me, " . . . the Prince would never allow it."

I detected no resentment, no resignation, just an acceptance of fact. She sensed my familiarity with the customs of purdah, and in responding openly, received me as a friend—not someone who spoke out of ignorance and pity.

"If there ever comes a day—remember my home is yours." What English word can express the warmth of the Arabic *"Ahlan wa sahlan"*?

"Thank you. You are so kind."

The hum of tires on gravel came from the driveway. The men had returned. Automatically she reached for a veil, then remembered she had none. We headed back through the trees to the far side of the swimming pool and away from the returning cars. I could hear Russ's voice, not quite the same as a native Arab. The time had come to leave.

Latifa remained by the pool. I said goodbye to her there. I caught a glimpse of her lavender dress, as she hurried through the garden. When I turned toward the terrace, she was gone.

Linda, Cynthia, Margaret and Sara were waiting for me. With regret we took leave of Princess Fahada and Hussa, hating to see this amazing day come to a close. I hadn't expected to see Amira Azziza again, but she joined us at the terrace steps with the assurance she looked forward to another visit.

Russ had driven the Land Rover over and kept its engine running. We piled in, and Sara shouted a final *"Fiamanillah! (Go with God)"*. Russ took leave of the Prince, then turned the car around without a glance toward the terrace. A final wave, as the Rover wound along the driveway, leaving the gates behind. The Prince's car had been in the lead. It suddenly veered away and headed back to the Oasis, as if on an urgent mission.

"How did you make out?" Russ asked me, when the Rover wheels hit the tarred surface of the Abqaiq road, and we had time to relax and reflect on the events of the day.

"Really great," I said, not knowing where to begin. "The women—wait till I tell you. So gracious! I can't believe this day really happened." Would he, or anyone else, believe it? As for Latifa, her story would be left for another time. "Where did you have dinner?"

"In the banquet room of the Palace. Prince Naiyf sat on one end of a setup on the floor, and I on the other. Call for the butler sort of thing. Look . . ." He handed me a small case. It held a gold pen and pencil set with the Al Saud crest.

"That's really nice," I said and meant it. But in my heart the red, white and blue WELCOME cake was the best gift of all.

A little farther down the road, we noticed a car parked on the rough shoulder and two men standing on the edge of the blacktop. Russ and I both had the same feeling.

"Doesn't that car look familiar?" I said.

"Our visit isn't over yet," he added.

The two men flagged us down. As anticipated, they were members of the royal escort. One of them carried a small cage made of sticks. He handed it to Russ with a grin. A pitiful grey bird fluttered against the bars, a length of white string tied to one leg.

"Guess this has your name on it," Russ said, passing the gift to Linda.

She accepted it gingerly. "How come?"

"Well . . . I suggested to the Prince that you might prefer one that could sing."

"Traded death for life . . ." I commented.

"Can you think of a better exchange?" he said.

The parked car drove off, and once again we followed the thin black line toward Abqaiq. The dark fringes of the Oasis gave way to open desert, and Linda asked her father to stop the car. She borrowed Cyndy's Swiss army knife and walked out onto the sand. Facing the last of the palms, she opened the cage, cut the string and watched the trembling flutter of feathers dive, then rise drunkenly toward the nearest palm. But, she hadn't completely given up the gift from the Prince. His gallantry would remain long after the starling had flown away.

Chapter Nineteen
THE VILLA IN DAMMAM

"Hey! The car's here!" Cynthia propelled herself down the hall and pounded on the closed bathroom door. "Lin—open up! I've got to comb my hair!" Several seconds of silence, then a faint click as the door opened.

"Again?" I overheard Linda toss at her sister. "This is the third time. What more can you do to it?" She came into my bedroom and fussily reached under her denim skirt to pull down the tail of her embroidered Swiss blouse.

"Does this look okay?" she asked, adjusting the tasseled cord that shaped the neckline about her shoulders.

"Well," I said. "It's a bit non-Saudi, but the Princesses will enjoy it. You'll do fine."

The end of the school year brought Linda home from The American School in Switzerland and a long awaited family reunion. Her year in Lugano had aroused an active eagerness for independence and a maturity that never dampened her joyous wonderment of life. Renewing her contact with Princess Fahada presented a challenge, and she refused to wear a long Arab style dress in favor of a short skirt that accentuated her western identity.

Amir Mishari's family frequently spent time in Dammam,

visiting the Governor and other relatives, including Great Aunt Nura who lived in one of the guesthouses on the Amirate grounds. Residing in Dammam offered the Princesses the opportunity to attend a private school for girls, along with Hussa who had not returned to her home in Buraida.

Ras Tanura on the Gulf was a mere hundred kilometers up the coast from Dammam, and we often received invitations from the Al Abdullah family to visit them. I realized our position was unique, and every visit deepened a growing kinship with the Kingdom, its intimate family life and close association with the Governor's family. Sometimes we hired a local taxi for the drive to Dammam, but more often Amira Azziza sent a car to pick us up.

"Do go and open the front door," I told Linda. " . . . so the driver will know we are coming." I finished puffing a fluff of powder to my nose. "Take a look up the street. Sara said she'd walk down."

I picked up my purse, added a few extra *riyals* just in case, and headed for the kitchen. Ahmed was finishing some ironing.

"I'm going to Dammam," I told him. "Mr. Nicholson knows. I'll be late getting back, so tell him not to wait dinner."

Ahmed's eyes narrowed. "Yes, *memsa'b*." He never understood why we visited the Saudis—and the Governor's family. It was better to stay clear of unpredictable events.

I turned away to avoid his censure and picked up a plate of freshly baked date bars. The cakes were always well received by our host family. Linda signaled from the front porch that Sara had arrived.

"Your hair will do, Cyndy," I called. "We must go."

"Okay," she mumbled. "But I can't get the clip straight."

"Don't forget about dinner," I reminded Ahmed.

"No, *memsa'b* . . ." He watched us leave with stricken eyes, as he flipped a dishtowel over his shoulder, certain the Al

Abdullahs would have us in jail before the day was over. The Saudis were not to be trusted.

We joined Sara in the waiting car. A truant gust of air caught my hair, forerunner of a threatening *shamaal* and the discomfort of blowing sand. The teasing fragrance of dried roses wafted through the Mercedes's air conditioning unit, and I knew Sara was there even before she greeted me. For a small fee the Indian Medicinal and Incense shop in Al Khobar would decant rare potencies into tiny bottles from storage jars, or weigh out various herbs and seeds on an ancient balance scale to relieve headaches or stomach disorders.

I relaxed in the car's cool comfort, realizing that each day's increasing heat would send Saudi families escaping to the heights of Taif or to the mountains of the Lebanon. Today was here to be faced, and I would enjoy it to the fullest. Anticipation recalled the slight figure of Princess Latifa hurrying away through the trees of the summer residence. I had not seen her since that day in Hufuf, but each visit carried the hope that she would be there.

Jassim Said on the Main Gate waved us through with a flourish. He secretly enjoyed our stealthy trips in a royal car. I wondered how many American women had been escorted in such a manner. None that I knew of.

Our growing association with the Governor's family was a delight and a problem. My desire to meet local families was more than satisfied, but I had to resist the temptation to talk about our distinguished friends. Small towns breed gossip, and nowhere more rampant than in a foreign land. I never mentioned these visits to anyone—not even to Fran. Sometimes she would ask: "Where ya been?", "Missed you last Tuesday", or "Don't forget coffee at Joan's next Wednesday." I knew that rumors of our association with the Al Abdullah family would prompt ARAMCO officials to terminate our visits. Skilled in tact and courtesy, the Government Relations people handled Company contacts with the Governor and with Saudi Government Ministries in Riyadh. Embarrassment prompted by an employee dependent would not be tolerated. There would be no mention of the Governor's *hareem*, just improper conduct.

The gate to the Al Abdullah compound swung open to admit the car. The gatekeeper did not look up but resumed his squatting position against the wall. I marveled at the long hours an Arab could assume this position without being permanently paralyzed.

Family compounds had emerged during recent years of providing modern homes for Saudi families. Constructed in Arab style and surrounded by high concrete brick walls, the homes featured arched doorways, flat roofs, heavy wooden shutters, windowless upper stories and rough plaster finish. Architecture had not yet progressed to pastel shades and lacey tiles decorating rooftops, shutters and doorways. Yards were sparse due to compromising privacy by hiring a gardener. The feathery mimosa was decoration enough, its lacey branches spreading over garden walls.

Azziza's family occupied the first of four homes within the compound. Such an arrangement kept married sons in close contact with the extended family and observed the pattern of equality for multiple wives. We followed the walkway to the front porch, noting that springtime brought tiny scarlet berries peeping through dark leaves of the ground creeper that controlled loose sand in open areas. The days of expansive lawns and flowerbeds were yet to come.

Amira Azziza stood just inside the doorway to greet us. Her graceful dress of orange silk cast an apricot flush over her broad cheekbones and high lighted the sheen of her free flowing hair. Usually she offered me a flaccid handshake, a western custom unfamiliar to the Arab, but today she pressed her lips to my face in a customary family greeting.

"*Ahlan*," she welcomed. Her warmness of tone high lighted her offered friendship.

Before I realized it, my acceptance of the gesture prompted

a similar response from me. She nodded approvingly, and we were whisked inside by the ebullient Lulu.

Sara touched me on the shoulder. "Did you see how Azziza kissed me? I tell you, I am a daughter to them. Do you believe that?"

"Yes, Sara," I answered, for I had felt a similar emotion myself. With Sara it was different. She was Arab, though not Muslim, and from a noble Jordanian family.

I felt enriched by Sara's friendship, but concerned that her desire for independence resulted in separation from her family. She yearned to be accepted as a westerner but retained much of her Arab inclination and inheritance. It was difficult to live within the two diverse cultures that existed in the Eastern Province. Confusion resulted and aroused questions about one's sincerity toward either. In the family of the Governor Sara had found a home. Her free spirit delighted the captive Princesses and brought them into closer contact with the world beyond their walls.

Azziza allowed this contact, obviously encouraged it, but clearly there would be a cutoff point in the not too distant future. The inevitable was apparent in a small framed photograph of an impish four-year-old girl and a tall boy in formal *thaub* taken at the time of their betrothal years ago.

"This is Fahada and Bandar, our cousin," Hussa had told me. As first cousins, the Al Abdullah women were a favorite source of wives for the King's brothers. Bandar was the youngest.

In line with her acceptance of Sara as a close friend in need of family guidance, Amira Azziza hoped her gentle influence might bring Sara to accept a husband of the Amira's choosing.

Each visit brought more understanding of this Muslim family. I felt at ease with them, but recognized our western presence in their Kingdom forced new wealth and economic advancement to pressure the validity of tradition and tabu. The Amira's greeting, spontaneous and sincere, reflected an inner peace and security our society had long ago submerged in preference for industrial advancement known as "progress". The unruffled tranquility of her quiet features was not an acceptance of her "dismal fate", as westerners saw it, but rather the visual expression of an inner peace and joy in human relationships upon which her life was built.

I readily accepted the endless expressions of concern for each family member, until I, myself, through the utterance of filial names, felt one with them, their well being having priority on each day's agenda.

" . . . and how is Aysha?"

"*Zain!* Very good."

"Praise be to Allah for his goodness!"

"And Cynthia is well?"

"Oh, yes. Today she has a holiday from school."

" . . . and Aunt Nura?" I asked.

"She has gone to Beirut for medical treatment and will be back soon," Azziza explained.

"May Allah bring her comfort."

The plate of date bars was still in my hand, so I beckoned a servant who whisked it away into the recesses of the house.

"Where is Amsha—and Hussa?" Linda asked, noticing the girls were not in the room.

She freed herself from Lulu's eager attentions and sank into one of the deep chairs clustered about a small table and tall brass lamp with ornate crystal shade. At Fahada's insistence she had brought photos of the American School in Lugano, a few snapshots of boy friends and the snow capped Alps at Zermatt, where she had skied. Lulu quickly sat next to her, eager to examine Linda's creative hair do of sausage rolls spilling from the crown of her head and interwoven with tiny ribbon bows.

Amira Azziza explained the girls were at school. Fahada had not returned to Riyadh and they would all be back soon. She tucked her sweeping skirt under her arm, as she moved across the floor, and instructed a servant to warn the driver he must soon pick up the Princesses. I admired the slender elegance of Amira Azziza, her quiet voice and spilling gestures. Fahada had the same regal poise as her aunt, combined with the enthusiasm of youth and the inherited leadership of warrior ancestors.

Umm Naiyf's villa was in the same compound, and she usually joined us on our visits. Today she was absent. Sara noticed and asked after her well being. She had made herself comfortable on a broad cushion with a slip cover of fine white cotton embroidered with blue thread in a floral motif. Her right arm rested on a padded bolster, reminiscent of a camel saddle set near the center pole of a *bait ash sha'ar* for the comfort of a guest.

"She is very busy and will join us later," Azziza said, further explaining as she sat next to me. "Her seamstress is in such demand and must finish Umm Naiyf's new gown by tonight."

Lulu looked up from studying Linda's coiffure. "She has sent a maid to Al Jamil's shop for more beads and gold braid. Umm Naiyf declares there are not half enough."

"Is she going to a party?" Linda asked.

"Yes," Amira Azziza said. "We are all going—to a royal wedding in Riyadh. The King's daughter will marry her cousin."

Lulu put her arm around Linda's shoulder. "I shall wear my hair like Linda's," she said. She piled long strands on top of her head and rolled them over her fingers to simulate waves and curls.

"Will Fahada go?" Cyndy asked. " . . . and Amsha?" Fahada's cousin encouraged a growing friendship with my youngest daughter.

"Oh, yes," Lulu said. "*Inshallah*, she will have a chance to see Amir Bandar." Then, after a thought. "She doesn't care. She says she will never marry him, but we are all hoping to see him."

"How will you know him, if you have never seen him?" Linda asked, her eyes wide with disbelief at lack of association with male friends.

Sara forestalled a reply. "I would never go," she said. "I refuse to live that way—to marry a man you have never seen. Not for me!"

Sara pushed herself up off the floor and turned away to cool the anger that flushed her face. She walked to one of the tall windows. I watched her fingers separate the polished slats of the heavy wooden shutters. She peered through them. There was nothing to see but the guardian eight foot high wall.

"You mean—she doesn't know him?" Aware of custom, Linda found facing it was something else.

The Amira's seniority took over. "He is family," she said. "That is all that matters." Then on a lighter note, "We do not go to Riyadh very often. Too much competition and rivalry. We prefer the quiet life of Al Hasa."

"Do you know the Naisairiyyah Palace?" Lulu said, entranced by the splendor of the coming event. "It is more beautiful than all the palaces of Europe! Gushing fountains—furniture of gold—chandeliers more brilliant than the stairway to Paradise."

She pulled Linda to her feet. " . . . and how we shall dance! I must teach you." She began the controlled, free flowing movements of a graceful, creative dance, emotional, passionate, until she gasped for breath. "You can't imagine all the beautiful gowns—some from Paris." On impulse she shook down her hair and tossed her head, long tresses scattering about her in wild abandon.

Linda dodged the flying hair, her curiosity rising with every pronouncement. "Will Fahada dance with the Prince?"

"Linda—it's a lady's party." Lulu's sidelong look suggested a daring conspiracy. " . . . but . . . *inshallah* . . . we could . . ." She cast a furtive look at Azziza then swung further into the room, dragging Linda with her. "We could throw on an *abbaya* and sneak down to see the men's party in the garden."

Two young women came in from the kitchen. They overheard Lulu's proposal. "I've done that," the one called Fatma said. ". . . and nearly got caught."

"No one's going *mutfarrajean*," Hamida said, loud enough for all to hear.

I had heard the word before but didn't know its meaning. I must ask Sara to explain. Perhaps it referred to the cloak clad ladies the day of the Welcome Cake?.

"That's fun for once," Lulu added. "I'd rather look at the gowns and guess which cost the most." Her expressive hands traced the outline of a ball gown over her plain cotton dress.

"Lulu . . ." Hamida exclaimed. "Your dress didn't cost twenty thousand *riyals!*" Hamida was a cousin and Fatma's sister.

"Some do . . . ," Lulu said. "I heard one of the Sudairi women paid twenty-five thousand for hers!"

My thoughts turned to years earlier when I was new to the Kingdom, and Russ had brought home a special gift. "For my bride," he had said. "From the Naisairiyyah Palace." At that time the Palace was in the process of construction, and many ARAMCO craftsmen helped with the finishing touches. One of them installed gold fixtures in the many bathrooms and on endless doors throughout the Palace, giving him access to the rooms and to *hareem* supplies stored in a separate area. Many costly items disappeared during construction due to mismanagement by supervisors and Princes, a fact that prompted Russ's friend to bring home a bolt of fabric from the *hareem*—for Russ's bride: yards and yards of black silk net heavily embroidered with metallic silver thread in intricate design. I had put it away, being sure I would never have the opportunity to wear it.

"Yes, I know the Palace," I said. "But I have never seen it. Someone brought me a gift from there."

"I didn't know that," Cyndy said. "What was it?"

"Material for a dress—black net with clips of silver."

"Perfect for a wedding," Lulu said.

Amira Azziza returned to the conversation. Her previously lighthearted participation now took on a tone of finality. "Soon Princess Fahada will be married. The arrangements are in progress. The Amir will meet with the King." Silence surrounded the group. "She has not accepted, but she will." Then, facing me, " . . . we invite you to come to her wedding."

"Oh, Mom," Linda cried. "May we?"

Before I could answer, Lulu set off a wild ululation, " . . . you see, you will have the perfect dress. Our seamstress will make it more beautiful than you can imagine."

"We will be honored, Amira," I said, ignoring Lulu's outburst. I was well aware that expansive speech was as good as the event taking place. Perhaps this invitation—though sincere— might never come to pass, and the momentary panic I felt at the thought of attending a royal social occasion was more wishful than actual.

"Soon we must go to Beirut for shopping," the Amira said. "Sara, will you come with us?"

Sara stood as if stunned, then closed the shutters and returned to face Azziza. "Yes," she replied, but it was obvious her thoughts were elsewhere. She dared to speak up. "Fahada wishes to be a teacher—to help others." Weren't these her own yearnings—to step beyond the codes for women?

Cyndy sat quietly, taking it all in. "What if you don't like him," she said in a steady voice. Her words hung in the air, lost in the ensuing silence.

Fahada's aunt leaned forward in her chair to face Sara, her expression devoid of emotion. "The Princess will marry her cousin," she said. That was all. There would be no challenge— a fait accompli—nothing unusual. "The celebration will take place here in Dammam."

I hoped a moment like this might not arise to offend our

hostess by overstepping the bounds of propriety and allowing our concept of human rights to question custom and tradition.

The Amira ignored Cynthia's challenge. The situation was not a question of rights but rather what would be. She watched Sara return to her seat on the floor, then reached across me to take Sara's hand.

"Dear, Sara," she said. "There are others who will become teachers. Do not worry. Our desire for schools will continue. It will take time."

A commotion at the front door announced the arrival of Umm Naiyf. She blew in like a fresh breeze, depositing her veil on the back of a chair and issuing a crisp order for coffee. The scent of India's "Best of Heaven" followed her into the room, for Umm Naiyf was addicted to perfumes and known to have rare fragrances delivered from Bombay.

Looking for a chair to settle into, Umm Naiyf prompted Fatma to take to the floor, relinquishing her seat next to the Amira. Hurrying had brought color to her high cheekbones, and she ran a finger along the line of her headscarf to loosen the pressure. With a deep breath and a sigh she bemoaned the problems inherent in acquiring a new dress.

" . . . the results will be beautiful, and we shall all envy you," Fatma said, and Umm Naiyf leaned down to kiss her curly head. Kinship greetings were passed all around, and spreading her knees, Umm Naiyf smoothed the folds of her dress to cover her legs, a gesture she had followed a thousand times.

"I see your daughters are well," she said to me, flipping long braids over her shoulders and surveying Linda's freshness with a studied glance.

Servants hurried in with the coffee service, and Amira Azziza directed the arrangement of small tables and divans so we could all settle down to enjoy the bitter cardamom that left a roundness in your mouth, cooling and savory. I had not been served first. The little cups had been poured along the line of chairs. I was no longer a guest. I was one of them.

"We were talking about schools," I said to Umm Naiyf, attempting to change the subject from marriage. "I visited one for girls in the town of Rahima near Ras Tanura. A former teacher from Jordan got Government permission to open the school."

"And was it good?" she asked.

"It suited the needs of the women and girls."

Amira Azziza responded with interest. "The goodness of Allah brought you a teacher," she said. "It is not always so. One day we will have teachers for Al Hasa, *inshallah*."

"That is true," I said. "This teacher understood the needs of the local families and abided by the rules of the Ulema."

"Yes," Sara spoke up, having regained her composure. "It was the same in Oman. Sometimes the Bedu women came with their daughters."

"Allah!" Umm Naiyf responded with gusto. "Go to the desert. That's all the education you need."

We all had to laugh, as she punctuated her words with a loud slurp of coffee and held the cup for more, its capacity being barely a thimbleful.

"Umm Naiyf claims to be a daughter of the Ajman," Azziza explained to me. "We cannot be sure. She has always lived with us. Sometimes I think she is a Persian. Many of them came to the Kingdom through marriage. Still she insists on visiting the tribe when it camps near As Sarrar. Do you know where that is?"

"I do," Linda said. "Mr. Nelson, our social studies teacher, showed us on a map."

"When I visit the Ajman on the desert," Umm Naiyf said, "I remember what it was like to find water and food for family and animals. There was little enough food to last the summer and to carry us through the winter. We learned from the desert and from tales of ancestors."

She sighed with nostalgia, eyes focused on the memory of some distant encampment. "Bedu life is the true freedom—though it may never give you a new dress."

Sara could hold back no longer and worked her body to the edge of her cushion. "What is a new dress if your children die? I showed the Bedu how to protect their babies, to clean their bodies and remove lice from their hair, to purify water and to keep animals out of the tent. That is what they need to know."

"*Inshallah*—one does with what one has . . ." Umm Naiyf turned philosophical. "Now we have many comforts and in time perhaps even more."

"Like a telephone—even a television . . ." Lulu interrupted with anticipated enthusiasm.

"Perhaps it will come," Umm Naiyf said, adding a note of warning. "We must never forget that one day the oil will be gone, and we will have to go back to the old ways."

Lulu laughed outright and shook her finger at Umm Naiyf.

"An *iffrit* is on your back! You know you don't believe such things. With all the little houses now built, the Bedu can live in town and have a better life."

"*Inshallah*—the King will encourage them to settle," the Amira added.

" . . . and will that be a better life—shut up in a small house, never to feel the breeze through the worsted walls nor to live your life in the freedom of the sands. Is this better?"

Umm Naiyf twisted in her chair to emphasize her words. Again the discussion took a questionable turn. Much had to be resolved before the acceptance of new ideas. Fortunately, Reema made a timely entrance with several children in tow. Sara called out to Aysha who had a little girl by the hand—one I had not seen before. The child seemed to be younger than Aysha with light brown hair and very dark round eyes. She wore slacks and a blue sweater, somewhat too small for her plump little body. She pulled away from Aysha's grip and hurried to snuggle against the security of Amira Azziza's lap, hiding her head.

"Haifa. . . . ," Azziza chided with a note of sternness. "Do not hide your face from our friends." She loosened the child's grip on her dress and encouraged her to face me.

"*Marhubba*—hello," I said.

The child came toward me and raised her serious face to mine. It was easy to offer the expected greeting, and I did.

"What is your name?" I said.

She lowered her lids, hiding her eyes behind a thick screen of lashes and refused to part the tight line of her lips. Aysha freed herself from Sara's embrace and dragged her friend toward the hallway.

Servants had gathered about the front door voicing loud directions to a driver waiting in the hall, and pushing him out the door with their shrill cries. The children jumped up and down with excitement, calling to Reema, who swept them up and shouted her way out the door. Haifa dropped a little pocketbook she clutched in her hand and tugged at Reema to wait. As she looked up, the veil of propriety slipped from her demeanor, and childhood's challenge of strangers darted at me from the security of distance and Reema's protective bulk. The intensity of her gaze would forever bind us in an unexplainable bond.

"The driver is going to pick up Amsha," the Amira explained. "Haifa loves to ride in the cars."

"Is she a cousin?" I asked, my thoughts lingering on the child.

"She is a daughter."

The sound of an engine catching fuel brought Reema rolling back into the room. She wiped perspiration from her brow with her apron. An expansive smile wrapped Linda and Cynthia in her affection, and she insisted they must come, too.

"The car will be crowded," I pleaded. "There will not be room."

"Of course they must come," Reema insisted.

Linda got to her feet. "I would like to see the school," she said. Her only acquaintance with Arab schools for girls was the sight of high cyclone fences wrapped in palm matting.

"Take two cars," the Amira instructed.

Lulu responded to the advantage. "Amir Naiyf is here. I'll tell him to go with them."

She jumped up, grabbed the veil Umm Naiyf had carelessly dropped on the back of a chair, and eager for intrigue, tossed it to Linda.

"Here! Wear it," she said with a flirtatious glance. "He'll speak to you." Her laugh held more than diversion for a moment.

I watched Linda catch it, then with a shrug she followed Reema out the door.

I was not best pleased when a young man appeared in the hallway, adjusting a *quttra* on his jaunty head. Holding the cloth across his face, he looked briefly into the *hareem*, gave Lulu a knowing glance, then headed for the cars.

"If you send me to a girls' school, I'll run away." Linda had said. She would take nothing less than the fullness that life had to offer. And it would all be hers, one day.

Chapter Twenty

OF LOVE AND MARRIAGE

With a burst of power the automobile engines started up. Chattering servants hastened to return inside the house. Reema paused to steady herself against the living room wall. She wiped her face with her apron, her breath coming in short gasps. Fatma noticed and took Reema by the arm.

"I'll help with lunch," Fatma said. She motioned Hamida to follow her into the kitchen.

Soon their flying skirts bustled back and forth, as the two young women spread a large flower printed cloth on the floor of the adjacent room and set out dishes and bowls overflowing with sliced melons and oranges.

Lulu stood in the doorway holding the front door ajar. She leaned forward to pull the door close against her back. With rapid hand signals she caught the attention of the two young men who would accompany the cars. A brief but animated conversation ensued, and the men took off. Lulu waited until the gate closed behind the cars and the villa's security reestablished before closing the front door. Noting that preparations for lunch were well under way, she plumped a cushion, pulled up her skirts, adjusted the gold stitched cuffs of her flowered pantaloons, and spreading her knees, sat near me on the floor.

"Linda and Cyndy are family," she said, then hesitated unsure of how to express her feelings.

"Thank you, Lulu," I said. "They think of themselves as belonging to Arabia and consider the Kingdom their home." I never felt quite at ease with Lulu, and wondered at her expressed interest. She appeared to be the instigator of the family with a flair for the dramatic. I set out on a safe course.

"They were born in Dhahran, you know."

Amira Azziza stirred in her seat, her interest aroused.

"At the Clinic?" she asked.

"Well—at the old hospital. It is now the Boy Scout House."

Umm Naiyf seized the opportunity to become involved, and her eager voice usurped any other conversation.

"A boy's house?" she questioned. "They don't live at home?"

"Indeed they do!" I said with a laugh. "The Scouts is a group of young people. They learn many things about themselves and about people of other countries."

Amira Azziza took up the theme. "Your visits bring friendship. That's what we want from America."

"And Linda and Cyndy," Lulu pronounced with some forcefulness. She pushed herself up from the floor, obviously irritated that the initiative had been taken from her. With a hard look at Umm Naiyf and with skirts flying, she whirled away.

Would I ever know what had been on her mind? My daughters, of course, but in what association? Were they Arab or American? Their birth certificates claimed them as citizens of the United States. But they felt otherwise.

What did they know of the United States?—only quick visits to hug Grandma Nickie in San Bernardino and to spend boring days shopping at Best's in New York. It was a challenge to guess the dress sizes needed over the next two years—and shoes. I never came out even on those.

Whenever the destroyers U.S.S. Laffey or Duxberry Bay tied up at the Ras Tanura terminal pier on routine visits to the

Gulf, we received invitations to go aboard the ships. The girls always wore their prettiest dresses to greet the sailors, who toured them around gun emplacements, submarine depth charges and winding up at the mess hall below decks for piled up scoops of homemade ice cream. The Stars and Stripes will always mean home, I kept telling my daughters, but they answered: "The U.S. is your country. Our home is Arabia."

I thought about this many times over the thirty years we lived in the Kingdom. They never lost a kinship with the country of their birth and felt positive and secure about their childhood years.

Azziza leaned close to me, the gold bangles on her wrist pressuring my arm. She confessed that Reema had been occupied all morning preparing a special lunch for our visit. A shadow of concern strayed across her eyes.

"Reema is not well," she said with a sigh. "Allah has not smiled lightly upon her."

"Has she seen a doctor?" I asked without stopping to consider what medical services might be available to her. There was The Woman's Hospital in Al Khobar, closest town to ARAMCO operations, but far from being up to western medical standards.

American expatriates suffered grave concerns over medical treatment for their families, fearful of unknown diseases spawned by this ancient, underdeveloped country. The effects of trachoma were visible in the blindness of local citizens, though special programs were in progress to fight the disease.

ARAMCO took care of the medical needs of its Senior Staff employees and dependents. When the Company opened its medical facilities to local employees, American families became paranoid that an Arab might be in a hospital room next to them. What were we denying Reema and others like her? The Royal family always had complete access to ARAMCO facilities. But—a servant. . . ?

Here was a subject dear to Sara's heart, and she joined us.

"You must take her to ARAMCO," Sara said.

"We have, but it is no use. She needs an operation."

Azziza rubbed her hands over her stomach, the tinkling of her bracelets adding realism to the gesture. "Her body is too large. There is something inside."

"A child. . . !" Sara exclaimed, clapping her hands and leaning forward to offer congratulations.

"All praise be to Allah for such a blessing!" Azziza intoned, then miserably, "No—not a *welad*—something else—I don't know."

"ARAMCO has excellent doctors," I said, hoping to dispel the Amira's fears for her faithful servant. "Who will take care of her?"

"Dr. Abdi. Do you know him?"

"Oh, yes. He is the best. Allah has directed the well being of Reema."

"*Alhamdulillah!*"

Reema's problems momentarily on hold, the conversation turned to other subjects. Would Linda be returning to Switzerland? Yes, I told them—to finish high school, then she would attend college in the States. Sara explained the different levels of western education. The wives didn't immediately agree. Education for girls was quite new—all right for the younger ones—not for girls of marriageable age.

The discovery of oil and all its attributes: the cars and busses, hospitals and schools, air conditioning and home appliances were force feeding new life into Arabia's traditional society. How would our daughters be affected by years of living in a country foreign to us, and eventually accepting another country equally foreign to them as home? What did they know of the States? Yes—America was my home, not theirs. Would they one day settle down or become global nomads? Amira Azziza's words often came back to me: "Home, family, God, country are indivisible—they are you."

"What about you, Sara," Azziza asked. "Will you go to

America?"

"Yes, of course—some day. But I will not live there," she hastened to add. "I shall live in Beirut or Europe—closer to my family in Jordan."

"Then, you must go to Jordan when you leave here," Umm Naiyf pronounced.

"No—I cannot," Sara said, emphasizing her words with sharp tones and a little sadness. She turned to face Azziza. "With such politics now, I could never leave there. They wouldn't let me go. I would be a prisoner of the government. I must have my freedom."

"And what of your family?" asked Azziza.

"In Beirut I would be near them."

THE GULF WALK AND WIDE WHITE BEACH OF
NEJMA

"But you could not be a part of them . . ." Umm Naiyf continued. "You can never have your family when you want what you call freedom." She looked full into Sara's eyes. A sigh of nostalgia crept into her words. "This exists only on the desert with the Bedu . . ."

Her full lips quivered, then tightened with controlled emotion, perhaps remembering years spent in a Bedouin tent. Eagerness conveyed her love for the closeness of land, family and God—the oneness of life—the security in trust—a peace acquired through mutual suffering and courage.

"Here is true happiness, Sara," Azziza said. "You must stay with us—let us find you a husband."

"No. I cannot. I must be free to pursue my own life—to find my own husband—one who is like me . . ."

Sara's sincerity of tone affected us all. I knew where she was coming from, her strength of will to defy tradition, against Azziza's quiet acceptance of what she knew must happen.

Unruffled, yet persistent, Fahada's aunt pressed her point. "Dear Sara, it is all the same—a man who is you and you are he—this is love. Family is stronger than love. A member of your family is no stranger although you have not met him. He is already you . . ."

Her gentle smile brought reassurance to her words, and I began to understand the Arab thought on love, marriage and honor.

Sara sat in deep thought, to be startled by a commotion erupting on the front porch to the women's entrance. Laughter and shouts heralded the arrival of the girls. They burst into the house. *Abbayas* flew in all directions, maids hastening to retrieve them. Even Linda dropped her veil on a low table near the door, receptacle for copybooks, pencils and loosened hair bows. Sara hustled off to inner chambers with Fahada and Amsha, where the girls could change clothes.

Hussa took a stance in the middle of the room and plunked her books on the floor. She walked over to greet me, and I awaited her usual challenge of western standards.

"*Ahlan*—how are you?" Her dark eyes glowed with youthful energy through heavy applications of *kohl*. Deft fingers tossed aside strands of hair caught in the tassels of her *abbaya*, as she flipped the garment over her head. I replied in English and asked how her day at school had been. Her prompt answer confirmed a desire to learn our language. I picked up one of her copybooks.

"Show me what you have done in school," I said.

"Oh—it is very bad. I am not a good student. I do not like the teacher."

How many times had I heard that cry?

"*Ya*, Hussa ," Umm Naiyf called to her. "It is necessary to pay attention in class."

"It will not get me a husband." Her laughter rippled through the *hareem*.

The pages of her copybook were precisely drawn, meticulously neat. The lettering was done in fine Arabic script, but the pages were lacking in quantity. Maps of the Eastern World were marked over in colored pencils, and a few pages showed carefully set numbers.

"Where is the United States?" I asked.

"Oh, it is too far away!"

Turning, she grabbed Linda by the hand, and beckoning Cyndy, dragged them both out of the room. They paused in the hall to speak to Prince Naiyf. Umm Naiyf swallowed a titter, enjoying my observance of her son. Aysha and Haifa had made a dash for the kitchen and now emerged to announce lunch was ready. Last dishes steamed on the "table", and Reema let out a deep breath as she rang a bell to summon the family women.

"Will you eat with your fingers?" Hussa addressed me on her return. I recognized an open challenge. "I eat with my fingers. I know they are clean."

After hurrying out to meet the cars, Lulu had disappeared into other reaches of the house. She soon returned, off guard and somewhat flustered, as if caught up in her own intrigue. She paused in the middle of the room, cooling herself below the rotating ceiling fan. She had something on her mind, I could tell, for she directed her gaze at me. I wondered what was absorbing her interest, and whether I could counter balance whatever she was up to.

Sara and several family women were already seated. Hussa and my daughters dashed in somewhat out of breath. Whatever it was that brought flushes to their cheeks, Lulu's mission would have to wait until after lunch.

The meal was particularly delicious. Reema smiled broadly, as she offered a large platter of spaghetti topped with chicken slices and mint leaves. Was this her special dish?

"How nice, Reema," I exclaimed, serving myself a full portion. "It is—*tammam*—perfect!"

Everybody was so hungry there was little desire for chit-chat. The older girls soon finished and retired to their rooms, taking my daughters with them. I found it difficult to avoid Lulu's eyes, and when lunch was finished, she hurried over to sit next to me.

Foregoing any preliminaries and taking a deep breath she said: "There is a Prince who wants to marry your daughter."

Her direct gaze ruffled my equanimity. In no way was I prepared for this!

"Do you agree?"

Her words came as a shock. Her expression betrayed no sign of amusement. Was she sincere or testing me? Were the girls playing a game and Hussa had taken Linda where the Prince could see her? A planned meeting? I cautiously worded my way through.

"Indeed, Lulu—that is quite an honor."

"He saw her picture, and he loves her very much," she raced on, her hand pressing firmly on my arm. "He will be very good to her."

A mother's instincts braced for caution. I must not offend. Latifa's gentle face swept before me. The restrictions on her life would never be my daughter's.

"Our customs for marriage are not the same as yours, Lulu," I said. "The Prince may not understand that."

What if it was Naiyf, the Amir's only son, and his mother sitting right there?

"Oh, do not worry," Lulu went on, her voice rising with excitement. "He promises never to marry another wife. She will be the only one, and he will take her to live in the States."

Still startled, I wondered when all this had been arranged. But, of course, that is how it is done in Saudi Arabia. The family draws up an agreement. The girl's opinion is rarely considered.

"That is generous. But Linda is too young to marry. She has many years ahead before she takes a husband." I watched for reactions.

Why did Amira Azziza and Umm Naiyf just sit there, making no attempt to enter into the conversation? Lulu spoke so clearly. For once I wished I did not understand.

"All girls must marry sometime." The Amira broke her silence. "Marriage is happier when the bride is young. She is more pleasing to her husband. Fahada is a little older than Linda, and soon she will marry her cousin."

" . . . she will have jewels . . . so much money . . . cars!" Lulu raced on. "Do you agree?"

I realized this was for real. The family had made their decision. If I agreed, a discussion of the contract would follow, perhaps including concessions to the bride. When all parties signed in the presence of the *Ulema*, the marriage would be in effect. The consummation would take place after several days of ritual and festivities. Islam does not recognize marriage as a sacrament. Power lies in the hands of the women, and the *hareem* had spoken.

"Who is the Prince?" I asked.

"When you tell me you agree, I shall take you to him," Lulu said. She lifted her hand from my arm, a smile of triumph lighting her face.

Chapter Twenty-One
THE HAREEM

The room that a moment ago seemed strained and teetering on the verge of disaster gave way to youthful exuberance, as Sara's vibrant presence returned, accompanied by Fahada, Hussa and my daughters. Crisp dresses sprouted hibiscus blooms and sprigs of purple bougainvillea, a pleasant exchange for school attire. In seconds empty chairs blossomed into well kept gardens, and the walls needed no further decoration than the girls' enlivened faces. How I hoped Latifa might be with them, but she failed to appear. The interruption terminated Lulu's proposal, and I breathed a sigh of relief. There was no ready answer to give her that would not offend. Amira Azziza excused herself, Umm Naiyf following, and the two women left the room. Had my disinterest in Lulu's offer upset them? I considered her an unlikely spokesperson for the family, but—then, how was I to know?

The time for afternoon prayers was closing in, perhaps the real reason for the ladies' departure. Cyndy confirmed the possibility, when she sat next to me.

"What have you been doing?" I asked.

"Oh—not much," she said. "Except Hussa had a long conversation with Naiyf—I guess . . ."

"Where?"

"In the hall. He just kept looking at us, and Fahada got mad and dragged Lin and me into her room."

"Oh."

"Lin didn't want to go—guess she wanted to talk to Naiyf— but she came anyway—and, you know what—we watched Fahada say her prayers . . ."

"Well—I don't know that you should have done that."

"It was okay—she said so," Cyndy went on, then thought- fully, " . . . it was different from the guys on the street. I mean, she kneels and touches her head to the floor many times—but first she put on something like an *abbaya*, only white, and wrapped herself up—all but her face. It was strange . . ."

"She blocked out all distractions," I said. " . . . leaving her face open to God."

"Yeah . . ."

"Remember the day we came home from Al Khobar on the ARAMCO bus, and the driver pulled off the road and walked out into the desert to pray?"

"Yeah—it was so hot, and my legs stuck to the seat," Cyndy said.

"He couldn't wait five minutes until we got to R.T," Linda said, as she and Hussa joined us.

Left out of any immediate conversation with her young relatives, Lulu continued the subject of marriage. "Linda, when you become a Muslim, you'll learn how to pray . . ."

"And why should I be a Muslim. . . ?" Linda retorted with a tinge of irritation.

A quizzical frown furrowed her brow. The gutturals of Ara- bic were difficult to follow, along with sounds not heard in the English language. The effusiveness of execution, plus the need to translate into your own language, added other dimensions— a challenge to anyone's desire for understanding. Ignoring Lulu, Linda crossed the room to join an animated conversation be- tween Sara and Fahada.

With a firm lip and shoulders braced, Lulu appeared poised to back off, though not giving up the pursuit.

"Fahada, tell us when you will marry your cousin," she called out with a loud voice.

Princess Fahada paid no attention to Lulu's outcry. She was enjoying a private discussion with Sara. That she heard was evident, for she threw Lulu an icy glance—one that would silence the most persistent of petitioners. Lulu circled closer for a more advantageous view of her cousin.

"I hear he has recently discussed the matter with the King."

Fahada did not respond. She turned her back on Lulu, and getting up from her chair, hooked her arm through Sara's. "Did you send for the shoes I wanted?" she asked Sara. ". . .the red ones like yours?"

There was precious little in the way of western clothing to shop for in Al Khobar and certainly not the luxury of a shoe store.

"There hasn't been time to hear from my friend," Sara answered. "But, she'll send them."

"Fahada—your cousin has asked for you! He is ready to marry!" The attacker refused to be cast aside.

With an awesome pride of ancestry, the Princess addressed her relative.

"Lulu, I shall first finish my education." Her tone of voice should have frozen all further talk on the subject. The Princess turned to me. "Mrs. Nicholson, did you know I have been teaching?"

"That is good news," I said. "Do you like it?"

"Yes. Very much. I want to complete my education and become a teacher."

"Your husband, His Royal Highness Amir Bandar, would never allow you to be a teacher," Lulu shouted, peeved at being ignored.

Fahada gathered control. It was plain she had had enough.

Lulu could be most aggravating. "You may have him, Lulu—that is, if he doesn't divorce you on the first night."

"Fahada! *Alhamdulilah!*" Hussa championed. "See, Lulu, you can never win over Fahada. I hear he is so handsome I would gladly be his wife!" She threw her arm to her forehead in a mock faint, and even Fahada had to laugh.

The question of shoes now out of mind, the Princess turned a serious face toward me.

"Mrs. Nicholson, do girls in America have to marry if they don't want to?"

"No—of course not," Sara interrupted. "Look at me. I am not American, but I live like a westerner. I am happy with my freedom. When I find a man I love, then I shall marry."

"I would like that," Fahada said. Her expressive face became thoughtful. A fleeting frown marred her brow, and her full lips tightened, deepening the flush on her cheeks.

"Oh, if only the King could see you," Hussa exclaimed. ". . . he would rush to marry you. What a life you would have!"

Everybody laughed, but Linda seemed puzzled, searching for some subtle innuendo behind the words. She looked at me as if to say: "Is marriage all they think about?"

"Humph! He is an old man." Fahada made a sour face. "What will you do, Linda? Will you become a teacher?"

"Well . . . I really like people very much . . . but sometimes they do strange things," Linda answered. "I think I'll study psychology and become a psychologist."

Sara's explanation brought a quick response from Hussa. "Then I shall be your first patient. I flunked school the last two years."

"And your marriage . . ." piped up Lulu.

"Maybe Linda can tell us why Nejela Al Yahyah keeps getting into trouble with the *mutaaw'ah.*" Fatma entered the conversation, as she returned from the kitchen and adjusted her skirts to sit spread knees on the floor.

Lulu seemed to be in fine tune with all the gossip, for she

bragged, "Maryam told me Nejela wasn't punished this time because her father promised she wouldn't do it again."

"He said that the last time, and she still does it . . ." Fahada added.

"What does she do?" Linda asked.

Lulu had a ready answer. "Walks down the streets of Al Khobar by herself—wears short skirts and no veil . . ."

"I think I saw her once," Cyndy said. "I was at Jamil's shop, and she was buying a picture frame. I didn't think she was Saudi."

"I've seen pictures of French ballerinas she has painted. She calls herself an artist and says she's going to open a shop," Hamida added.

"Wow! Maybe she's a woman's libber," Linda offered.

"I don't know about that," Fatma said. "I don't go shopping often—you can't look at fabrics and things without your *abbaya* slipping off your head . . ."

" . . . and the veil hanging away from your face so you can't see anything," Hamida concurred, running her fingers through her short curly hair, damp from kitchen duties.

"I really don't mind . . ." Fatma conceded. "I feel protected."

"Nobody knows who you are," Lulu added. "I giggle and stare at the men to annoy them. It's a game."

"Sometimes I wish it wasn't," Fahada said. "I'd like to go to Beirut with you, Sara, and not wear a veil—though I think I'd miss it."

"Well, you wouldn't have to wear one in Paris," Lulu said. "Go to Paris to buy your wedding dress."

"Lulu! First I shall be a teacher. I have no intention of getting married. I shall make choices for myself."

"Me, too," Linda agreed. "I want to be my own person— you know, be recognized for myself the way men are. Isn't that what you want, Sara?"

Sara had been rather quiet, not offering opinions of her own. It was one thing to speak of such freedoms for herself, but certainly dangerous to encourage rebellion among her Saudi friends.

"Yes," Sara said. " . . . and I agree with Nejela—you have to stand up for your beliefs—maybe it's part of women's lib—but it's something I had to do."

"*Alhamdulilah!*" Hussa cried. "I'm all for it."

"Me, too," Fatma added.

"I don't know what that's about," said Hamida, shrugging her shoulders, as though such ideas were beyond their world.

"Sara knows—and Linda . . ." Fatma said.

"I'll show you." Never at a loss for histrionics, Hussa took a stance in the middle of the room. "You have to start with a march . . ." She stood up straight, pulling her skirts around her. "You have to shout about what you don't like and march around where everybody can see you." She beckoned for Fatma to join her.

"I couldn't do that. I don't feel that way," Hamida said. "I don't want to change anything."

"You don't have to," Hussa said. "I just want to show you." She tried to hold her skirt under her arm but it kept slipping. She squirmed to keep it in place. "If you don't like long skirts, you just say so."

She gave an ineffective twist to tuck the folds of her dress tighter under her arm. Sara joined in and did likewise, with Fahada following. Linda's dress was already too short, so she began pulling clips from her hair. Hussa pushed her to the head of the line to be the leader. Hamida and Fatma brought up the rear, not wanting to miss the fun.

Laughter and exaggerated gestures punctuated the march, and more than one participant tripped over skirts that would not stay in place. Hussa grabbed a cushion cover of Damascus silk from a chair and waving it aloft cried: "Away with the veil!"

"No!" Linda cried. "You say: Down with the veil!"

Mixed cries of "Down!" and "*La!*" (No) bounced off the

ceiling, as loose fabrics that could be reached ended up as flags of protest.

The noise brought Amira Azziza hurrying in to see what was going on. She dodged her parading relatives and sat next to me on the far side of the room.

"Our daughters hear about these new ideas. They want to experiment with them," the Amira explained, as though embarrassed at the upset.

"I understand, for it is the same with my daughters."

Azziza went on: "They ignore the fact that we cannot suddenly break from tradition. We have survived the past. We will not throw that security away. It is our lifeline."

I sensed Azziza was trying to justify the differences we both had to contend with in opposing ways.

"Change does not always fit," I said. "We adapt to our needs and to the situations we face."

"You know," she began. "We live by the laws of Islam. We women are ready for change. It will come. But we will not defy those laws that have protected us. To denounce one part of our religion means we can get rid of it all—and that we will not do."

Not our way—theirs. What did I know of tradition—the ancestry of a culture as old as the sands? We were the product of diversity—grabbing on to the way of the moment. Today it was technology weaving its web around us, and we had no past generation to advise caution. We had nothing to leave behind— just to go forward in the face of change.

Hussa called to me as she passed by with a mock gesture of cutting her hair. Azziza smiled, amused.

"It is a game. One day it will not be so. Yes—we women would welcome change—we are ready—but we shall wait until the men are ready."

How long, I wondered, aware that the strength of the *hareem* could wait it out until the time was right.

Amsha's younger sisters, Aysha and Alia, tagged at the end

of the line. Hussa signaled Cyndy to participate. But Cyndy made her own choices and elected to remain neutral.

"I could never imagine Arab girls daring to do something like this," she whispered to me.

"Why not?" I answered with a new found sense of people being people. "How are they different from your sister?"

"Yeah, Lin challenges everything. But—Arab girls can't do that."

Azziza overheard. "Not to be observed," she said with an understanding glance at Cyndy. "We voice our opinions even as Linda does—we will gradually gain what we want within the priorities."

"I don't get it," Cyndy whispered. "What does she mean about being observed?"

"Well—letting people see you do something," I said.

"What's bad about that?"

"I'm really not sure," I said. "It's how Muslims—especially Saudis—perceive people seeing them do something they shouldn't."

"So—it's all right not to wear a veil in Paris, but not in Beirut."

"France is not a Muslim country."

In truth, I could hardly explain it myself, and this was not the time to try and do so. The conversation was getting too personal for my ability to continue without Azziza overhearing and uprooting so delicate a subject. Again I was thankful for a timely interruption, for someone was always coming or going.

This time the beat of a drum drowned out the marchers, as Reema joined us. She held a small pottery drum under her arm, warming it with her body to tauten the skin, testing the tone with the rap of knuckles. She flopped into a chair and spreading her legs, set the drum between her voluptuous knees and began a staccato beat with fingers and wrist in a rhythmic tattoo. The little girls jumped up and down, clapping hands.

"Sara! Sara! Dance for us. You promised," Aysha cried.

" . . . you must—you promised . . ." echoed Haifa.

Reema broke into a long wail on a quartertone, then trilling her tongue, ululated in a high pitch to catch the attention of her audience. The marchers were ready to give up and toppled into chairs, catching their breath between outbursts of laughter.

"Sara—dance," Aysha pleaded, pulling her out of her chair and onto the floor.

Legs apart, hips out, arms raised high and back, Sara began to exaggerate the subtle convolutions of the belly dance. The beat came faster, accompanied by a wail—hypnotic, sensuous, delirious. Sara pulled her skirt tight about her hips, an exaggerated aura of ecstasy distorting her face, as she wriggled and bumped to the cheers of her audience. I found myself cheering, too, for the adept use of muscles so seldom seen. No Hollywood *hareem* dancer could have been more suggestive than Sara's accentuated antics for the entertainment of ladies in seclusion.

"More! More," Aysha yelled.

"Dance again, Sara," Fatma insisted.

"Sara, teach me to dance . . ." squealed Haifa.

Fahada reached out to pull Aysha on her lap. "Hussa, it's your turn," she said.

Hussa took a deep breath and worked her way out of the chair. "All right—but I'm not as good as Sara."

She began to dance. Strands of unruly hair dangled about her face. Hussa tried to bring them under control, her body reverting to ungraceful angles and stumbles. A miserable failure. She relinquished the floor, murmuring, "I shall be Linda's first patient."

"Yes—now, Linda, it's your turn," Lulu challenged.

Linda took Aysha by the hand. "Come on, Aysha," she said. "I'll teach you my way."

Slowly, the child followed Linda through the quick rhythms of rock and roll. She appeared to have too many feet, but lots of effective bumps and rolls.

Everybody agreed that Sara was the best.

"Sara—you must dance again," Fahada encouraged.

Sara made a valiant effort to comply but finally flopped exhausted into a chair. Gasping for breath, she moaned, "I am too old . . ."

Chapter Twenty-Two

A REQUEST

The day had woven a web of peace and security, soon to be ruptured by my need to return home. The passing hours held reminders of tasks yet undone, even as the sun's last fragile rays called out for prayer. I didn't want to get involved with Lulu again and hoped departure might snap the thread and unravel her proposal.

I leaned forward in my chair to gain Hussa's attention, just as a car could be heard entering the gateway. The perfect moment to ask for transportation. This day's intimacy had confirmed the basics we shared, devoid of frills that time and need had implanted. I must move on to my tomorrow, even as this family sought guidance from its past.

Between dying drumbeats, fragments of conversation drifted in from the hall. The child Haifa hurried across the room toward the open door, and I caught sight of a young woman removing a veil. She allowed a servant to retrieve the *abbaya* that slipped from her shoulders and with a step of urgency entered the room.

I immediately recognized the Princess Latifa. The walls of the salon seemed to slip away, and I stood again on the fringe of a pool bubbling through the undergrowth of a desert garden. That unfulfilled moment now returned, augmenting my desire to see the Princess again. Her presence in this environment troubled me, and I needed to be assured of her well being—why, I could not explain.

Amira Azziza welcomed Latifa with a half smile, her gaze lingering to accept the truth of the moment, as Haifa clambered to be picked up. I watched Latifa give the child a tight hug and acknowledge Azziza's gesture of welcome. Then she quickly smoothed her hair, shook out the folds of her long dress and surveyed the room, intent on looking for someone. With a glow of recognition and another attempt to neaten her hair she hurried to take a seat next to me.

"I heard you were here," she said, ". . . and came as fast as I could."

"I am glad you did," I answered. "For I was hoping to see you." I held back the urge to express my pleasure at her presence, for that was not the Saudi way. "How are you?"

"Oh very well," she replied. There was little assurance in her voice, for she seemed more concerned about the quiet reaction of her relatives. A last tucking back of loose strands of hair, a settling into her chair, then complete concentration on me.

Although her face reflected pleasure at this meeting, there was little resemblance to the lighthearted confident young woman I had encountered in the gardens of Hufuf many months before. Her simple Arab dress, dark green cotton with barely a row of ruching for trim, sleeves still showing signs of having been rolled up, and local leather sandals were far different apparel from when I had left her at the pool. Had life with the Prince deteriorated, or was I reading too much into her unplanned arrival. I often wore a simple free hanging *thaub* at home for coolness and comfort. Obviously, she had not expected to come visiting.

All her youthful charm was there, from the way she held her chin up to the soft smile lines at the corners of her mouth, tremulous as she hastened to apologize for an appearance that failed to meet standards for social etiquette.

"And your daughter . . . ." I asked, hoping to ease her concerns and conform to common courtesies.

"Thank you, she is well. How are your daughters?"

"Well—I really don't know—Sara has been teaching them the belly dance."

Latifa's eye glowed with appreciation. "What would we do without Sara!" A sudden flush of red filled her lips and relaxed the taut muscles across her face.

Reema had taken a break and set the drum on her lap, for in spite of much persuasion, Sara declined to continue. Urged on by the children, her plea for mercy was interrupted by the return of Umm Naiyf. She had put on her new dress and quickly became the center of attention with exclamations of how handsome she looked, the skirt just the correct length, though there could be more braid around the neck and sleeves.

"Everybody at the party will be envious." Hussa proclaimed. "They will want to make off with your dressmaker."

Umm Naiyf did indeed appear quite regal, in spite of the severe lines of her headscarf. The acclaim of her relatives brought a softness to her face that reflected a gentleness I had not observed before.

Latifa expressed polite agreement with little enthusiasm for the gown. She seemed to be keeping a distance between herself and the Amir's family. Had the women made acceptance difficult for her?

Umm Naiyf understood. I sensed her feelings transferred images I could only imagine. What was it like to be an outsider in a closely related family? She strode forward in that deliberate manner of hers to greet Latifa with sincerity, showing off the profuse decoration of shimmering beads on the sleeves of her gown and inviting Latifa's approval.

Umm Naiyf had not been a relative of the Al Abdullah family. The Amir married her when she bore him a son, an event that sparked petty jealousies among the other women. In time her relationship with the Bedu more than paid her dues to the royal family, for the loyalty of the Bedu Sheikhs assured the continuance of the newly formed Kingdom. Umm Naiyf savored her position. Her expression of welcome was genuine, for she understood Latifa's predicament. I sensed Latifa's concerns bore no relationship to Umm Naiyf's history. Today offered something she wanted: a few moments to touch base with reality.

" I apologize for my hasty appearance," she said. "I didn't know you were here until Amsha called me a short time ago. She is such a lovely person. I enjoy her friendship."

"I was about to ask for a car. I'm glad I didn't, for I would have missed you." I said, realizing Latifa had made a special effort to see me.

"I don't get out very much," the Princess said. "I have much to learn about the Saudis."

"That's why I enjoy visiting you and your family."

"I am not truly a Saudi . . ." she confessed.

"You are special!" I said.

She laughed. "Well—I don't know about that." The lilt of her voice was as I remembered it.

"Who is the child?" I asked, for Haifa had returned to climb on Latifa's lap.

"My daughter," she said, pushing back strands of straggling hair from the little girl's face. "In a family like this . . ." she explained. " . . . it is difficult to know just who is the mother—there is so much love showered on the children."

The bold little face with its strong chin and dark eyes was hardly a miniature of its mother's.

"I must apologize," Latifa hurried on. "She looks so awful. I put out a dress for her, but she would not wear it—and her hair is so tangled . . ."

"I have been watching her," I said. "She seems quite happy."

"Yes—today she has children to play with."

Haifa sensed we were talking about her and scampered off to join Aysha and Alia.

"See how anxious she is to be with them."

With a sigh Latifa gazed longingly after her daughter, then quickly faced me to apologize for her own appearance. She glanced at her hands, rubbing the palms together as if anxious to explain their condition.

"I have been dusting my house, and my hands smell of lemon oil." She hid them against her skirt.

The Al Abdullah households were overrun with servants. There would be no need for the Princess to clean her house. Few ARAMCO wives did that. Why, even the houseboys had houseboys!

Although her attitude toward me was positive, Latifa was far from relaxed and noticeably uncomfortable. Twisting in her chair, she cast furtive glances at her family members, then returned her attention to me, ignoring any relationship she might have felt. The desire to spend a few minutes with me was stronger than any infringement on protocol as wife of the Amir. I tried to make light of her concerns.

"Don't worry," I said. "I often perform duties I don't normally do. Servants are not always efficient."

"I don't have a servant." Then a hasty explanation. "That is the way I want it. Sometimes a woman stays with me, but today she went to Hufuf. I like to take care of my home myself."

"Cleaning up after *shamaals* and humidity is not my favorite task," I said, attempting to make light of the situation. "I'm happy to have Ahmed get rid of the sand dunes that pile up in the windows."

She seemed suddenly withdrawn. Perhaps I had said the wrong thing, or she felt abashed at not clarifying a situation she found difficult to explain. It was but a fleeting gesture, for with self-conviction she offered an explanation.

"You see—I have my own house. It is very nice and not too

big. I like to take care of it myself." Then, an after thought, ". . . besides it keeps me busy."

Umm Naiyf had left her chair and was about to sit closer to us. She nodded a greeting to Latifa, and carefully arranged the drape of her new dress as she sat down.

Seeking friendship with the Al Abdullah family prompted me to take things as they came—neither to pry into personal affairs nor to ask leading questions that might be rebuffed. Amira Azziza's invitations to visit were more than I had hoped for. Latifa was something else. I felt a personal responsibility toward her. Any deeper relationship would depend on the Amir.

"Latifa," I asked. "Have you been ill?"

She didn't answer. In composure she appeared sad, wistful and extremely thin. Hollows accentuated the cheekbones, and dark pigmentation beneath the lashes deepened the sea green hue of her eyes. Chill winds from the north had crept into her soul despite the brilliance and warmth of Arabia.

There was no laughter in her demeanor—just an on going struggle to accept and to be a part of the society that controlled her every movement. The submissions of Islam demanded her individuality. She could have been my daughter—nineteen years old perhaps—and she had chosen a lifestyle sprung to engulf her.

"Are you sure you are well?"

"Oh, yes . . ." a fleeting smile brightened her face. "I am quite well."

"You seem to have lost weight since I saw you in Hufuf."

"I am thin," she admitted. "Does it look so awful?" She sat erect and pulled her dress close about her waistline. The garment was far too large.

"Well—no—but . . ." I rested my hand on her arm in a gesture of trust, a response to her silent plea: can you hear me although I speak no words. Had we been alone, I might have spoken up. My silence prompted her to take the lead.

"I know it does show, but I can do nothing about it."

"Surely, ARAMCO doctors could offer some advice."

"I went to the American Clinic," she said. "The doctors were kind, but I was unsure about letting them examine me, because it was not proper to remove my veil." She paused, and I acknowledged that such procedure was common practice among Muslim women. She seemed to feel more at ease and continued. "They said there was nothing wrong—that I must try to eat rich foods."

"And do you?"

"I try." She hesitated, then continued. "You can't imagine all the food that is delivered to my house. It really doesn't do any good. I try, but I have no desire for it."

I searched my memory for some tasty dish she might enjoy. What in the world provides more sheer satisfaction than Oscar Davidson's delectable smorgasbord?

I suggested: "How about a milkshake—use molasses instead of syrup—and there are custards you can bake with lots of whipped cream."

"I don't understand. What is a milk-s-h-a-k-e?" She laughed at her struggle with an unfamiliar word.

"It's ice cream—milk—syrup—all whipped together—with an egg for added richness."

"Just an egg?" She seemed truly puzzled. "You cook it first?"

"No. Just mix it in."

"And it tastes all right—this raw egg?"

I had to laugh at the seriousness of her doubts. She shrugged it off with an air of fatality.

"Anyway, I would try it if I could, but I have nothing in my kitchen—all my food is delivered from the Palace."

I never doubted the strength of will that brought this young woman to her chosen situation. Her soft spoken and genteel manner were attraction enough, as well as being a cover-up for the frustrations of learning to adapt to a closed society. It was not all unfamiliar to her, but like Sara, she was walking a double line. The distance she maintained from her Saudi relatives, made me suspect she might open herself to me. A nod, a smile, a traditional greeting for the young Princesses, and that was all. How could I tell her it was loneliness, not illness, that undermined her strength? I decided to take a chance.

"Latifa, do you remember I invited you to come to Ras Tanura?"

"Mrs. Nicholson," she said. "I have not forgotten." There was longing in her words.

"Now—will you come?"

She didn't answer immediately, struggling to pit desire against the improbable, selecting a choice, not an excuse for the truth.

"That is more impossible than before."

I dare not ask why, nor consider the consequences.

"My husband has been living in Dammam for several months, and we may never go back to Hufuf," she said, accepting a fact that had no relationship to her.

"Is it better—living here in Dammam? There are more shops and places to go."

"I do not go shopping. Everything is done for me. But I do see my child more often than before. At the minute she is staying with me."

"That must make you happy." How I wanted to ask why Haifa was not living with her mother.

"Her grandfather has been quite ill. You know he is the Governor."

"Yes."

"And my husband has taken over affairs of State."

Umm Naiyf had moved away, not understanding our conversation. The center of attention had returned to Amira Azziza. She was giving orders to the servants and otherwise directing her large family. Linda kept trying to gain my attention. The time to leave was not far off. Only a few minutes remained to spend with Latifa.

"Do you mind if I ask a question?" I said. Perhaps she antici-pated what it would be.

"Please do. I will give you the best answer I can."

"And you wouldn't mind?"

"No." She seemed eager for me to ask. It might be something she could not say.

How I wished we could be alone and speak of things not possible in a family setting. I wanted to befriend this young girl, not as the wife of the Amir, but as someone in need of support and understanding of where she was coming from, and to help her face the trials that confronted her.

"Why is your daughter not living with you?"

"When I lived in Hufuf, it was convenient for her to stay with her grandfather."

No—this was not the real reason. I knew something about the rights of husbands and children—how they may be taken from the mother at seven years old, especially boys, and after a di-vorce. For some reason the Governor took the child to live with him. I decided to try again.

"Did you know that Amsha came to Ras Tanura—and Hussa? They have been to my house."

Her eyes widened. "Amsha has?" She fell into deep thought. "Then . . . perhaps I shall ask again." There was little assurance in her words—a desire cut short by doubt—a seed seeking fertile soil. Could it take root?

I decided to ease her troubled thoughts. "Latifa—is there some-thing you want—anything I may do for you?"

"Yes . . ." she answered without hesitation. "There is one thing I would like very much. I wish to continue my French studies, but I need a teacher. Mrs. Nicholson, do you think you could find me a French teacher?"

Something to do—to occupy time—to provide companion-ship. How much a teacher would offer her.

"I shall try," I assured. "I shall do my very best."

She leaned toward me, gratefully accepting my offer and spoke freely as though she knew I understood her situation. An unspoken explanation lay between us.

"She would have to come to me . . ."

"Yes . . ."

"I could send a car for her . . ."

"Would it be better for her to speak Arabic or English?"

"Oh, English." Her amused smile carried overtones of relief together with a "thank you" for a much wanted gift.

The activity in the room had quieted down. Several of the family members had left. Children still scurried around, and Haifa came to tug at her mother's dress. Above the convening silence I heard Sara in conversation with Fahada. Linda and Cyndy said their goodbyes to Hussa and Amsha.

"We better be going," Linda said. "Fahada has ordered a car for us."

The time visiting with Latifa was far too short. I regretted the need to leave. In a gracious farewell, Azziza confirmed we would meet again, but for the moment a guest from Bahrain required their presence at dinner. Umm Naiyf and Amira Azziza walked toward the door together, pausing to cast a long look, almost a directive, at Latifa.

"I am sorry this is such a short visit," the Princess said. ". . . but I must leave."

"I will not forget about the teacher," I assured her.

"Thank you." Her smile was all the thanks I needed. At the moment I gave little thought to further details, or how to keep in touch with the Princess. Somehow I would fulfill her request.

Fahada beckoned our car had arrived.

"Sara, are you coming with us to Ras Tanura?" I asked.

"No. I'm spending the night with Fahada."

A final word with Latifa. "Will you attend the dinner tonight?"

"No . . ." she said. There was a note of sadness in her voice, as gathering courage and independence she walked through the door with the other two wives.

Chapter Twenty-Three
THE FRENCH BOOK

One of the joys of living in the Kingdom of Saudi Arabia was going on long vacation. Every two years we closed down the house, not as simple a job as it sounds. Housing was still on the short list, and we were required to relinquish our home to a newly arrived family until our return. It meant packing up all our personal belongings, stacking them in a back bedroom along with toys and games, bicycles, extra horse gear on hand, my sewing machine, and ironing board. A last mighty shove for rugs and refrigerator, then slam and lock the door!

Fran promised to find a family who would hire Ahmed for the period, and she herself would take care of our mares. All we had to do was leave for three months of travel. Goodbye to work and school. The girls would make up lost classes on their return. Don't forget tickets, passports, health cards and travelers' checks. Count all the hand luggage and call a taxi. "Cyndy— you can't take all that stuff!" Then, off to the airport for our first destination. This time it would be India. The world was ours for the taking, and its riches of people and cities would replace the bleakness and austerity of "home".

The two years of waiting between vacations seemed even longer in spite of my contacts with the Al Abdullah family. We had been held over for an additional six months, so that our leave extended to three months. Anything could happen in that time, and I wondered if we would ever see the Princess Fahada again.

My efforts to find a French teacher were without success, and I wanted to let the Amir's wife know I had not forgotten her. However, long days of preparation for our departure—compounded by much excitement and social obligations—left little time to devote to our Saudi friends. During quiet moments I thought of Latifa and her loneliness and vowed I would find a French teacher upon my return at the end of summer. It was a relief to know we would escape the dreaded heat and humidity of our small town, and anyway, most of the royal family departed for the cool mountains of Taif or the Lebanon. At the last moment I tried to contact Sara to give a message to Latifa, but she had gone on a shopping spree to Beirut with Princess Fahada.

It was a more serious event than vacation that threatened our association with the Governor's ladies. While visiting friends in Palo Alto, California, Russ pointed out a story in the San Francisco Chronicle concerning the Kingdom of Saudi Arabia. Among other events of political interest there was an account of Haile Selassie's visit to the Eastern Province, followed by a brief mention that His Highness Saud Al Abdullah, Governor of the Eastern Province, had died and that his brother, His Highness Mishari Al Abdullah, former Amir of Hufuf, was now Governor. The new Amirate Palace in Dammam was nearing completion and would soon be ready for occupancy.

Nostalgia surged through me. What had happened to my friends? Sara would still be a teacher at the school, but what of Amsha—Hussa—Lulu? Would they be shut away from us forever? And Latifa. . . ?

We were too involved in our own affairs to be concerned for long: friends and relatives to visit—reservations to be confirmed for the long trip back—endless days of shopping for the next two years: clothes, shoes, linens, and birthday presents—all to be packed and shipped according to ARAMCO'S shipping system. At least, it wasn't going to cost us anything to send our purchases!

We flew into Rome on our return, and I realized the wonderful days of freedom and diversity were coming to an end. In less than two weeks we would be home. The vast wastelands that stretched as far as the eye could see as we flew over the Arabian Peninsula, the turquoise waters of the Persian Gulf, the wind that whipped golden sands about our plane made me ask myself: "What am I doing here?" This desert is not where I want to spend my life! Yet, I had chosen it.

Ali Shorty met us at the Dhahran Airport, and once again we sped over desert roads to our home on the Gulf. The first thing was to start up the Land Rover for a quick dash to the Farm to check on the horses. True to her word, Fran had done a good job in caring for them. We were barely unpacked before Sara hurried over to catch us up on all the events and happenings during our absence. First and foremost—she was in love. Azziza had found Sara a "husband".

"No—I will not marry yet . . ." Sara said. "I am too happy just to be in love! Oh, he is so handsome—and he loves me!"

"Sara! How exciting! Who is he?" I asked on hearing her extraordinary news.

"He's a Saudi Prince. His name is Hammad, and he comes from Taif."

Taif, I recalled—the summer residence of the King.

"He is a captain—a pilot—in the Royal Air Force, and he has his own plane. He flies down every week to see me!" Sara tripped over her words in her anxiety to tell me everything.

"How exciting!" I said. "Will we meet him?"

"Of course. But tonight we are going for dinner and dancing at the Officers' Club at the Airbase." (The United States maintained a military base at the Dhahran Airport.)

It seemed so romantic, and Sara appeared to be truly in

love. In Saudi Arabia marriage was an affair of the family, and Azziza's influence would tighten that bond. Sara was in danger of losing the rights she had fought for.

"Do you still see the Governor's family?" I asked.

"Oh, yes," she said in answer to my question. "I am a sister to Fahada."

"Does Amsha still live in Hufuf?"

"Oh, no," Sara said. "Now that her father is Governor, her family lives in a new villa in Dammam. It is much easier for me to visit them."

What of Latifa, I thought. Would there be a chance to see her again?

I renewed my search for a French teacher. I could explain only that a Saudi woman wished to study French in her home and would pay well and provide transportation. It was a hopeless task. No one was interested. A French woman in Dhahran said she would do it on a limited basis—purely out of curiosity. I crossed her off. The next best thing would be to get some French books. A Lebanese shop in Al Khobar provided an English/French Dictionary, a workbook and a child's book of fables. It was a start but not nearly enough.

I called on Evelin Alarie, French instructor for our Senior Staff School. She agreed to lend me the textbooks used in her classes for Nejma students.

"I really shouldn't . . ." Evelin said, handing me the books.

"This family will be so grateful," I told her. "You know Saudi women don't get out very much."

"How do you get to meet them?" she asked.

"Well, they're relatives of a clerk who works for Russ."

"And you visit them?"

"Once in a while . . ."

"Will you take me sometime? I'd love to meet them," she said with all sincerity.

I thanked her with a half promise to take her one day. Anything for the books.

Now, how to get them to Latifa. In the first place, I had no idea where she lived and could not have approached her without an invitation. Again I depended on Sara. She came by after school, and I asked her if she would take the books on her next visit to Fahada.

"But I never see Latifa," she said. "She lives somewhere else."

"Couldn't Fahada ask a driver to take them to her?"

"Well—I don't think that would be possible."

"She does live in Dammam, doesn't she?" After all, I expected the Governor's wife to live with the Governor!

"Yes, of course!" Sara sought further explanation. "Well— she has her own house on the Palace grounds. She is the first wife now with Amir Mishari. Azziza and Umm Naiyf really don't mind—after all, they are getting old . . ."

I began to understand—or did I? How did one deal with three wives? By law a man must treat his wives equally. A dress for a dress—a night for a night. How many men could handle that? Did I really want to know the entanglements that must arise—the demands of family members? No wonder Sara had little to say. If she couldn't deliver the books—who could?

I didn't dare approach the Amirate Palace guards—a most inappropriate action for a woman—nor could I mention the Governor's wife to any male Saudi. Maybe the answer lay with ARAMCO. I decided to try.

The ARAMCO Government Relations Department handled all matters concerning the Governor and the local Saudi Arabian Government headquarters, Officials and Ministries. It had the reputation of considering its operations the most important in the Company. To accent their unity all the men wore bow ties.

I telephoned the Assistant Director and asked if their representative could deliver a package and a letter to the Amirate on one of their visits to the Government headquarters.

There was a long pause, then a cautious response. "Can

you tell me what it concerns?" Mr. Whitehead asked.

"Oh—I assure you it is quite personal," I answered.

"You did say the Amirate?"

"Yes. The letter is to go to the Amirate—actually, the Amirate Palace," I added.

There was a long silence before the director spoke again. "This is highly irregular, Mrs. Nicholson."

"Oh, believe me," I hastened to explain. "There is nothing official involved. No complaint or favor of any kind. It is just a personal letter to a friend at the Amirate . . ."

"I am sorry. We cannot do what you ask—it is completely out of policy . . ."

Out of policy to offend the Governor's wife? I thought. If he only knew! Why, ARAMCO bent over backwards to grant the Governor's every wish. Mr. Whitehead couldn't bend, and I couldn't explain further.

"That's all right," I countered. "I have other contacts. I don't need your help . . ." and I hung up, rather pleased that I had left him hanging and probably wondering what an American dependent was up to!

I sought advice from Russ. He reminded me of Adnan—a young clerk in Government Relations who sometimes filled in as a messenger to the Amirate. Adnan frequently visited us of an evening to help Russ with his Arabic. He was also willing to deliver my letter. I explained it was for a member of the Governor's family—addressed H.H. Amir Mishari Al Abdullah/ L (his wife would not be further identified)—and should be handled discreetly, without fanfare and preferably given to the Governor himself. Adnan grinned broadly and promised to deliver my message on his next official trip to Dammam.

Some two weeks later, I was surprised and honored to receive a visit from Amir Turki, of Rahima. I could not imagine why he had come and with some sense of fluster invited him inside. Russ was not at home, but I could handle the situation myself.

"Am I speaking to Mrs. Nicholson?" he queried.

"Yes—won't you come in?"

"I have a letter and a package for you from Dammam," he said, handing them to me. "The writer hopes for an answer."

My heart raced with excitement. From Dammam. That meant Latifa.

"Do call on me if I can be of further service," the Amir said. I hardly heard him, so anxious was I to read the letter. With a flourish and a smile, he wrapped his cloak about his shoulders and returned to the waiting limousine.

To me, the Amir's visit signified that my contact with the Governor's wife would remain unofficial, yet approved by the Governor himself. Eagerly, I unwrapped the package. The small white box inside contained an exquisite lavaliere of perfect Persian Gulf pearls wired to a heart shaped frame of gold on a fine gold chain. It was a rich gift. I was more enchanted with the letter in which Latifa expressed her pleasure at having me visit her the coming Friday. As I fastened the pearls around my neck, I remembered the Arab custom of giving a more valuable gift than the one received. The books were not a gift, merely the fulfillment of a request.

On the appointed day, Cyndy and I prepared to go to Dammam. Linda had returned to Switzerland the week before. We would take a local taxi and arranged for Ali Shorty to drive. I checked my store of gifts and selected a coloring set and pencils for Haifa. It might help the language barrier, for the child spoke only Arabic. I also wore the pearls.

Ali was the most reliable of the Ras Tanura taxi drivers. In true American fashion the oil roustabouts nicknamed him "Shorty" in keeping with his diminutive size. As Ali Shorty he was known to all of Nejma. We considered him the safest driver and were always glad when he met us at the airport on our return from out of Kingdom vacations.

He often told me of his Bedouin family, and how he visited them on the desert when they camped nearby. I felt I knew his family, for he spoke of his brothers and his elderly father. When I asked about his mother and sisters, he spoke of them without hesitation, even though it was not his custom to do so. I learned of his mother's illness, his sister's new baby—a boy, *alhamdulilah!*—how three camels had been lost, but luckily were found—of his youngest sister who was no longer a child. Ali was very much the desert Arab, a member of the Bani Khalid tribe whose *dirrah* was Al Hasa. He had a profitable business driving a taxi and had picked up a little English along with extra *riyals* from Americans who appreciated his carefulness on the road. To him the Americans were more than customers—they were his friends.

There was only one way out of Ras Tanura, so I waited until we were half way to the Dammam turnoff from the Dhahran-Ras Tanura road to mention our destination.

"Ali—today I am going to Dammam . . ." Most often our trips were to Al Khobar for shopping, to Dhahran for visiting, or to the airport for vacations.

"Dammam?" he queried. "Why you go to Dammam?"

I chose not to be too specific until we were in town. "I am going visiting today," I said.

He seemed to think for a moment, then said, "I know—you go to the *suq*—*wajjid* Bedu things you like to buy . . ."

I made no comment.

"Cyndy—you like to go to the camel market? I show you everything—even ride a camel . . ." he laughed.

"Sounds fun," Cyndy said. "But I'm wearing my best dress."

We reached the Dammam turnoff. Several young girls, heavily veiled, their black cloaks billowing, were skipping stones on their way to school. Like Ali's sister, they were no longer children.

"I know—I take you to the gold market . . ."

"No, Ali—today we go to the Amirate," I said.

He didn't answer. I waited another minute. "The Amirate, Ali . . ." I repeated with emphasis.

He gave the car a quick spurt of gas to bypass a heavily laden donkey cart. "The Amir of Dammam lives there."

"No . . ." I answered. "Not that one. The Amirate Palace of the Governor."

". . .Al Abdullah?" His tone was horrified, unbelieving. His hands shook on the wheel, and his visage reflected in the rear view mirror was tense, frightened. I could tell by the sudden slowing of the car that something was amiss. Then he made a quick turn to the left and off the main road. Concerned, I asked if he knew how to get there.

"Yes—I know . . ." he muttered.

"I think it's near the sea." I continued. "We should go back to the main road."

He pulled to the shoulder and stopped the car. "You say Al Abdullah?" he repeated.

"That's right—the Governor . . ." I was beginning to lose patience. Although I had no idea of the exact time we might be expected, we still had to find Latifa.

"Please, Ali . . ." I said. "Just turn around and get back on the coast road. It can't be far ahead."

He seemed not to hear me, but slumped in his seat, hands off the wheel.

"Ali!"

"No . . . ," he said. "I not take you there!"

Chapter Twenty-Four
FINDING LATIFA

I accepted Ali's fear; yet hoped to convince him everything would be all right. I also had to reassure myself that we would find the Princess Latifa. What could go wrong, when she had invited us to visit her?

"I not take you there," Ali repeated. "It is not good."

"There is nothing to fear—believe me."

I had no way of knowing if that would be the case. My American connection could not bring into focus atrocities I had heard about. All that was in the past—what about the unknown?

"You not in any trouble?" Ali asked.

"No—no, of course not—nothing like that."

"Bedu afraid of Abdullah. He is very cruel man. No—I not take you there."

I was well aware of the Al Abdullah family's powerful influence on the desert Arab and on the local population of the Eastern Province. With a handful of warriors Abdullah Al Abdullah and Ibn Saud, first cousins, had fought side by side across the Arabian Peninsula to solidify the tribes in peace toward the goal of a united country.

The Bedu fought back to maintain the old ways: self perceived aristocracy and the strict preservation of tribal honor. The laws of the desert were irrevocable, cruel for the survival of the whole. Fiercely proud, the Bedu claimed their rights as desert dwellers, more often than not waivering in their loyalty between Prince and independence. Abdul Azziz and Abdullah attained their goal of peace in 1932, but cruelty was often the pathway to achievement and implementation.

Eighteen years later, when we first made Arabia our home, brutal law enforcement was firmly entrenched. I had seen the great concrete chair plastered into the outer wall of the Al Kut fortress in Hufuf where Abdullah had meted out punishment after Abdul Azziz became King and his faithful cousin the Governor of Al Hasa. Many were the tortures and beheadings, the lashes and expulsions carried out on law breaking citizens and rebellious Bedu. Fear was well entrenched in the populace, who believed all the tales of horror.

"Look, Ali," I said in an effort to convince him—and myself. "It is all right. We are going to visit his family. See—here is a letter asking us to come."

I took Latifa's letter from my purse. I knew he would not be able to read it, even had it been in Arabic. Perhaps he would recognize the official crest of the Al Saud.

"Now—do you know how to get there?"

"Yes. I know."

We proceeded in silence. What did I really know of this country's struggle for peace? Of the Al Abdullah family? Of Latifa? One thing was real: the kinship I felt for her—an unexplainable need to see her since that first brief encounter—half real, half fantasy—many months ago. Ali and his fears were not acceptable in my world. We must go on and find the Palace of the Governor. There would be no turning back.

Our way took us directly toward the sea and the outskirts of Dammam. I had a vague idea of the Amirate's location. Russ had driven me past it some years before, when Dammam was little more than a mud brick fishing village. The area did not become the seat of government for the Eastern Province until 1957.

I accepted Ali's fear. I also had to overcome my own concerns for the unknown before I could convince him our visit would be all right. Changes facing the every day life of the local citizens had yet to be proven. The past was still today and tomorrow. Words were easy—acceptance of the future questionable. He looked up from staring at the road ahead and caught my glance in the rearview mirror.

"Someone will meet us—you'll see," I said.

"I not take you there.".

Just beyond the shore in the shallow blue green waters of the Gulf stood the ragged remains of an old Turkish fort, one of several along the Al Hasa coast built during the Turkish/ Portuguese occupation. The invaders had never penetrated the waterless and formidable interior of the peninsula. This they left to the Arabs. The immense forts and isolated towers stood as reminders of their presence. Local citizens tore some of them down, piece by piece, to use salvageable bricks for garden walls, mud houses and irrigation dams. The fort at Dammam, that once had risen from the sea, now remained a memory, save for remnants of a retaining wall where numerous urchins clambered and fished.

We were approaching the oldest part of town, and Ali picked his way along the shore and through the sand flats, avoiding the perimeter street that paralleled our way. We followed a rough cart path, swerving to avoid ruts, donkeys, and pedestrians and straddling open sewer ditches dug into the land from houses to the sea.

Among crumbling structures along the frontage road, a handsome building came into view, pure white against the overall natural dun brick construction of the town. Four levels ascended, one on one. Plaster lace work in sword and palm tree design graced arabesque arches and sagging balconies. The hand carved shutters of the *mushrabiyah,* where many pairs of eyes once gazed on the world below, hung on loose hinges. Deterioration reclaimed the structure from its days in Time, when with grace and confidence, it had defied the advance of its conquerors.

"That is the old Palace," Ali said. "Now Abdullah has a new one."

I did not prod him further, as we continued on our way, which I was sure he knew. Signs of modernization came into view: streets undergoing repair, newly planted oleander bushes along walkways, and stacked sewage pipes awaiting construction of a modern waste disposal system. New homes indicated the local citizenry was gradually moving into this improved area, where western structures and influence made a difference. Twenty years—could that be all since the Kingdom faced a new life? Twenty years—a grain of sand in Time that marked the rhythm of passing years, when prophets, pirates and raiders had lived as one.

"See, Cyndy, what a difference change can make where once there was no change," I said.

"It's just an old building, Mom, like a lot of others among the ruins of the world."

No, not exactly, I thought. Had oil been left in the ground, had people like us not come, there would still be majesty and pride staring at the ruins of a pirates lair that Time had returned to the sea.

Ali swung the car back toward town and turned onto a wide newly surfaced street. He slowed the taxi to survey the town and entered a broad driveway in front of a flat roofed building flying the national flag. A high cyclone fence surrounded the yard, and uniformed men loitered around the gate. Ali stopped short of a day guard's shelter—a light wooden shed outside the fence. The building appeared to be too primitive for the Governor's headquarters. Why had Ali stopped here? He sat at the wheel with the finality of having delivered us to our destination.

I waited for what might happen next, certain this was not the Governor's Palace. The guard approached. Ali stared straight ahead, hands on his lap. It was up to me to respond. I asked for directions to the Al Abdullah Amara, indicating a residence rather than the seat of government. The man ignored my question and leaned forward to scrutinize the occupants of the taxi. He flipped his rifle from shoulder to shoulder, bringing my nerves on edge. I was familiar with the term "loose fingers". The man beckoned for a second guard who started toward the taxi. With a hasty "thank you" I tapped Ali on the shoulder and told him to drive away.

"That was not the Amirate," I said with annoyance.

"No—it was the police station."

"Why. . . ?"

"I think you make a mistake."

"No, Ali. I did not make a mistake."

We continued in silence. Shops and houses gave way to extensive salt flats that edged a distant grove of trees.

"Those trees," Ali said, " . . . that is the Amirate of Abdullah."

THE MAIN GATE OF RAS TANURA

A thickly wooded area appeared ahead, tree trunks hidden behind twelve foot high walls that repelled sand flats and the sea. It was a pleasant contrast to the starkness of the old city, though I felt apprehensive of what might be encountered there. Buoyed by my ultimate purpose in coming, I disregarded the ominous threat of the wall that denied access to the Amirate grounds. It extended farther than the eye could see, interrupted by closed gateways guarded by armed soldiers. We drove the length of the walled grounds to get our bearings and to evaluate the possibilities of finding Latifa.

A high archway framed in burnished wood broke the length of the wall midway. It cored out the base of a three-story building, part of the wall itself, and created an open ended arcade. The building's slanted roof and smooth plaster finish added a new dimension to the flat roofs and rough flung jus exteriors of the local buildings. Instead of shops, the sides of the arcade were lined with long benches. Here sat petitioners and villagers, fingering prayer beads, while awaiting an audience with the Governor. The guards accosted each man as he approached, directing some to sit on the benches, while allowing others to proceed through the arcade and to enter a garden just visible at the rear of the building.

Swinging cloaks, activated by the long strides of the men, flashing gold trim below heavily bearded faces wrapped in red head scarves, threatening guards with rifles, swords and *kanjars* ruled out any thought of gaining admittance to the royal compound.

We pulled off the road and parked near some trees to review our situation. This was not the entrance we sought. Which one of the many gates along the wall might lead to the Amara? We decided to examine them again. Each was armed and shut tight, reaffirming our first impression that the gates held no clues as to where they might lead.

"Look, Mom," Cyndy said. " . . . you gotta ask!"

"Yes—but where?"

Ali remained silent. He was going to be of no help.

"Why not ask the last guard we passed and see what happens?"

". . . and if nobody expects us, it will be embarrassing." I pictured myself being rebuffed and brought in for questioning, for what American woman had ever demanded entrance into the Amirate, unaccompanied and unveiled.

We drove back to the central archway and parked off the street. Groups of men continued to enter and leave the grounds.

"Ali—this must be the government entrance," I said. "People are expected to come here. Why don't you ask the guard how to get to the Governor's residence?"

With reluctance he did so, but the guard threatened him and told him to move on.

"If I could show him the letter," I mused.

"Maybe we should just go home," Cyndy said. "Do we really know what we are doing?"

The situation was not hopeful. No guard was going to tell us what we wanted to know. We were invited, expected. There must be a way.

"We've come this far," I said. "Let's try again. Drive slowly, Ali, and if we come to the correct gate, somebody may be on the lookout for us."

We drove past three additional gates, the guards staring at us with drawn rifles. Finally I concluded, as Cyndy had, that our only choice was to return to Ras Tanura.

"See—there's a narrow dirt road at the end of the wall," I told Ali. "Let's turn around and go home."

"That is good," he said and hastened to comply.

As we entered the dirt road where the wall turned toward the sea, we passed a final gateway into the Amirate grounds. Through the grillwork we could see flowering gardens, a driveway bordered with scented jasmine, broad banyan trees, a mosque and a succession of low walls, all indicating a residential area. Ali stopped short of the guard's cubicle outside the gate.

"Now, what do we do?" Cyndy asked, as if this one was going to be no different from the others.

"Looks promising," I said. "Let's give it a try."

It was useless for me, a woman, to inquire, so I asked Ali to question the guard.

"No," he said. "I not go any closer . . ."

Encouraged by the view of the garden, I prepared to do it myself. I edged along the seat, my hand on the door handle. Before I could exit the car, reality held me back. As Cyndy had expressed: did I know what I was doing? Anywhere in the world it would have been a simple thing to ask a question. In Saudi Arabia, under the circumstances, it might have been life threatening.

The envelope in my hand was an invitation, not a passport through barriers of tradition. What authority did I have to pass through that gate and gain admission to the Governor's *hareem*? The guard was the first line of defense. Only those of proper status and credentials would be screened before entry. I had neither.

What I did have was the image of an unbeliever: a foreign woman, improperly attired, shamelessly unveiled, unaccompanied by a male relative, unfit to be admitted to the Governor's private domain. I had no *hareem* ring—the password of other days, by which the eunuch recognized the bearer.

I could not show him the letter, which he would not be able to read, for no male would acknowledge any reference to female family members. Had I really thought my visit would be as simple as walking next door?

I slumped back on the seat. "Lovey," I said. "Let's go home."

"But, mother. She's expecting you. We could at least ask if she left a pass."

"Maybe . . . I don't know." The world of the Arab was still far from my understanding. I was not going to press my case with any gun crazy guard, when I knew Ali was trembling with fear in his seat.

"I think it's going to be okay," Cyndy said. "Look, Mom . . ."

Hurrying along the driveway from the far end of the garden, a man in white *thaub* and red *quttra* appeared to be waving at us. Ali saw him, too, and instinctively put the car in reverse.

"No, Ali . . ." I said. "Wait a minute."

The man came closer, beckoning and smiling.

"See—we are expected!"

Begrudgingly, Ali changed gears and inched the car toward the gate. Instantly, the guard was on the alert. He stood in front of the taxi, rifle raised. I expected Ali to back out and make a run for the road. Instead, he froze, just long enough for the man in white to reach the gate. He called out to the guard. A brief conversation ensued. The guard turned away from us, pushed the gate open and returned to his post.

The newcomer barely raised his eyes to Cynthia and to me. "*Marhubba* . . ." he greeted, then instructed Ali to drive ahead to the first inner wall, while he ran alongside the car.

The driveway paralleled the rear of the Amirate building, through open areas of rock lined pathways, spreading plane trees, blossoming mimosas and oleanders. From time to time Ali slowed the car to a stop, refusing to go on. I tried to reassure him there was nothing to fear, until guards of immense proportions popped out from nowhere and challenged us at rifle point. Their stance and visage were more fearful than the weapons. Another moment of anguish until our guide, still following on foot, caught up and indicated the car was to go ahead. Our benefactor's broad smile and gestures of welcome gave assurance we were expected, though nothing could erase the pain in Ali's eyes.

The low walls seemed to separate buildings and private gardens. We passed a mosque where several men were entering to pray. The government buildings stood far to the right.

We kept clear of them, but I could see no other structures that might indicate a residence. The perimeter walls seemed to grow taller, as we continued, and rose to a height of thirty feet. They met at right angles, creating a dead end to this section of the grounds. A sense of peace and harmony elicited from fragrant shrubs among the trees, the oppressive walls laced with the vivid blooms of scarlet and purple bougainvillea—a note of hope in an otherwise uncertain passage.

We could proceed no further.

"*Tafadhaly*," our guide said, smiling as he opened the rear door, indicating we had arrived.

Only then did I notice a small pedestrian gate, alongside a wide automobile gate, where the driveway curved to meet the wall. Neither handles nor latches were visible from the outside, creating the deception that the openings were a continuation of the inner wall, that at this point was about eight feet tall. Slender palm fronds waved above the gate, and delicate banners of the mimosa expressed a warmth of welcome. Ali opened his door to assist us in alighting.

"No! Not you," bellowed a thunderous voice, and a gate guard stepped forward with a threatening gesture.

Poor Ali cringed in his seat. The guard approached and indicated the car should be parked near a large eucalyptus tree.

"*Memsa'b*," he whispered. "I not stay—I just go."

"Yes—all right—you go . . ." I reached to open my purse.

"No—I just go!"

I recognized his agony. "Okay. See you in Ras Tanura."

He backed as fast as he could down the long driveway, and I heard his motor gun, as he exited the outer gate. A moment of concern crossed my mind. How would we ever get home? Somehow I felt Latifa would find a way—if we ever reached her!

A brassy clang aroused me, as somewhere a bell kept ringing.

"*Tafadhaly*," our guide repeated, directing us toward the pedestrian gate. A rattle of keys indicated someone had arrived on the other side. Quickly, our guide stepped away, and the guard entered his cubicle, as though not wanting to see who-ever might be behind the opening door.

Chapter Twenty-Five

THE DOLLHOUSE

Cynthia stepped through the partly opened door, and I followed—into a world that was neither Arab nor American. The flagstone walk where we stood edged a garden of trees, the serenity of their deep shade reached out toward the sea, to be forcibly cut off by the forbidding walls. Beyond and unseen lapped the turquoise waters of the Gulf, where rising mists carried the odor of seaweed and sodden tar over the wall.

We seemed to be alone in the garden, until a grating sound indicated the gate closing behind us. The rattle of heavy keys compelled me to turn around. Having hidden behind the gate, Haifa now pushed with all the weight of her young body to get it closed. She pressured a key into the lock, then slipped behind us, extending a mischievous smile.

Today she was the little Arab Princess in a tale from Scheherazade dressed in apricot silk dotted with seed pearls. But the dress was of western design, and her lace trimmed socks and white slippers were not native to Arabia. Like a butterfly testing the sweetness of a blossom, she paused momentarily to look at us, then flitted away, skirting a bed of saucy periwinkles toward a diminutive house set in the shade of feathery *ithl* trees.

She beckoned us to follow, as at that moment Princess Latifa appeared on the terrace.

"*Marhubba!* It is so nice to see you! I am so happy you came!"

She stood there on the terrace, her white dress of softest silk enveloping her in a cloud. Simple elegance from the finest boutique in Paris. For a moment it all seemed to be a dream— this storybook house and its occupants set in a secret garden— the replica of an engraving from Hans Christian Anderson somehow trapped into reality out of the intense imagination of a fairytale.

"Please—do come in . . ." Latifa welcomed. "I'm afraid you must be too hot after your long trip."

What was there about this young woman that drew me to her? In all the strangeness she was familiar, and I felt a bond with her that had no reason to be. A Princess of the royal family or a displaced child—was she both?—giving me the feeling that somehow I would share her life—whatever that might mean.

We ascended the tile steps to the terrace, the little house invitation enough. Its single story was constructed of white stone and wood paneling with a low peaked roof. Above the door, a sunburst of jeweled glass gleamed from its frame of carved mahogany. Misgivings fled, for here was a warmth of welcome that dispersed all fears.

Haifa hid behind her mother, now and then peeking around, as we came closer. Latifa extended a hand, and Haifa gave her the keys. The heavy metal cast a shadow where it touched her dress, reminder that the outside world stalked her paradise. I expressed genuine surprise for the unexpected appearance of her Dollhouse.

"Do you like it?" Latifa asked. "It was built for me when we moved to Dammam."

"But—it is lovely . . ."

"Then, please, tell me what you think of the inside . . ."

She led the way, the child following. The rattle of keys was apparent now, as she selected one from the bunch in her hand and unlocked the front door. We entered through a fusion of color from the stained glass window that drenched the hallway with light. She quickly locked the door behind us and set the keys on a table in the entry hall. We could have been entering an old world European villa, but the warm skin tones of the child and her intense brown eyes revealed her desert heritage.

"Please—*tafadhalu,*" she said. "Make yourselves comfortable." Latifa directed us to a pair of Danish style divans upholstered in deep purple. They were arranged on two sides of a low table, where a bowl of pink periwinkles doubled their pleasure through a reflection in the glass tabletop, extending their daintiness to include crystal candlesticks with lavender candles.

Danish teak end tables and chairs bordered a tall leaded window that faced us, its long lace curtain interrupting the flow of floor to ceiling paneling, where exquisite Dresden figurines languished or stared from glass cases against the polished wood. It was all so airy and peaceful that I was certain the Persian carpet beneath my feet bore kinship with Aladdin's own. A scrolled rosewood screen secluded the adjacent dining area, and on the wall behind us, two polished brass fixtures directed light through crystal shades onto a perfectly executed cloisonné portrait of His Royal Highness Crown Prince Faisal, who had recently replaced his brother Saud as King. This was the home of a family, a nuclear family, which expressed the tastes and individuality of its members.

Recalling the villa of Fahada, I half expected a bustle of servants, slaves and retainers to emerge through the sliding wooden panel that led to the private area of the house, but there was no sound save our own voices and the low hum of an air conditioner. Haifa leaned against her mother to whisper in her ear with a nod toward Cynthia.

You know," Latifa began, as she hugged the child. "She is somewhat disappointed that your daughter is a big girl and not exactly her size for playing with. She was looking forward so much to someone her own age. It is my fault because I should have reminded her."

"Perhaps this will cheer her up," Cyndy said. She handed Haifa the paper parcel she had been carrying. The child's face lit up, as she discovered the coloring book and pencils, anxious to release the hours of fun waiting there.

"Did you have any difficulty finding us?" Latifa asked.

"We found our way through Dammam," I said. "But there was a small problem at the entrance gate."

Her smile was one of embarrassment. "You see, really no one is allowed in. There are always people seeking favors of the Governor—even through me . . ."

I interrupted her pause. " . . . and I didn't look like a proper person to come visiting."

"I hope you weren't upset," she said.

"No. I felt certain I would find you."

" . . . thanks to your guide," Cyndy added, looking up from helping Haifa color a Persian cat.

"I left your name with the guard," Latifa explained. "But when you didn't appear, I sent Saeed to find you . . ."

"And he did!" Cyndy added.

The sliding door to the inner hallway was somehow ajar, and a figure wearing a long white robe strode past, the stiffness of the garments rustling as it went. I felt certain the person was a man, but what male would be striding through the private quarters of this house? The high walls and guards, her obsession with unlocking and locking the front door left no possibility for a stranger to invade her home—and, yet . . . Latifa must have been aware of the presence, for excusing herself, she left the room. Haifa dashed after her.

"Who was that," Cyndy exclaimed, setting a blue pencil back in its box.

"I don't know," I answered, equally puzzled. "A servant, I guess"

"Kinda strange . . ." Cyndy commented.

A soft glow came through the stained glass window above the front door, illuminating the crystal prisms of a cranberry lamp hanging in the hallway. What a mixture of reality and mystery seemed to hover over this little house, I thought, and the circumstances that brought me here. I could only be ashamed of my antics concerning the picnic for the Royal Hareem and hoped Latifa would never hear of them. Yet, wasn't that episode a link in the chain of events that led me to her?

"You were so kind to send me the books," Latifa said, as she reappeared, unperturbed over the interruption.

"I wish I could have done better," I told her. "I shall keep inquiring about a teacher."

She had attended school in Italy and considered Italian her first language. English was very easy for her, as was Danish, which she learned from her mother. Although she liked French, she needed further study in grammar. Arabic, which she now studied every day, was a bore, the pronunciation impossible, and none of it made much sense. I had to laugh, for I found Arabic equally difficult.

"It seems we all study French," I said. "It is the language of the world."

" . . . and a good thing it's not Arabic, or I'm afraid most of us would fail!" She looked at me with open amusement, quite in control and at ease. "I often visited Jordan with my father," she explained. "I felt at home there—as if it held the answer to my wishes. Do you know what I mean?"

"Perhaps the way the desert has a special meaning for me," I said.

"Yes, like that." She smiled. "Is that why you came to Arabia?"

"No. I came to get married!"

We both laughed. It was an absurd answer and we both knew it. Yet, it was true for her, as well as for myself. Somehow it broke the formality of a first visit, and I hoped for an opening to learn more of her background. I don't know what made me feel she wanted that. Sometimes just talking about things makes them more tolerable. I missed my father and sisters in California. My mother had died in 1948, and I never would have left her. Were such feelings also Latifa's? No matter our age, we remain basically the same person, though time and experience temper our tolerance.

"I used to make movies in Hollywood," I said, knowing that city of magic attracts most people.

"And did you like it?"

"Yes. Every day was a trip into another world—one that took you away from sameness into adventure and romance."

"I think I would have liked that, too."

"Do you know of the actor Valentino?"

"No."

"He made movies about Arabia—a handsome *sheikh* who carried women off into the desert—silken tents—incense—romance . . ."

"And you thought Arabia was like that?"

"We made make believe. Reality is something else."

"Yes . . ." she said, a veil of remembrance misting her face.

"It wasn't Valentino but a painting I had that attracted me to the desert. A narrow cart track wandered through sand hillocks and sage brush, disappearing into the pale lavender distance—on and on wherever your imagination wanted to go . . ."

"Well, it wasn't a cart track that brought me here," she said, her eyes bright with amusement. " I fell in love . . ." She offered no more.

There was so much I wanted to ask her, but questions can be dangerous. I knew nothing of her circumstances and very little of a woman's life in Saudi society. What I did sense was her need for contact with the life she had given up; yet never weaken the ties that had brought her to this country. The musical cadence of her voice, combining cultured English with the singing inflections of other languages, belied any disturbance she might be feeling, for she carried the conversation into areas of her own choosing.

"I have not always lived in Arabia—but I have told you that," she began.

"Yes," I said.

"Well, you see, although I grew up in Europe, I came from Jordan. My father is Jordanian. I don't remember living there, for I was very small when we left. My mother wanted to return to her country of Denmark." She paused, as if thinking how to continue. "I never wanted to visit in winter because of the snows and bitter winds."

"We went to Copenhagen once," Cyndy contributed, watching Haifa color a ribbon around the cat's neck.

"And did you like it? Did you think it is a nice city?" the Princess asked.

"We were there only a few days—on vacation," Cyndy said. "But I remember how cold it was on the canal trip."

"Yes," Latifa added. " There was really no use to look forward to spring, for the snows didn't leave until summer."

"But it was beautiful." I said. " . . . the green forests, the clear blue lakes, the crisp air . . . and the Little Mermaid."

Latifa had to smile. "After Arabia you'd think so!"

I sensed that her demeanor was not just to entertain a guest, but a reflection of trust—of a willingness to expand our understanding of each other. At this moment, it was difficult for me to accept her as an Arabian Princess—the wife of the Governor. She could have been my daughter who had drifted beyond her childhood home into a society that could hardly hold reality for her. Then, unexpectedly, a leading question.

"You know—sometimes I look at Haifa and I cannot be sure she is really my child. Do you think she resembles me?"

The child looked up, as though sensing we were talking about her. The impish face bore little similarity to her mother. She had a firm chin and warmer skin tones, the shape of her face rounder with full lips. Her eyes were of the deepest brown, alert and quick changing, and her dark straight hair already longer than her mother's.

How should I answer?

"It is really too soon to tell," I began. "Girls resemble their mothers as they get older."

Latifa was quick to reply. "Your girls don't look like you—except maybe Linda—but I would know they are your daughters . . ."

"And, of course, Haifa is your daughter, too."

"I know she is—that her blood is my blood—but I cannot see anything about her that is me!"

The child was her daughter, yet not a copy of her mother. She was completely Arab.

"Look at her smile—exactly like yours," I assured.

". . . and the funny little way her lips purse when she's thinking.."

Latifa laughed. "Do I do that?"

"Oh, yes. You may not see too much physical resemblance, but she is you, exactly!"

"I think you are just being kind." Latifa reached for the child to hug her, but Haifa wriggled away with a frown, perhaps sensing we had been talking about her.

"*Ya, Mon . . .*" the child said. She stood up and pointed toward the sliding door.

It had again slid open, and the figure in white hurried past. Latifa excused herself, and the two followed the figure down the hall, closing the door behind them.

"There must be someone else in the house," Cyndy said.

"Can't be a serving woman—she wouldn't hide. Besides I'm sure it's a man." I said, with some uneasiness.

There was no point in speculating who the intruder might be, so in the absence of our hostess, we again studied the room. I wanted to remember everything. The usual collection of foreign nicknacks—jeweled glass lamps, Russian papier mâché boxes and hand painted porcelain plates—graced all the empty places. But where we Americans polished our brass coffeepots and used them for decorator pieces, the one in this house would be confined to its own coffee hearth.

CYNDY PLAYED THE PICCOLO IN THE RAS
TANURA BLUE DEVIL BAND

"Look at her great T V," Cyndy said, her voice carrying a note of envy.

The subject of television was rather a sore spot in our home. TV's had recently been admitted into the Eastern Province. They didn't always work, had few programs—mostly religious and in Arabic—and were highly censored. Once in a while there'd be a movie from India, those highly popular in Beirut and Cairo. But just when the action got interesting, and the hero with glazed eyes reached forward to kiss the heroine, the censor's scissors jerked him away. Hardly worth watching!

When Latifa returned, she carried a platter of little cakes and some small Limoge plates decorated with hand painted violets. After setting them on the table, she left to return with a coffeepot—not Arab but French—tall and slender and of fine porcelain. Haifa followed with the cups and silverware.

"I should have asked if you prefer coffee or tea," Latifa said as she set the pot on the table.

"Coffee is fine," I said.

"Really, I must apologize for not making the cakes myself, but everything comes from the Palace," she said, pouring the coffee. "I prefer to make my own, but I do not always have the necessary ingredients."

"They look delicious," I said. "Many times our commissary is out of items I need for meals—so, that is how it goes."

Haifa and Cyndy shared the refreshments, our perfect hostess satisfying our every wish. The incident of some stranger in the house was of no concern, for she deftly handled whatever problem there might have been. I led the conversation to my lack of transportation and asked if she could get us a taxi.

"We have many cars," she replied. "There will be one to take you to Ras Tanura, but it is not time yet." She set her coffee cup back on its delicate bed of violets, then looked at me as though accepting my trust. "You know," she said without hesitation. "Haifa is not the daughter of the Governor."

I must have raised my head in surprise, for she rushed on not waiting for my response.

"I was married first to the Amir Mohammed Al Abdullah, the son of Saud Al Abdullah who died recently." She paused as if waiting for my reaction.

"Yes," I began, startled at her revelation and trying to put pieces of a puzzle together. "Yes—I recall the late Governor had a son—an only son, I believe."

"Yes, that is right," Latifa affirmed. "Perhaps you also know that he died a tragic death in London three years ago . . ."

Chapter Twenty-Six
THE ITALIAN ROSE

Of course! Fran had told me first. She had hurried over to Murrawiyyah's stall where I was saddling up—with that "wait 'till you hear the news I've got" kind of a walk that was Fran all over. It didn't mean too much at the time, but now the tragedy struck home.

"The young Prince Mohammed Bin Saud was Haifa's father." Latifa's calm composure did not betray that the horror of the incident had any remote connection with her. She glanced at the child, busily turning pages to seek a new source of pleasure.

Was the tragedy stored too deeply to ever gain moments of reflection? It is the nature of the Arab to move on and build anew. Once gone, there is no lingering mourning after death.

"Oh, Latifa . . ." I said. "I didn't know. I am so sorry."

Again she faced me, lips separated, as if willing to say more, but instead she looked down to pick up her coffee cup.

"Then I married Mishari Al Abdullah, Amir of Hufuf and brother of the Governor. I lived in Hufuf, while my daughter remained at the Palace in Dammam with her grandparents."

"And that's how it was when I first met you."

"Yes." Latifa paused, her attitude one of relief. "Now that I have my child, I will not entrust her to anybody. I am afraid to let her out of my sight. There isn't always something for us to do here that she likes, but we are together."

A million questions rushed through my mind. How did it happen? What did you do? Why didn't you go back to your parents? If I asked, might she not terminate our budding friendship she obviously wished to continue? In a way she answered for me.

"It was all so ugly. I don't want to think about it."

She refilled our cups, inviting me to have another cake. Haifa dashed out to return with a full glass of orange juice. The figure in white strode past, just as the child slid the hall door closed. Latifa made no effort to leave.

"We of ARAMCO knew how sad it was for the Governor—Saud—his only son. There was no mention of a family." I said, exercising restraint.

She didn't answer, for she knew, as I did, there would be no reference to a wife. The event had been discussed up and down the halls of ARAMCO and at morning coffees. Any details—if known—were hushed up. It was not a good subject upon which to speculate. One didn't dwell idly on local politics.

Oil! What tragedies have accompanied its benefits. A country suddenly burdened with enormous wealth—the world clambering at its door for a stake in the riches—temptation for those who had never tasted the sweetness of freedom. Young men accepted as royalty—honored and hosted by the world—too much of what they had never had before, now giddy with celebrity status: pockets full of cash—expensive cars—flowing alcohol—easy sex—all out of control, and so a false step and tragedy.

"It must have been difficult for your parents," I suggested, seeking more answers.

"I don't want to talk about that," she said with a positiveness that offered no return.

I could only imagine a story often retold—always new. A

handsome Prince—a young romantic girl—an escape into the sun. Why had she married her husband's relative? A man years older than herself? The earlier romance of luxury and travel replaced by the austerity of Islam. I recalled another day—another place. "I am married to the most wonderful man in the world!" But, it couldn't have been that in the beginning. Arab society claimed its own.

Russ had once told me of a Saudi clerk who lived in Rahima. His brother had died, and the clerk had taken in his brother's two wives, another sister and eight children. Together with his family that made six women and fourteen children to care for. How could he ever earn enough to feed them all!

"He came to find me and the baby," Latifa was saying. "I had never met him. He was so kind, and I needed that kindness. He had come to take me home—and I went with him."

Home to security—to honor—to the teachings of the Koran. An Arab family takes care of its own. The grandfather wanted the child. Returning to Arabia would bring her close to Haifa. Marrying her husband's relative became a love match—and who couldn't love Latifa? She was a lady of elegance, education and beauty—delightfully young and vulnerable and in need of human relationships. In this different world she had not yet found a place with his family. In a sense I was a link with her past. Only she could bring herself into the future. Could I tie the two together?

I searched my mind for a flag of remembrance. Finally it came. "I met the Amir Mohammed," I said. "On a certain night in Ras Tanura—many years ago. In fact, Cyndy could have been only five years old."

Latifa had been holding her emotions under strict control. Now she aroused the past with eager interest. It was not all locked away—the days of first love.

"How was it that you saw him?" she asked. "Are you sure it was he?"

"Yes, I am sure," I said, recognizing here was a subject not altogether repressed. "I saw him on several occasions at ARAMCO gatherings but never really met him until this night."

"What night was that?"

"It was an unusual situation, and I think you'll appreciate it," I said.

"Please, tell me . . ."

"Well, it was Christmas, and perhaps you know we Americans may not openly celebrate the holiday."

"Because we are a Muslim country . . ." she interrupted, eagerly listening to my every word.

"Yes. It had been previously arranged with the Saudi Government that we could have Christian services in the privacy of our homes or in prearranged public buildings within our community. Sometimes a minister joined us from Bahrein. He was given a visa as a teacher—which was all right, because that was the only way he would be allowed to enter."

Again she interrupted. "I think it is rather sad that Americans are thought to be without respect for God, because no one ever sees them pray."

"As we see Muslims do," I added. "Five times a day. Believe me, the many difficulties we face are lightened through prayer and our love of God."

Haifa shook her mother's elbow. "*Ya, Mon . . .*" She pointed to the sliding door, again slightly ajar.

This time Latifa remained seated, her expression one of annoyance rather than concern. But Haifa ran off, disappearing down the hall. When she returned, she briefly whispered in her mother's ear, gave me a pointed scrutiny, then waited for a reaction.

"Please excuse me," Latifa said, as she got up. "There is something I must attend to." She again disappeared down the hall, Haifa tagging behind.

"What's going on?" Cyndy asked.

"Probably the woman has returned from Hufuf," I suggested.

"Maybe we shouldn't stay," Cyndy said, returning the colored pencils to their box.

When Latifa joined us again, she appeared to be somewhat agitated. "I do apologize," she said. "Shall I reheat the coffee?"

"It's fine," I said, wondering what might be amiss.

"Please—tell me about Mohammed . . ." she encouraged.

I decided to cut my story short and then ask for a car as soon as possible. "Since we would be without a minister this Christmas, I decided to put on a pageant with the school children that would tell the story of the birth of Christ. Because we expected most families of Nejma to come, we would need a larger space than our homes and were allowed to use the dining room of the Surf House—provided we did not allow any Arabs to enter."

"You mean—that would be wrong?" she asked.

"Yes—in the eyes of the Government. And if any local people came, all future Christian services would be shut down."

"I see." She appeared thoughtful. "I don't know what is the Surf House. . . ?"

Haifa returned and promptly emptied all the pencils on the table. With an authoritative gesture she pushed a red one toward Cyndy, who had not finished coloring the pantaloons of a clown.

I continued my story. "The Surf House is our Recreation Building. It has a lounge, bowling alley, library and dining room. We set up the dining room to be a theatre with screens around the entranceway to block the view of anyone who might walk through the rest of the building. The young actors had to gather in the outer hall, until I could cue them in to do their pantomime. The children were beautifully dressed as glittering angels, pink cherubs, long robed shepherds and rich Wisemen." I paused. "Do you know the story?"

"Oh, yes. I was not always Muslim."

"Then I shall tell you about the Prince."

I took a sip of coffee, and she refilled my cup. The details of that night were clear in my mind, but I would keep them to myself. I would not tell her that one of the boys, against my directive, had hung the children's Sunday School cross on the screen that separated the kitchen from the dining area. It was in full view of the audience. I would not say that the Muslim distrust of Christianity was an aftermath of the Crusades, and that to them the cross represented Crusader atrocities committed against the Arab. Thus my fear of it being seen and the risk of losing our Christian privileges.

"Well . . ." I continued the story. " Mary and Joseph entered, and angels proclaimed the birth of the baby Jesus. Little cherubs in pink costumes carried a large gold paper star . . ."

"I can just see them . . ." Latifa said. " Mrs. Nicholson—you are so clever!"

I laughed. "They were cute. Cyndy was one of them."

Cyndy looked up as if to say, "I was?"

"Although concentrating on the action, I was vaguely aware that all was not going as scheduled in the outer hallway. Loud voices and a commotion of movement indicated a disturbance of some kind. A man from Government Relations burst in and told me to get all the children inside immediately and then rushed out again. I could hear him telling someone in the hall: "You don't want to go in there, Your Highness—it is just for children." Then I heard a reply in Arabic. Latifa—can you imagine how scared I was?"

"Well—I don't know—tell me . . ."

"Because if an Arab entered, our Christian celebrations would be shut down."

"Oh . . ."

"The shepherds were supposed to come next—instead I found myself face to face with a tall, smiling young man in authentic Arab dress! Oh, how handsome he was! No shepherd—especially not ours—was ever dressed in such elegance!"

"It was Amir Mohammed. . . ?"

I nodded. "He asked me if he could stay and watch the children. In spite of my concern, I had to admire him. There is something about Arab dress that is flattering to men."

"You really think so?" she said with a smile.

"Yes, I do! Why—I almost fell in love with him myself!" I couldn't resist. "Anyway, when the Prince asked again if he could stay, I managed to stumble 'Of course!' For what else do you say to a Prince? The Relations man tried to get him to leave, but he wouldn't. They were afraid he'd turn in a bad report to the Governor."

"And. . . ?" She asked.

"He stayed until the end, smiling at the children, then turned to me with a gracious, 'Thank you,' and left."

Latifa seemed far away from her Dollhouse—in London, perhaps—remembering.

"He loved children very much—and, of course, he never said anything."

"Not a word to anyone."

How grateful I had been for his tolerance and understanding.

A bell clanged in the back room, and Latifa hurried to answer it. As she did, the sliding door was left open, and again the white robed figure paced past. It left me with an uncomfortable feeling, though, I couldn't say why. On her return, she again apologized for not being able to entertain us without interruption. Her statement assured me the intruder was a man, for I knew women have a right to privacy when receiving female friends. The knowledge reinforced my uneasiness, and I suggested it was time for us to leave.

"Oh, no . . ." she insisted. " . . . you have only just come!"

The Arab makes such a statement, all the while expecting that you will depart! However, I felt Latifa was absolutely sincere, and it would be polite for us to remain a little longer. I had brought a box of photographs Russ and I had taken on the desert, thinking they might interest her, as they do most people who have not experienced the vastness and ever changing beauty of the Arabian wilderness.

"You know more about Arabia than I do!" she exclaimed. "Just see the many places you have been. I have been only to Hufuf where I lived, the Palace in Dammam, and once in a while to the ARAMCO clinic."

"But—that isn't enough!" I exclaimed. "Couldn't you get away, if you wanted to—say to Beirut or Cairo?" I realized there was little she could do in Dammam other than visit family.

"Yes," she said. "I could go—but I keep putting it off."

"Couldn't you visit your parents?"

"I could—but. . . . ."

"Why?" I plunged on, unthinking of where I was going.

She changed the subject. "I must tell you that a short time ago I was invited to a royal wedding in Riyadh. I would have been gone for three days. The Amir's family urged me to go, but I didn't want to." A moment's pause followed by a determination to share her concerns. "Do you think I should have gone?"

How best could I answer that sincere question—offer guidance through a lifestyle I really knew very little about? What were her checks and balances—the requirements of the Amir? My answer would reflect complete concern for her.

"Latifa . . . you can't just stay in your lovely little house by yourself day after day. You need companionship, especially since you were raised with a sense of freedom. By going to Riyadh, you would have met more people and seen more of your country at the same time. Yes, I certainly think you should have gone."

She remained silent for a moment, twisting her cup on its saucer. A serious note puckered her brow.

"It is very difficult for me," she confessed softly. "I do not feel at ease. It makes me uncomfortable to meet people. When

I made this country my home, I promised to abide by the customs and to live as a Muslim wife is brought up to live."

My heart went out to her, and I reached for her hand. "Believe me I do understand, and I know it cannot be easy. My adjusting to the customs of Saudi Arabia presents far less restrictions than for you. I wanted so much to see you, but there was no way I could do that. Even ARAMCO couldn't break the barriers."

"Is it really that bad?" she sighed. "Yes—I know it is."

"Couldn't you get away some time? Visit your parents?"

"Yes, I could go—with permission from my husband. But there are many reasons why I don't. I know I will want to do all the things I cannot do here. I would want to go shopping, to the cinema, see all the things I did as a child—then when I got back here it would only make it that much worse, because I would miss doing those things more than ever. That is why I do not go—because I would rather not do those things any more. Do you think that is wrong?"

Her voice had become strained and hesitant, as though concentrating on some time long ago—bringing it back, yet forbidding it entrance.

"Oh, Latifa! Yes—I do!"

"Then . . ." in a little girl's voice, " . . . what should I do?"

I felt plunged into a sea of darkness, swimming tenuously toward the light, to reach a safe haven on a subject I knew little about. "Where is my way out?" her words had implied. I reached for an answer.

"Let me tell you what I think," I said, seeking a solution within the restraints as I knew them. "The struggle you have with yourself seems to come from fear of losing your identity as an individual. This you will sacrifice for the sake of being a true Muslim, to respect the wishes of your husband—but subconsciously you still want to be the person you were, the person your husband married. Do you understand what I am trying to say?"

"I think I do . . ."

"With courage and confidence, you should be able to maintain your identity. Visit your parents and go to the movies, shop without an escort. Enjoying these small liberties should sustain your need to be yourself, when you return to Dammam—to the one you love, and who loves you."

Her response was quick—the root of her fears.

"To do that, I would not be living as a true Muslim."

"No, Latifa. That is not so . . ." I hastened to pick up the thread. "What you are as a Muslim is in your heart. Islam is not the same in all countries. That is because it incorporated local customs, and in Saudi Arabia they are most restrictive. The Amir must know they are difficult for you, and any refractions would not be observed when you are out of the country. I don't know if he would be that tolerant. I do know he built you this lovely home, as you wished it to be, and furnished it according to your liking—in fact, upholding the requirements to give you surroundings according to your standard of living. Do you accept that?"

"Yes."

"Then, if you have the courage, ask and see what happens."

"I do not think I could," she whispered to herself, though I felt sure she would not discard my proposals.

The rustling figure slipped past the open door and down the hall. It neither paused nor looked in—the action was more like a reminder of its presence. The clanging bell rang loudly and long.

"*Sayaarah* (car)!" cried Haifa, running toward the front door. I heard the clink of keys, as the child unlocked the door and ran down the steps toward the gate.

"The car is here early. I do not know why," Latifa said, hastily adding, " . . . but you do not have to go."

Obviously, somebody had ordered the car for our departure.

"It is time for us to leave. My husband will be expecting us."

"No . . ." she said. "We can sit on the terrace for a few minutes." Latifa picked up some small folding chairs leaning against the foyer wall and set them up on the terrace.

"For a few minutes . . ." I agreed.

A late afternoon breeze bounced the fronds of the palms and rustled through the compact leaves of the banyan trees. A few dusty oleanders hung on to life in the dry, salty ground. Beyond the terrace over the wall lay the sea, sultry, disturbed, stretching past the ragged shell of the fort, past shallow sand bars to deeper waters and lands afar.

Haifa came running back, confirming that the car was indeed waiting behind the gate. The date palms, once laden with ripened yellow fruit, were now dragging empty, knobby tendrils where once life had swollen to full richness and capacity.

"The garden isn't very much now," Latifa confessed. "It needs attention. Once I did have an Italian gardener. He tried to plant some flowers. See here." She got up and walked over to an empty flowerbed, where one lone dry stalk still hugged the rough wall. "It was a very pretty flower—it only ever had one lone bloom—and it had a name—yes, he called it the Sophia Loren rose . . ."

"I guess for the Italian movie star," Cyndy said.

"But you see it is only a dry stalk now. It could not live here and remain lovely. It died."

"*Ya, Mon!* The car is here! The car . . ." pleaded Haifa.

"Yes—we must go. Thank you for a wonderful afternoon. I shall always remember it, and hope that one day I may see you in Ras Tanura."

"*Inshallah* . . . if it is the will of God."

At the gate she told me Saeed would drive us home. He was the Governor's personal chauffeur and a careful driver. Haifa turned the key in the lock, then she and her mother stepped behind its shadow as the gate slowly opened. Cyndy and I walked through, knowing that the two hidden figures could not be seen by anyone on the outside. The gate clanged shut. A key turned in the lock, and Latifa, the rose, and the Dollhouse were gone.

The guards paid no attention to the Governor's car as we drove the length of the driveway and out onto the dusty street. My thoughts were of Latifa and the rose—it was so like her—slowly fading in a walled garden by the sea—transplanted from one culture to another, incompatible, demanding, so that perhaps even love could not keep the bloom alive.

Chapter Twenty-Seven
THE G. T. O.

It was not unusual for Sara to visit me after school, but when her normally ebullient spirits seemed to be dragging on the ground, I realized something other than the classroom was causing her distress. She flung an armful of books on the Kuwait chest in the hall and dropped with a sigh into my favorite rocker.

"How about a cup of tea, Sara," I said. "You look like you could use one."

I retrieved two tiny gilt trimmed Arab glasses from the kitchen cupboard—no such luxury as a china cabinet—and set them on their saucers. The expectation they generated should have brightened anyone. It took five minutes to start the water boiling, soak out the initial bitterness from a spoonful of tea, then drop the damp leaves into the bubbling water. The sugar I would add later, for the beauty of Arab tea is its sweetness.

"Have you seen Fahada lately?" I asked, observing that Sara was slowly taking control of herself.

"Her mother returned to Riyadh, and I spent the night with her. There's talk of marriage again." Sara said.

"And what does Fahada say?"

"What can she say? Everything is arranged for her."

I had no ready answer, so I returned to the kitchen to add the sugar. Sara followed.

"These Saudis. . . ! I get so mad at them!" she said.

"Now what?"

"Hammad and I went dancing at the Officers' Club. Well, a *mutaaw'ah* cornered him. You know how awful they are. He banged on the table so everybody could hear and told Hammad he—a Prince—shouldn't be dancing in public with a bad woman! I wanted to scream at the man when he pulled my skirt and yanked my hair, then called me shameful because I, an Arab woman, didn't wear a veil!" Tears filled her eyes.

"Oh, Sara, I can imagine how you felt. I've had my legs rapped with a stick in the *suq*. It just makes you mad." I dropped a few dried mint leaves into the pot and returned with the brewed tea to the living room. The spicy scent was relaxing enough to swing her into a different mood.

"Nejela Al Yahyah has been on the streets again," I said, pouring the tea. "In a short skirt and no veil."

"I know," Sara said with a shrug.

"I saw her myself," I said. "We were both at Jamil's looking at his newly arrived silks from India. She's an artist, you know, and intends to open a woman's shop of her own designs."

Sara screwed up her face. "She can get away with it, because her father backs her, and he is an influential man."

"Don't forget you did it in Oman on your own—got Bedouin women to send their children to your school."

She did not comment.

"Maybe one day things will be different for women," I added. "Now, tell me—what does Hammad think?"

"He told his mother about me. He is pledged to his *bint 'amm,* and she will never consent to our marriage." Sara picked up her glass, but overcome with anger, quickly set it down.

"I told him to stand up to his family, but in my heart I know it is useless, because they are all one person."

"It's always been that way," I agreed. "The desert taught

them in unity is survival."

She brushed her hand across her eyes to stem the tears. "This is not ancient history. It's the twentieth century!"

"You ran away from these practices," I reminded her. "Have a little patience."

"It's all so unfair! He doesn't have to marry her to be a good Muslim! That's Saudi custom!"

Why hadn't Sara realized the vulnerability of her position? I could answer that—love is blind to reality. How could she ever live in a fixed up room in the family home shared with other married sons—the mother in control: never any privacy— the women protected from the attentions of strange males, for treasured, they belong only to the family.

"Sara—are you sure you want to marry him?" I asked.

"Oh, yes," she said. "I know he loves me." She extended her arm. " . . . look at these bracelets—this ring—these earrings. Every time I see him he brings something like this."

I fingered the rounds of gold bangles on her wrist.

"They're truly lovely," I said.

The tears returned. "He says he loves me because I am lively and dress the way I do. He loves me because of these things; yet cannot marry me also because of these things." She slumped in the chair. "Next time he visits his family, I know he will marry his *bint 'amm* and never return . . ." Two large drops spilled over, streaking the flush of anger coloring her face. The truth was in her tears.

"Dear Sara . . ." I said. "Don't upset yourself. Enjoy your time spent with Hammad and hope for the best . . ." I, too, felt the inevitable closing in.

"More tea. . . ?"

She passed her arm across her eyes to smear the tears caught in her lower lashes. "I will face what comes," she said with painful determination. "It will not be the first time." She pulled a tissue from her purse, gave her nose a hearty blow and even managed a smile. "I almost forgot what I came to tell you. The

Al Abdullahs are having a family party. They have asked you to come."

"How nice," I said. "When is it?"

"Fahada will let me know. One of the girls has finished a year of school, so everybody is celebrating."

"Of course we will go! Just think what education is doing for girls."

It was one thing for King Faisal to open schools for girls. After all, his wife Iffat had started one in Riyadh years before. But to install education in the small villages was quite something else. The twentieth century's intrusion was not accepted over night, nor did it have a means of implementation. In a joint venture with the Saudi government, ARAMCO agreed to pay all costs and to erect the buildings throughout the country. The curriculum, staff and instructors were to be determined by the government ministries. The schoolhouses for selected villages were there, but the basics for operation were sadly lacking. With no furniture, no books, and no teachers, the school in Sahat in the Qatif Oasis never opened.

Suhayla Abdul Goddar, wife of a Jordanian ARAMCO employee, and qualified teacher from Amman, offered to become the director of the one in Rahima. With dedicated effort and local recruitment of staff, she opened the school. I had been invited to attend the first open house. How proud the students were of their achievements.

Behind cyclone fences laced with straw matting, the girls had learned the Koran by heart and applied its teachings to everyday life. With it as their textbook they learned to read and to write. Simple drawings in paper pamphlets emphasized the need to keep goats out of the house, to cover the baby's crib with netting—if available in the *suq*—to protect the child from flies and disease. The children discovered the value of washing hands and to brush lice out of their hair. The older ones displayed their handiwork of fine embroideries and canned foods, how to use a stove and sewing machine. Reading, math and science were incorporated through practical application. Best of all was the individual development brought home to instruct families. In our small township of Rahima, education for girls made a difference, as it did when many more schools opened across the country.

When the day for the Al Abdullah party came, Sara joined us, and we took a taxi to Fahada's villa. The immediate family women were milling about dressed in their finest. Umm Naiyf was resplendent in another new gown, richly decorated with shimmering bugle beads. I felt somewhat out of place in my short Thai silk dress, but there would be guests I hadn't met, and I wanted to be accepted as an American—not someone dressed up to imitate their culture.

To my delight Latifa was present, outshining everyone in a pale yellow gown glittering with rhinestones. A filmy bit of gossamer sprinkled with pearls crowned her head, and the most valuable of jewels she might have worn was her smile.

"I knew you would come," she said. " . . . and this is one party I couldn't escape."

"Who are all these people?" I asked, observing several women milling about in the salon.

"I don't know—just family. Right now there seems to be a problem with transportation. My husband is hosting the Amir of Bahrein, and the Amirate cars are all in use."

"Are we going somewhere else?" I asked.

"Yes. To the home of Amir Samir Al Abdullah, my husband's brother. Fahada's mother is making arrangements."

I looked about the room—all women relatives of the Al Abdullah family, rulers of the towns and villages throughout the Eastern Province. I knew of Mohammed from Buraida, father of Hussa—Mansur of Sakaka in the northwest, whose famous camel corps guarded the endless stretches of pipeline that carried Arabian crude to Sidon in the Lebanon for shipment to refineries in Europe. Another brother was Amir of Jubail, and Amir Turki of Rahima was almost an old friend.

Amira Azziza joined us, offering a friendly smile to Latifa, as she addressed me. "We have arranged for you to go with Fahada," she said. "I must leave now, but I shall see you at Amir Samir's."

I thanked her, and she returned to stand near the door with Umm Naiyf.

"I must go," Latifa said, with a less than painful expression. "I shall see you there." Her shoulders lifted then settled, as with resignation she joined Azziza and Umm Naiyf. The three wives left together to share one car—equality in all things.

"Are we going to ride in the lavender car?" Linda asked after everyone else had departed.

"But we don't have it any more," Fahada answered. "I got tired of it. So after that I had a Mercedes." Excitement bubbled in her eyes.

"Was it lavender, too?" Cynthia asked.

"No. It was silver. I didn't like it." A petulant expression pinched her mouth.

"You are spoiled," Sara chided.

"I wish I had a car—any car," Linda sighed, enjoying a week's respite from school. To her mind, our Land Rover was a truck.

"Oh, Sara. Wait till you see my new one." Alive with excitement, Fahada tossed on an *abbaya* and veil preparatory to going out. As we headed for the door, she quickly pulled the veil aside. With the family gone, this fearless Princess revitalized to become the eager girl who had sneaked out of the Palace in Hufuf to speak to a couple of young Americans.

"It goes like the wind," the Princess continued. "I drive it along the Abqaiq road to Half Moon Bay, and when I see a car, I race it. Other cars try to keep up, but I pass them all! This is the one I really love!" The challenge of danger somehow removed the elegant Princess from her ivory tower.

"I hope you have an excellent driver," I said.

"He does what I tell him! I am the driver!"

"What kind of car do you have?" Linda asked.

" . . . a G.T.O!"

There was such daring in her tone that I envisaged some high powered racing vehicle. Even the Pontiac sports car was a strange companion for an Arab Princess.

"Is it lavender?" Cyndy asked.

"It is gold! You'll see how it streaks down the road passing everything in sight!" She leaned closer to us, extending her expressive hands. "See—I am not interested in jewelry. I want cars—fast exciting automobiles! I must have them."

The thrill of the hunt enlivened every gesture, every inch of her being. A true daughter of the House of Al Saud. She could not capture the capitol city of Riyadh with a handful of camel corpsmen, as her grandfather had done in years past. She could not ride the sandy wastes seated in an ostrich plumed *maksar* on the back of a camel, long hair streaming and black eyes flashing to incite the tribe's young warriors to victory against an enemy—as maidens did in years barely out of reach. She might have—had not the twentieth century broken barriers impregnable for three thousand years. The land changed—villages changed—new replaced old—but people did not change. It took a slow, patient time, such as the hours we spent appraising, studying each other, questioning and hopefully understanding. Blood had not changed. Fahada was a daughter of the desert, hampered by confinement in a capitol city instead of dwelling in a worsted tent on the open desert where her spirit flourished.

Cars—fast, flashy cars—were today's answers for her captive longings. Her voice echoed the tribal cry of warriors carried on the winds of morning—full and vibrant. The cry of victory! I could hear her shouting down the hall, then the muttering of fearful voices and the scurrying of many feet. She returned composed, satisfied. "When I go to America," she said, "I shall pick the car I want!"

I visualized her in a showroom on Fifth Avenue. What a

moment that would be! A servant signaled our transportation had arrived. Fahada adjusted the veil over her head and shoulders, and we followed her outside.

It stood on the dirt street—a flash of gold in the burning rays of the afternoon sun—the G.T.O.! A young man in white *thaub* and *quttra* gathered up the cloth he was using to polish the hood and hastily opened the car doors. Fahada sat in front with the driver, and the four of us squeezed into the back seat. The engine roared. Dust spewed behind where wide-eyed children gazed in awe. An old man following his sheep home gathered them close in fear of this latest work of Allah.

Through the rough streets of the town the driver carefully dodged the evening traffic of goats, vendors and uncertain motor scooters until we reached the Dhahran-Ras Tanura Road. The car jumped out and my heart with it. The wheels whipped the tarred surface, passing everything in sight.

"It sure takes off," Linda said, wriggling for a spot to sit on. "How fast are we going?"

Obviously not fast enough, for Fahada urged the driver on. I prayed for a clear way ahead. The throttle hit the floorboard. The Princess threw off her veil, despite Sara's remonstrance. In the dusk, I was sure there was a shadow on the road. A camel? Who could tell, for all landmarks vaporized as we passed.

"Look!" cried Cynthia. "That's Daddy!"

It couldn't be—yet the "Jerboa" (Cyndy's name for our Land Rover) approached and was gone as we raced on. I remembered Russ had an early morning meeting in Dhahran and would spend the night there. Had he seen us? What would he think? How could anyone identify objects that passed so swiftly? We turned left, slowing to negotiate a sand drift blown across the road. A motor scooter carrying two young men weaved uncertainly toward us. The car skimmed past, and both men fell off. Fahada looked back. The men were setting up the cycle. It had been too close. We gushed ahead. Vehicles were sparse, but each one a danger in our path. Suddenly Sara screamed a warning.

CITIZENS OF THE TOWN OUT SHOPPING FOR
BEADS AND SILKS FOR A NEW DRESS

"An Amirate car! The veil!"

It was too late. As we raced past, the occupant of the government car must have recognized the G.T.O. and observed the woman's haste to cover up.

"You are too reckless," Sara warned.

"It was only Turki from Rahima. He will not say anything." Fahada wound the ends of the veil around her throat to hold it in place.

We turned off onto a rutted road, where ten foot high walls of rough brick edged either side, and stopped in front of a solid iron gate. A guard swung it open, and we stepped over the ground bar and into deep sand.

A two story building sprawled ahead, its dimly lit windows opened to the breeze stared like fading eyes in the twilight. I shook the sand from my shoes and walked up the tiled steps to the porch. Several women and children stood in the entryway, including Azziza, Hussa and Haifa, now charming in a pale blue dress with layers of lace. The child watched us with amused recognition, her hand in the grip of a striking young girl wearing a shimmering green satin dress. Haifa nudged her, and the girl came forward to meet us. Fahada introduced her as Duha, the honoree of the evening's festivities.

Duha invited us into the women's salon and introduced us to those ladies already present. I caught a glimpse of open rooms, starkly bare and unadorned save for the variety of colorful gowns floating through. Along one wall, half submerged in deep gold chairs, reclined half a dozen older women. Their shapeless bodies sunk into the contour of the *setas*, they sat almost in a stupor, having long ago used up conversational resources on subjects worn out with reiteration.

Tonight there was something new—the graduation of a daughter—but the ladies would find it difficult to accept the fact that girls had left the *hareem* to go to school in the town, and that proud Duha had successfully completed her first year. I recognized the Great Aunt, who acknowledged my presence with a piercing stare. She seemed about to speak, but her attention followed the warm and smiling "*Marhubba*" of my short-skirted daughters. Her darkly hennaed fingers accepted my extended hand, as if it were a betrayal of her own culture, though she may never see our western faults take place in the world of Islam. On the floor at her feet, crouched the faithful slave—the parchment texture of her dark skin ridged and ancient, fragile as the burned out ashes of a campfire before the wind blows them away.

The elderly faces, cornerstone of the family expressed a

sense of pride, contentment and peace. Toddlers pulled at their skirts, granddaughters kissed their wrinkled cheeks, then skipped off to find their cousins. I was aware of Princess Latifa behind me.

"I see you arrived safely . . ." she said.

"You mean—the G.T.O.?"

She nodded. "Come, we may sit over here."

We made ourselves comfortable near an open window, while Sara ran off with my girls to join Fahada and a group of young relatives, busily engaged in selecting records for a portable phonograph.

That first visit to the Dollhouse had opened up other opportunities to spend time with the Governor's young wife. We spent many happy hours together behind the walls of the Amirate Palace, and her place in my life as a daughter grew through mutual respect and need. Latifa seemed to welcome her new life, and our topics of conversation broadened to include philosophy, literature and art. She confessed that she stayed by herself most of the time and had yet to become acquainted with the many branches of the family, though she was learning to enjoy the friendliness of those who visited her.

"There is something good about this life," Latifa said, as we watched the ladies pause in their activities to pat a toddler on the head or to reach out to save another one from a fall. "I have a lot to learn . . ." she continued. "Here—everybody has a home—you are always wanted—you are never alone—you meet your life with those who love you."

Her words were the keynote to an awakening acceptance of what she could not change. I listened in silence.

" . . . even through divorce which is common," she continued. " . . . or the death of a husband, there is always a male member of the family to bring you home . . ."

The echo of her own tragic days in London.

"But the dissention, the jealousy, the intrigue," I said. "I can't imagine so many women living together in harmony."

"Of course, that happens, too. After all, they are human!" she admitted. "But it is of little importance."

Not wanting to delve deeper into such possibilities, I looked about for Duha. From the moment we entered the house I was aware of the unusual necklace the child wore, and curiosity got the better of me. I beckoned her to come our way and she did, along with several of her young friends. Proudly she fingered the triple strands of oversized baroque Gulf pearls that lay against the satin of her dress, pinkly iridescent and irregular in shape, not peeled and polished by the artisan to jewel perfection. A long silk fringe straddled her shoulder, the termination of cords that tied the ends together. I had never seen anything so extraordinary nor so beautiful. Surely, it couldn't be a graduation gift.

"No," Duha said. "It belongs to my mother, and I am allowed to wear it this one time."

"It has quite a story," Latifa said. "I know only part of it."

Duha's fingers caressed the surface of the pearls. "The necklace belonged to my grandmother," she said. "It was a gift from Ibn Saud."

What fantasies ran through my head—Ibn Saud—the first King who gave his heart and his name to his country. I must hear the whole story. Would the women follow the tradition of men, born of lonely desert nights, and retell for the young and pride of family the courageous deeds of ancestors?

Tales of bravery and tribal honor were woven into the Ardah, the dance of men that culminated a festive occasion. I had seen it performed in the village of Sahat on the 'Id Al Fitr holiday after the month long fast of Ramadan. Men and boys from the hamlets and villages within the nearby palm oasis of Qatif joined in the joyous celebration along the Gulf's shores.

Line after line of dancers, linked shoulder to shoulder, faced each other. Those who had swords raised them high, and directed by the poet in song and verse, demanded proof of honor from their opponents. The smallest boys picked up sticks and imitated the movements of their fathers, for tomorrow they would be the ones to perform the Ardah.

"Our hearts are strong," they sang. "Bold as the flare of the coffee fire that leaps in the morning breeze."

There will be no such dance tonight. But, would I learn about the pearls if I asked—perhaps touch the heart of this gracious family and its essence of royalty?

"Duha—may I ask you something?"

Chapter Twenty-Eight
FAMILY HONOR

But Duha had other plans. She directed my gaze toward an oversized portrait of a man, a flat and faded print in brown rotogravure set in a thin gold frame at the far end of the room.

"You know who this is?" she asked.

"Yes," I said. "That's Saud Al Abdullah, the former Governor."

"My uncle," she exclaimed with pride of kinship. "And do you know this one?"

She turned to indicate a series of five windows, shutters open to the breeze, that followed the curve of the bay. The diffused orange glimmer of a lowering sun sent a pink half light creeping into the room and cast an eeriness over the second print of a man, whose heavy brows and ink black eyes seemed to challenge the invasion.

The blistering stare of that faded print—hung almost to touch the ceiling—held the power of ancestry over the room and denounced the efforts of women to pursue education outside the home.

I didn't have to search for a name. I knew.

"It's Abdullah Al Abdullah," I said. "The great liberator of Riyadh."

"My grandfather . . ." Duha said, surprised at my knowledge of her family's history.

The man's hawklike features, almost completely submerged in a bushy black beard, were well known to me through hours spent in ARAMCO's Arabian Research Library tucked away at the end of a long corridor in the Dhahran Administration Building. Here was a treasury of original papers, documenting the physical and cultural aspects of the Eastern Province, hand recorded by the first American engineers to explore the original California Standard Oil Company (CASOC) Concession Agreement. The face belonged to a warrior, and in the words of Latifa: "My father-in-law . . ."

In spite of the harrowing experience of my arrival, I felt humbled by this family's pride of history. I was delighted to be with Latifa again, even though I had spent many happy hours with her in her Dollhouse since that first formal visit. She seemed more at ease in the presence of her family, and we enjoyed observing the older women who kept a silent watch on younger ladies exchanging personal problems, and on the teens gliding in and out, anxious to share secrets in some private place. But first—a polite greeting.

"This is Juad, daughter of the Prince of Oman . . ." The eyes were those of a siren, haughty, enticing, and, oh! so exquisitely etched in her soft hued face. The mask and veil had taught women the power of the eyes.

"My cousin Sulfa . . . my aunt Fatma . . . my niece Laila . . ." related and inter-related—promised in marriage at birth, their future secure, the family intact. Alas, the daughter rejected, or when all male cousins have been spoken for.

It was a different world through a locked door, even as Alice reached her enlightenment through the rabbit hole to wonderland. I admired the cheerful togetherness of women on this night of celebration, their strikingly beautiful gowns designed for their own pleasure and never to be a lure for favors in a chance encounter with a male. It was happening around me; yet might there exist other hopes within hidden dreams? Dreams were my world, made up of secret longings in the search for a mate.

I could empathize with Sara and Latifa—one seeking escape—the other integration—yearning for individual freedom. Here peace and harmony reigned, the excitement of a festive gathering, the opportunity to look your best—fine feathers worn to outshine each other, not to attract the male.

"See, prayer time is not yet finished," Latifa whispered. "The elderly ladies must have arrived late."

It was then I became aware of a young woman directing two servants, former slaves, who refused to leave the only home they had ever known, to arrange small prayer rugs in front of the windows—facing west—facing Makkah. The individual rugs, barely the size of a small tabletop, enshrined palm trees and a mosque in brilliant colors—almost too gaudy for their intended use.

My interest was drawn to the young woman, for I envied her graceful movements, reflective of desert maidens walking long miles in search of brushwood for the campfires. She wore the short Bedu mask of iridescent calico typical of South Arabia. Her dark hair was arranged in eight thin braids, the custom for Bedu women on festive occasions, and the soft drape of her scarlet gown rippled over her slender figure. I watched her assist Great Aunt Nura to stand for the evening prayer—the fourth of the day—but not before she had slipped aside her mask and left her face open to God.

"Perhaps I should move away," I said to Latifa. "My presence might embarrass them."

"I wouldn't worry about it," she answered.

"I see the clerks and gardeners pray every day," I said. "But here it is so personal."

"It's rather curious," Latifa said. "The older ladies are never late for prayers, but tonight they appear to have waited until you came—for what reason I can't imagine."

The evening sky darkened over guardian walls and arch-ways. A deep lavender blush silhouetted the minaret of a mosque and gave rise to the slender crescent of a new moon with one brilliant star blazing the heavens. One by one, the older women knelt to honor Allah in the Islamic tradition of no ritual, no third party between you and your God.

> "Here am I, oh God, at Thy command.
> Here am I.
> Thine art praise and grace and dominion
> Here am I."

I felt absorbed into the timelessness of life, the infinity of God. The centuries that mark life's changes are the games we create, mazes of our own making wherein Time beats its drum in rhythmic epochs for our own obsession. The ravaged desert with its siren's singing, challenges man's openness to God— Allah—who is always there, even unto Paradise.

An endless chain of years lives on within these walls. Out-side, those who rush madly through the maze tear at the tradi-tions, the history, with tools of technology and riches—the *djjal* of the desert legend: a demon riding the necks of men, taunt-ing them toward distant glitter to a final nothingness of an-guish, so they cannot answer the words of the Koran: "What have you done with the boon of life?"

The room was warm, the languor enervating, the strange-ness subduing. The dried brine of the sea slipped in with the evening breeze, repugnant and sour. And with it something else, unnoticed until now—the wild, free, fierceness of the desert—the Prophet's answer to glittering dresses and idle talk. It came into the room in the form of a child. She was such a tiny thing, the little girl poised in the doorway—with the alert-ness and timidity of a gazelle. A Bedu child—a child of the wind, a child of freedom in search of the red sands she could not find. Lost, she was, in this impressive gathering, a vision of long loose tangled hair, silver bracelets and turquoise nose stud, strings of colored beads brightening her faded flower patterned dress. A leather amulet holding words from the Koran protected her from the Evil Eye. The face, thin and wheat colored, was all eyes—startled, enlarged by brown shadows of hardship beneath their trailing lashes.

"Who is she?"

Duha heard me. She approached the child gently, coaxingly, as she would a wild bird. She picked her up and carried her to me. But the little one looked at my strangeness with centuries of separation in her tortured eyes and screamed—as others had done before at first sight of us—and like a skink wriggled free and into the sand layers of obscurity.

"She is Bedu," explained Duha, as though that were the answer to everything.

The prayers finished, a somber faced servant entered carrying a brazier of burning incense. The thin veil of grey smoke plumed and drifted about the room, as each guest waved the scent of roses about her face and clothes. Haifa blinked her eyes and choked on a giggle, the fragrant vapor tickling her nose and leaving her momentarily breathless. Three times the incense burner made the rounds of the room, before the servant squatted in front of Amira Azziza and set the brazier on the floor in front of her. Activated by ageless repetitions, the tall wooden burner, painted red and dotted with brass nail heads and circles of chipped glass, seemed to have a life of its own that demanded an immediate response.

Azziza got to her feet, gracefully lifted the hem of her skirts and stepped over the brazier. The fumes rose under her long dress, circling her body with their feathery warmth, nuances of perfume and implication of custom. For a few moments she stood there, the guests enjoying her contentment, then returned to her seat. The sudden movement of air from her silken garment sent the fragrant smoke spiraling, and the charcoal sputtered and glowed in its tin cup.

Next, the brazier was set before Umm Naiyf, bypassing those women in between. A smile of anticipation, sensuous, enjoyable accompanied her straddling of the burner. Squatting, she hung over it in a kind of ecstasy.

What if it stops by me, I thought, as I watched the whirling vapor approach ever closer? Would I be singled out as a guest—in spite of my short skirts? What did it mean—this ceremony of the wives I might inadvertently be a party to?

The bearer paused in front of Princess Latifa, the charcoal eyes glowing red through lids of grey ash. The fumes spiraled like a formless snake, beckoning, enticing, demanding. Stony faced the woman waited. Latifa made no move. The passing seconds seemed endless. The servant grew impatient. She signaled with her hand, but Latifa remained seated. The pressure of eyes closed in. Then, slowly, elegantly, in perfect command of every movement, she arose. Her youth, her beauty, her confidence faced the room without a tremor. She lifted so slightly the drape of her yellow dress and stepped gracefully over the brazier. The smile never left her face, as she accepted the approval of her relatives, even seemed to enjoy it. She would be one of them—in her own way. The ritual continued in silence, the servant left the room and animated chatter resumed.

"Is the smoke cooling?" I asked in all innocence, as Latifa returned to sit beside me.

Was it my imagination, or had the sparkle of rhinestones on her dress enhanced a light in her eyes. With a glint of amusement she was about to answer, when Sara interrupted.

"The Prince enjoys it, too . . ." Sara said, as she joined us.

It took a few moments to ingest the meaning of her words. The ritual of the incense became clear, and a blush of understanding warmed my cheeks. Equality in all things. I tried not to picture the details, and Latifa quickly changed the subject.

"Now, *inshallah*! we shall have dinner!" she said.

The contentment in her smile answered my concerns: she alone shared her husband's love.

A tall gaunt woman entered and elected to sit on the edge of a straight-backed chair. I watched as Duha joined her and began to plait the long loose hair that fell freely down the woman's back. When she had finished, Duha untied the heavy tassels of the pearl necklace, placed the heirloom in the woman's hands and began rounding up the children for dinner. For a brief moment the lady held the pearls in her hand, allowing the strands to drip over the rough skin of her palm, then rolling the necklace into a ball, she deposited it in the deep pocket sewn into the seam of her dress. She stood up, pulled a brass bell from a second pocket and rang it vigorously. Its deep tones reverberated throughout the house to announce the evening meal.

Fahada and my daughters had been gone for some time—no doubt engaged in intimate discussions with close friends among the older girls. When they reappeared, I asked Linda to see if Sara could find out something about the Bedu child. It was Amsha who related that the child belonged to the Al Murrah tribe that roamed the great desert area of the Rub Al Khali, better known as the Empty Quarter.

As we followed the family into the dining area, Amsha told us that Duha's father, Amir Salim Al Abdullah, had married a Bedu woman, daughter of a tribal chieftain. At one time the woman's mother had been the wife of Ibn Saud. It was not uncommon for the King to marry a chieftain's daughter, if only for the duration of his visit on the desert. Such a union lent honor to the tribe and cemented the bonds of loyalty. The Al Murrah had befriended the King as a young man during the years he sought to unite the Bedu. He considered this tribe his own.

"The woman who called us to dinner is Duha's mother," Amsha continued. "The child you saw must be a relative, perhaps of the Amir's other wife—also of the desert but a daughter of the Ajman."

"And do they get along?" I asked, intrigued with such relationships.

"Only they know . . ." Amsha laughed. "The Ajman were once bitter enemies of the Al Saud—now they are both peaceful and loyal to the King, as I'm sure the women must be."

We had arrived at the dining room, and Amsha glanced around, as if looking for someone.

"We are all envious of her beauty . . ." she said. "That is a trait of the Ajman women. I wish I had a face like the one behind her veil."

"I'd like to see what she looks like," Linda said. "Do you think I could? Is she here?"

"Why don't you ask?" Sara said, perhaps wanting to see the results herself.

Amsha pointed to a lady on the far side of the room, but the beauty of her features was hidden by a light veil.

A sumptuous feast was spread on the floor before us, completely covering the embroidered cloths that had been laid to receive it. Two large trays on pedestals held center stage, supporting the charred bodies of whole roasted sheep laid out on beds of saffron rice. The pungency of sesame, pepper and cinnamon assailed our senses from roasted chickens and hard-boiled eggs that edged the trays. Numerous small dishes of ground lamb with pignolas, hot vegetable stew, sliced tomatoes and cucumbers circled the area together with heaping mounds of bananas, oranges and apples interspersed with wedges of pink melons and platters of glazed sweets dripping with syrup. All but the lamb and rice were set in individual servings, so that the entire floor seemed covered by an endless array of dishes.

Hand washing over a great metal tub was in serious progress. We stood in line to await our turn. The somber faced woman of the brazier was chief officiator of the proceedings. She poured water over my hands from a tall slender spouted ewer. It dripped into the tub, grey and foaming with thick soap curds massing in the hard water. I took the soap offered by a servant and passed it on to Cynthia. Another woman poured the rinse water. As I turned to leave, she hawked at me in her loud voice, and made me wait for two more rinses to come! A young girl offered me a fringed towel, and a second grinned widely, as she doused my hands with cologne.

I was delighted to see Hussa, here on a visit from her home in Buraida, some three hundred kilometers north and inland of the peninsula. She entered from the kitchen, rubbing her hands with a towel that she deftly tossed to a servant. With a quick step forward, she signaled us to fill the seating area she had claimed for herself. It was no mean accomplishment for me to sit with feet tucked under, and with ripples of laughter Hussa flipped her glittering skirt over areas my short one failed to cover.

I was glad to see Cyndy feeling at ease with her Saudi friends, for she sat next to Amsha who piled Cyndy's plate with food. Hussa had Linda and Sara in tow and squeezed them into a place occupied by a distant cousin. Lulu wanted to join their group, but Amsha's scowl sent her away. I had not forgotten Lulu's efforts at matchmaking and was glad the subject had not surfaced again. In fact, I dismissed it as a prank of curiosity over my reaction. I felt she had no authority to speak for Amir Naiyf, if he were the Prince involved.

In spite of the formality of the occasion and the questioning eyes of Juad who sat across from me, I felt at home with this family—almost as though there might be a place for me, too. Perhaps Latifa's gesture was a part of it, for her desire to sit with Azziza indicated an effort to reach a turning point in her life.

Now and again I looked up through doorless archways into the back rooms that contained a minimum of comfort. Cushions, rugs, and palm matting covered the terrazzo floor. Shelter, food, water were the basic needs of the Bedu, and conservative princely families of the Eastern Province followed the puritan traditions of the desert: the obligation of man to face God and himself without the distraction of possessions.

Stacks of *hubbuz*—flat rounds of unleavened bread—stood close at hand, and I followed Hussa's lead, as she tore off pieces from a slice, and folding them between her fingers, squeezed up morsels of savory meat from the various dishes. A pair of calloused bare feet, soles blackened by years of application of henna, planted themselves between the trays of lamb. The owner, a buxom servant woman, hiked her flowered skirts under her belt, pushed up her sleeves and hacked at the carcasses with a long knife. Soft rolling fat flopped against her arm, as she delivered pieces of the succulent meat by knifepoint onto every plate.

The elderly ladies finished first. They had been quietly enjoying the evening meal, now and again glancing at me with an intent other than politeness. As they got up to leave, it became incumbent upon the rest of the family to do likewise, finished or not. After the final hand washing, we returned to the salon. The light night breeze had cleared away most of the incense, but the fragrance of roses clung to the walls and seeped into the chairs. Through the open shutters, brilliant Arabian stars studded the night sky, paling the descending moon.

The older women cornered Sara and insisted she sit with them. It was clear they had something on their minds. We studied each other from across the room, as cardamom coffee, sweet mint tea, and the rich full Arab *musbutah* (thick coffee) were served to all. I felt an impasse was about to take place, for the Matriarch Nura seemed to be interested in me. Clearly she had something on her mind—not tales of valor, but questions for Americans she had little opportunity to meet.

Again the same question: "Do you have sons?" And the fervent hope that: "*Inshallah*, you will have grandsons!"

I asked whether the young graduate would return to school. No. Duha would prepare for marriage. She would go with her aunt to the Rub Al Khali, that vast sand area of South Arabia to live with her Al Murrah kinsmen and prepare for marriage to an Al Murrah Prince. I knew the Saudi custom of selecting mates equal in family status to assure the well being of a daughter. It was their way—not mine, and I wondered where the conversation might lead.

A quietness settled over the room, not one of relaxation and well being experienced after a delicious meal, but one of waiting—a moment suspended in Time. Something unexpected was about to occur, but I was not prepared for the question Great Aunt Nura directed at me through Sara.

"Why do you Americans allow your daughters to run off and marry anyone they choose?"

Had I heard correctly? Sara's expression confirmed she had delivered the desired message. But—how to answer this power play from the core of Saudi society? Fragmented thoughts cluttered my mind. The answer must not denounce Saudi custom, nor fail to uphold the morals of my own society—good or bad as they might be. Could I find a meeting ground for understanding?

I surveyed the faces around me: the Matriarch Nura, defender of tradition, Fahada taunting rebellion, Duha, quietly acquiescent, Juad, challenging our presence, Sara, uncertain in transition, Latifa, seeking to blend two worlds, and my daughters, uninhibited by demands of custom. "What words of wisdom from the philosopher, Khalil Gibran: "Our children come through us, but are not of us . . ."

Latifa had joined me after dinner, and I looked to her for support. "What shall I say?"

"The truth," she answered. "Let them know who you are."

I faced my challenger who waited patiently from her deep velvet chair.

"Our lives are different," I said. " . . . and yet we are the same. I have wished to meet you for a long time. I felt we wives and mothers wanted the same things for our families." I paused, waiting for Sara to translate. The ladies leaned toward her, their intent expressions absorbing the words but showing no response.

I went on. "You are a very old and respected country, wise in the ways of survival. We are new—experimenting as we go—and, yes, it is true. Sometimes our daughters choose their own mates." There—I had said it—fully aware of the pitfall that nothing brings greater disgrace to a Muslim family than a shameful daughter, and the sacred trust of fathers and brothers to protect their virgin women.

A flash of recent history came to mind—the flower children of San Francisco—defying the "system" and taking control of their own lives. How to explain this phenomenon heard around the world? I hardly knew its impact myself.

A rustling of fabrics and eager mumblings competed with Sara's attempt to answer questions, as the ladies pawed at her for clarification of my words. I noticed that Juad, well versed in English, had moved closer to Fahada and was now engaging her in serious conversation.

"Did I say too much?" I asked Latifa.

"Well, I don't know," she answered with a smile of support. "They are trying to sort it out."

I was aware of Linda nudging me, a glare of disapproval in her eyes. "Mom . . . ," she said. " . . . do you know what you're doing? Don't mix up their lives."

"Sweet Linda . . ." I thought. Ever the champion of those in need. But wasn't it I who sat in judgment? I was about to say something, when Sara spoke up.

"They want to know what you do to preserve family honor."

Family honor . . . For us was it respect of family? Yes. Pride? Yes. Security—love—all of these—not honor in the Muslim sense. How I wanted to say: we do not put family honor on the backs of our young daughters—but dare not. I looked directly at Nura and tried to simplify my thoughts for accurate translation.

"We, too, have a code of honor but approach it differently.

Instead of keeping our daughters in seclusion, we prepare them to accept responsibility for themselves. We recognize that individuals have human rights—the freedom to express themselves—different as we all are. We teach them to use good judgment, to consider values, to accept trust—for trust is the obligation of freedom."

I paused. Had I said the wrong thing? Could they envisage ideas that were not their own? I would try to say it in a different way.

"We are honored to share Duha's achievements with you. She has brought further prestige to your noble family. Just as we are proud of Linda's efforts at school in Switzerland. Through education at school and at home they learn the value of good judgment, dependability and trust—the strength of who they are and the family they belong to. The family stands behind them, for it is stronger than the individual—a haven to come home to. We recognize that marriage encompasses the spirit as well as the body—and that spirit must be free."

The eyes of the Great Aunt never left my face. Her brow below the veil frowned. Then, a half smile of enlightenment as she said: "*Bismillah!* May Allah the Compassionate, the Wise guide your footsteps."

I thought she was about to leave, but instead she leaned forward to ask another request of Sara. "We shun the exposure of women as shameful—is this then so of your daughters?"

"I think women are proud of how they dress and always try to look their best," I said. "For the body is a beautiful and graceful thing when taken care of. It delights our husbands as well as ourselves."

I hesitated. I should not have said that. Did my words imply acceptance of veiling instead of suggesting the right of young women to enter the world beyond the *hareem*? I gave Latifa a quick glance, then hurried on.

"We sense that character is formed within each of us—not determined by what we wear. Of course, the circumstances of where one lives make a difference. Our open society allows freedom of expression. The individual determines what that will be, based on the values she accepts for herself and those established by her family. One may speak only in generalizations, for there are exceptions to every rule."

I waited to allow the ladies to digest Sara's words. Nura looked at me as if expecting more—and there was one idea I wanted to express.

"Although, as you, we are a family, each member is different, and that difference seeks its own kind. For us the bonds of matrimony are sacred. The young couple must choose wisely, for in God's presence they vow to live only unto each other. Our bond with God is love. We understand you make a marriage contract with family. We make a contract in partnership with God."

Why was the room so silent? Was this the moment of being rejected? Had I weakened the togetherness of differences I had been trying to achieve? Was everything gone?

Nura leaned forward in her chair, adjusted the heavy shawl about her shoulders, then reached out to pat Sara's hand. With a tired smile, she collected her voluminous skirts about her, and leaning on the arm of her companion, got to her feet. She paused to steady herself, taking a moment to survey her gathered family. What was she thinking as she moved forward?

She paused for a moment to give me a nod of that proud head, and I felt embarrassed for my short skirts. She moved on to greet Fahada, obviously sure of the traditions this daughter would continue. Nura managed an enigmatic smile for Linda, as though this child represented the future that was slowly making demands of her country. But Duha, that bright and loving face, would hold the family's honor through innovations. Duha lowered her eyes, as her aging aunt kissed her on both cheeks. Then, Nura moved on, to steady herself in front of Cynthia. The hands that had nurtured a lifetime of children reached out in a tenderness of goodnight. The fingers trembled, as the Great

Aunt leaned forward to place her salutation on the damp pink cheeks. Then, she and the other ladies were gone—no doubt to retire to the rooms above and to enjoy the breeze from the roof.

I turned to Latifa. "Did I say too much? Were they offended?"

"I wouldn't worry about it . . ." she said. "They'll think about the things they understood and dismiss the rest as not concerning them. See—we are about to have tea again. I'm sure you could use some."

And she was right. Most of the guests had departed to other areas of the house. A few Bedu women in their dark cloaks and calico masks stood near the kitchen entryway. Soon Duha would be among them. Her mother had returned to sit on the same upright chair, fingering the pearls she had retrieved from her pocket.

Now was the moment of opportunity. With such pride of family, surely it would not be amiss to ask . . .

"Latifa," I said, somewhat tremulously. "Dare I ask Duha to tell me about the pearls?"

"Well, I don't know. Why don't you ask?"

I did. In response, Duha brought her mother to sit with us. She seemed quite happy to do so and even set the glistening jewels on my lap. Our circle of listeners enlarged, and I pushed the difference of custom from my mind. Simply put, what did it matter as long as you got to where you wanted to be?

Chapter Twenty-Nine
THE WARRIOR'S BRIDE

"Our family has a long history," Duha's mother began. "But I shall tell you what I know about the pearls."

I settled into my chair, listening, as the veil of memory misted Muna's eyes. Latifa, too, awaited the woman's words, for here was a part of her life she had never known.

"Do you know the Rub Al Khali?" she asked. "Have you been there?"

"I know of it . . ." I said. " . . . sand mountains that range across South Arabia. It is called the most feared desert on earth."

". . . . my home," Muna sighed. She surveyed her intent audience. "I hope you will understand what I want to tell you."

"I will explain everything," Sara said.

So Muna continued. " . . . years ago, the young Prince Abdul Azziz came to us—the Al Murrah tribe—for rest and comfort during the years he first raised an army with the hope of restoring his father to power and creating a united country that would replace tribal warfare with peace."

" . . . *Ummi*," Duha interrupted. " . . . what about the pearls?"

"Have patience child," Muna said, bringing Duha to sit closer to her. "But, not all tribes wanted peace. They raided each other's camps. What you didn't have you took. Many wanted to keep the old ways, but the Prince knew that tribal unity was the only way for a better life. The area of Al Hasa had yet to be overcome, and with the support of his loyal cousin, Abdullah Al Abdullah, he kept his band of warriors together."

"My grandfather," Duha interrupted.

"There was no honor in battle . . ." Muna continued, immersed in her story. "The Prince recruited men from the tribes. Sometimes they deserted him and joined the enemy. That is what happened when the young Prince found himself and his small band of desert warriors in retreat fighting Ajman rebels on the fringe of the Rub Al Khali. Many of his men were wounded, and he had been struck in the groin by a bullet . . ." She paused.

"The pearls . . ." Duha urged, shaking her mother's arm.

"I am getting there," her mother said with a smile. "The impatience of children. Some day they will know that time has neither beginning nor end. It is told that a large encampment of our people had settled near Saffur. Scouts from the Prince's army alerted our Sheikh that the warriors were headed our way."

Muna paused—her face a vision of remembrance. She seemed to have returned to the sands—far away from the Al Abdullah villa in Dammam. Her voice was different when she spoke again—no longer her own, but the voice of memory. She knew the desert so well—the ways of her people—and her voice seemed to carry me along with her to a day long ago . . .

* * * * *

Saiyda awoke—confused. How long had she been sleeping against the limestone boulder at the base of Jabal Hamdin? Could it be night? She adjusted the strings that held a coarse veil across her face. No—it was not night, though shadows darkened the scrub brush scattered near where she sat, and a purple haze deepened the red hue of distant dunes where her family camped. In spite of stiffened muscles, she got to her feet and hurried part way down the slope away from the *jabal*, her long skirts dragging a trail behind her. She paused to scan the arc of the horizon and its immediate surroundings.

"Hessa!" she cried. No movement caught her gaze across the empty landscape. "Hessa! *Yella!*" Saiyda called again. "We must start back!" Only silence responded, save for the first whisper of the evening breeze stirring the grains on the tops of sand drifts.

A large pile of gathered sticks and brush lay heaped nearby—firewood the sisters had been gathering since early morning. Mother had impressed upon them the urgency of needing plenty of firewood to keep pots boiling for cooking the sheep and for medicinal needs in expectation of the warriors' arrival.

Saiyda could wait no longer. Hessa must have headed home or run off on some purpose of her own. It was not the first time her sister had disappeared over some frivolity, when there were chores to be done for the camp. Somehow she must get the firewood home, as well as carry her little sister Nada still asleep at the base of the large outcropping of limestone. Saiyda turned back to awaken the child. There would be no stopping to dig for mushrooms or search for the tiny scarlet spider, Daughter of the Rain. Children of the great deserts learned early to care for themselves, and at twelve years Saiyda was equal to most any demand.

Nada was awake and calling for her when she retraced her steps to the *jabal* and began making preparations to return home. She unpinned the soft veil of netting studded with bits of silver that covered her hair and fell down her back to the ground. She folded it into several layers, knotting the ends together to form a sling. She would carry Nada, as her mother did the newest baby, in a sling over her shoulder.

Saiyda unwound the length of rope about her waist and used it to secure the sticks into a bundle. She fastened the other end around her waist, set Nada in the sling and started walking, dragging the firewood behind her. It was slow and hard work, especially when the bundle of sticks caught on outcroppings of limestone or on brittle thorn bushes. At such times, she would have to stop, set Nada on the ground and release the bundle so she could proceed another short distance.

The desert had its own life—a myriad of contours changing with the vagaries of wind and flood: sudden drops in the surface, dry wadis with loose stones and soft sand pools, and the beginnings of dunes, harder than the rocks, as wind blown sand packed about dead roots and scattered chunks of limestone. Between Jabal Hamdin and Wadi Saffur along the line of the red sands, Saiyda knew there were no treacherous salt flats to cross. She kept to the soft sand areas that fringed low sandhills, rather than drag the bundle over a rocky stretch and pick a zigzag course between the stony flats.

From time to time she paused and set the child on the ground to give her a sip of water from her gazzelleskin bag. Then she removed the headscarf that fit snuggly under Nada's chin to allow the air to circulate about her neck and ears and to dry the damp skin. She pulled back Nada's unrestricted wispy hair and secured it in the back with a light thorn from the *arfaj* bush.

"Now you look like me," Saiyda said with a laugh, swinging around so her long dark hair flung about her head like the wheel of a donkey cart. "Can you walk, little one? Let's see how many bright stones we can find."

They started off again, Saiyda sighting the direction she wished to follow. There would be no scampering here and there, as they had done in the early morning hours. She wondered where Hessa had gone. What was more important than bringing the firewood back to camp? She paused to scan the distance again, hoping for some sign of her family's encampment: a shepherd bringing home the ewes after a day's grazing; a scattering of the camel herd foraging for the last of dried summer grasses until the rains came, even a thin black line that would be a *bait ash sha'ar*, her father's tent. Still in that infinity of vision, there was nothing different in the sameness of the landscape. The humid clouds hung in darkening circles, gathering in the trails of grey and white moisture that tormented the scorched sand with its weighty burden.

Saiyda settled Nada into the sling and trudged on. She found herself stumbling from blocked vision and tossed her veil on top of her head. It didn't matter. There was no one in sight.

An opening between decreasing levels of ragged limestone revealed a vista of uninterrupted flat land to the south. Moving slowly across it and proceeding east toward her direction came a compact caravan of camels. A few of the animals had split off from the main body, causing small jetties of dust to rise as they scattered in different directions, heading for their own family encampments, clans of her tribe, located a kilometers distance from each other.

A DESERT FAMILY AWAITS THE RETURN OF ITS
WARRIORS

Camel herds spread out over vast areas were no novelty to Saiyda, but rather an important aspect of her life and an indication of tribal wealth. But these were not animals being led home by a herder. Each camel carried a rider, some slouched low over the hump. Those riders in the lead carried banners and battle flags of green and white held proudly aloft even though the pace indicated a weariness of both man and beast.

Just the night before, while she and Hessa lay wrapped in their orange blanket pretending sleep, Saiyda had heard the elders gather in her father's *mejlis*, and through the curtained tent wall, she had heard the men speak of battle losses and the intent of the Prince to regroup his forces and to attack again. Though how soon this might be was uncertain, since it was rumored the Prince himself had been wounded.

"The warriors!" Saiyda exclaimed, setting Nada on her feet. "See how many!" She untwisted the rope about her waist, pausing to rub a sore spot the rope had worn just above her hip. "Can you walk, pretty one?" she encouraged. "Let's run to the big rock. See how it looks like a camel's head!"

A surge of excitement filled her with anticipation. Jamil would be coming home! She was promised to her first cousin, even though he had been gone for many months with the Prince's army. How she looked forward to being his bride and to wear the red silk dress locked away in her mother's trunk. But first—the firewood. ! Where had Hessa gone? Why wasn't she here to help?

Saiyda straightened the bundle of firewood to start it dragging behind her, then taking Nada's hand in her own, the girls proceeded down the incline. She loosened the strings of the mask that were hooked over her ears. How good the air felt on her damp skin, even though it was as moisture laden as the pools of perspiration clinging under the fringes of her hair. They reached the camel's head outcropping towering above the wadi.

"See! We did it!" she exclaimed "Soon we'll be home!"

Then, in sudden panic, she jerked Nada to her side. An involuntary scream died in her throat, and she fumbled for the mask to cover her face. There was nowhere to flee, so she stood rigid, clutching Nada's hand in her own.

Without warning, two camel riders swung slowly across her path. Draped *quttras* covered the men's faces, all but the eyes. The leader stopped his mount and gazed at the two girls. Saiyda's black eyes blazed with indignation and suspicion, challenging the set stare of the stranger. His attitude was one of weariness, yet struggling to hold the alertness of a hawk on the hunt. She was well aware of desert politics, and her fear gave way to unrestrained alarm. These men who rode in the shadow of the hills were enemy scouts following the retreating warriors. How could she warn her tribal family of impending danger? She must get away.

Saiyda lifted Nada into her arms and started backing up. Her feet became entangled in the rope tied to the firewood, and she fell to the ground, Nada tumbling face down and crying.

"Sir," Saida cried . "You frighten my little sister." Her bold stance dared the men to accost her, contrary to the law of the desert.

The lead camel swerved. She noticed how the rider shuddered and slumped forward as if in extreme pain. He managed a few words.

"We give you the peace of Allah. We have no wish to distress you."

Saiyda stood up, untangling her feet from the rope. She brushed the tears from Nada's cheeks, as thick with sand, they slid slowly down her chin. "Go!" she cried. "Leave us!"

"You carry firewood for the camp of Sheikh Abdullah Bin Khalid of the Al Murrah," the second man said.

So. Her judgment was correct. These men were enemies wanting to search out her father's camp! She pinched her lips into a hard line. No daughter would speak of tribal secrets to a stranger.

The second rider swung his camel closer. "Speak up! Are you a daughter of the tent of Sheikh Abdullah? It is Amir Bin Saud himself who seeks the comfort and care of the Sheikh's people."

Saiyda stood to the full height of her twelve years. The words were a trick to extract information. Didn't the great Amir Al Saud ride below with his battle weary warriors? Her lips would remain sealed to these betrayers of her father's honor!

The leader pulled on the rope of soft wool around the camel's neck and swung his mount away from the girls. A streak of bright red seeped alongside a darker one that reached the length of his rumpled *thaub*. He shivered as if in pain, and his fingers clutched the long lance supported by his shoulder.

"We intrude upon the *hareem*," he called to his companion. "*Yella!* It's a poor tracker cannot find a haven in a *shamaal* . . ." He turned away to hide a gesture of weakness. His head slumped on his chest.

"Water! Give me your bag!" the companion cried. He jumped to the ground ready to snatch the gazzelleskin where it lay in the sand.

"No—leave it for the lass. We have offended her enough . . ." The words were little more than a whisper.

Bright red stains appeared on the rider's robe and in the sand. Fresh bleeding. Even an enemy has the right to be cared for. Without hesitation Saiyda offered the water to the wounded man. She reached on tiptoe, pulling herself up by the black sheepskin saddlecloth. He leaned to take the bag from her and loosened the tucked under flap of a *quttra* from the side of his head. She saw a youthful face, bearded, sun browned, a large full nose—even a kindness in the eyes not revealed before. Then his body pitched forward, and the water fell to the ground.

Saiyda reached for the sling that dragged in the sand from her shoulder and ripped off a section of net from the bottom of her veil. Deftly she scooped up a handful of sand, piled it on the piece of veiling, then knotted the fabric to form a pouch. She had not forgotten her youngest brother's encounter with a fox he had chased when it ran off with a lamb. There had been deep gashes in his thigh, and the flesh was torn at the ankle. She had helped her mother care for him. Even an enemy should not be denied help.

The man lay slumped over the camel's neck, his face turned from her. She approached the camel. Her hands groped beneath his robe to stuff the compress against the wound. A jellied stickiness on her fingers indicated she had located the injury—a ragged line of flesh just above the genitals. She barely had time to set the compress in place, before she was thrust to the ground.

"*La, hareem*! None of your tricks!" the second man shouted. He pushed her against the pile of wood, and striking the camel's belly with his fist, turned it away from the girls. Then, he mounted his own camel, and the two men headed toward distant sandhills.

* * * * *

Muna paused in the telling. Our group of listeners had enlarged, and we moved closer together. I decided to join them on the floor. Haifa had left her friends and sat close to her mother, now and then giving a sidewise glance at Cyndy.

"Go on, *Ummi* . . ." Duha said, as she looked at the necklace of pearls on my lap. And her mother continued.

* * * * *

Saiyda and Nada reached camp with the firewood. Still no sign of Hessa. There was far too much confusion and jobs to be done with the arrival of the warriors to worry about her sister. Mother shouted orders that kept her busy running to deliver water to her father's *mejlis* for coffee and to carry bowls of soured *laban* for the Amir Saud and elders gathered there. She would not go in, but squatting, deposited the bowls along the inner side of the curtains, as far as her arm could reach.

Sometime during the night Saiyda felt a disturbance of the

orange blanket in which she slept. Hessa had returned to share it
with her. The girls were used to sleeping together, and Saiyda was
glad for the closeness and companionship of her sister. But—
where had Hessa gone?

* * * * *

Haifa shook her mother's arm. "Where did Hessa go? Why
didn't she help?"

"Hush . . . if you don't interrupt, Muna will tell us." Latifa
answered.

"Come and sit with me . . ." Linda coaxed, but the child
snuggled closer to her mother.

* * * * *

The full moon had come and gone, and still the warriors
camped with Sheikh Abdullah. They became restless and threatened to disband.

"His wound has turned our leader into half a man," they cried.
"He cannot lead us any more!"

Muna put her arm around her daughter and included the other
children in that warm embrace. Her forceful tone enlivened her
words, as she continued.

"Imagine the rage of the Prince when he learned of this outcry. Rising to his full height, he shouted to Sheikh Abdullah that
in spite of his slow healing wound, his men must know he is a
whole man.

"In the name of Allah!" it is told he shouted. "Prepare for my
wedding. Tomorrow I shall take a bride!"

Chapter Thirty
SAIYDA

Muna's words seemed to fade away, and I heard the voice of history telling its own story:

* * * * *

Saiyda and Hessa trembled and wrapped the orange blanket close about their heads, for the full length of the tent shook with the force of the Prince's fist on the central rope that held the roof upright. His anger was a frightful thing to see, and his will would be done.

"See to it that I have a bride," the Amir directed Sheikh Abdullah. "And spread the word throughout the troops that a celebration is in order. Tomorrow I shall wed, and the next day the march begins again."

Shocked—surprised—elated—the Sheikh's family rushed to make preparations. Which daughter would be honored by the Amir? Which one would please him most?

"It must be Hessa," the Sheikh's wife declared. "Hessa was born to please a man—her flower is ripe and her bed matured to nurture his seed. Allah set her in my womb to please a great man. Let it be Hessa."

* * * * *

Muna paused and signaled for another serving of tea. She sipped slowly, gathering courage for the story to come. Sara, too, enjoyed the break, for she had described to us every word that Muna had said.

"Of course," Muna commented, " . . . being the bride of the Prince would have been a simple thing. But—Hessa had other ideas."

We all shifted position at Muna's words, anxious for her to continue.

* * * * *

Next morning the troops were alerted to the coming marriage. It meant their leader had healed, and the march would resume. They entered into preparations with great vigor, offering assistance to the family, running errands between camps and building campfires. They cleaned rifles and lances in preparation to dance the Ardah for their Prince.

"It will be an honor to become the bride of the great Amir," Saiyda told her sister. "I am glad you will be the one, for I shall marry Jamil." She felt a twinge of envy when her mother brought out the bridal dress to air, wrinkled and smelling of sandalwood. One day it would be her turn.

Several women rushed to prepare Hessa for the wedding. First, they washed her in a large tub filled with precious water stored in goatskin bags and dragged into the tent by small boys. All night the women helped the shepherds refill them at the well. A solution of zinc and arsenic stored in mother's trunk removed some of the bride's superfluous body hair. They painted Hessa's hands with henna paste, leaving a golden glow to her skin. And finally the youngest girls helped to weave tiny purple flowers into her braids that Nada and her cousins had found in the sand about the camp. Later, the women would adorn the bride with their silver necklaces and heavy bracelets to enhance her worthiness, but no one noticed the tears that fell from Hessa's eyes.

When the girls were left alone, Hessa faced her sister. "I cannot do this," she confessed. "You, Saiyda, must take my place."

* * * * *

Muna sighed and took a deep breath. The events to follow were critical. Would her listeners understand.

"Oh, no . . ." Linda said. "Why would Saiyda do that? She loved Jamil."

"Just as Hessa was in love with Ali." Muna said. "Instead of gathering firewood, she had gone down to the wadi and hurried to the well, expecting Ali to be there watering the camels. But Ali was not there. Her disappointment was great, for she was very much in love with him." Muna turned her attention to me. "You see, even our demands of purity cannot hold back the urge to mate." She sighed and hugged Duha closer.

"People of the desert protect the group, not the individual," Muna continued. "Hessa's desire to wed Ali was a personal issue, not critical to her clan. We cannot know the exact conversation that took place between the two girls. We do know that Hessa persuaded Saiyda to take her place as bride of the Amir. Perhaps she told her sister that the fault of being a woman had started, and she was unclean. The bride of the Amir must be pure, or the family would be dishonored and an outcast. Saiyda must have been stunned by her sister's words. There was no choice. She agreed to take Hessa's place. It was the only way to uphold family honor."

* * * * *

The girls planned to make the switch. Wrapped in an *abbaya*, Hessa ran among the tents to hide from the groom, as was the custom before a wedding. While everyone searched for her with cheers and laughter, the girls exchanged clothes and covered themselves with long veils. The Prince would not remove the facial mask, they thought, for the bride had the right to refuse on the first night. Only the girls would know the difference, for tomorrow Hessa would resume the role as bride, and the Prince and his warriors would be gone.

They had not counted on the Prince. When he entered the bridal tent, he noticed the girl in the red dress wore a veil with silver studs. In her distraught state, Saiyda had picked up the familiar garment she wore every day. He noticed the torn edge where she had used the cloth to staunch his wound.

* * * * *

Muna paused to sharpen her memory. Her story telling held us spellbound and transported me to a *bait ash sha'ar* pitched on some desert fastness on a night long ago.

"That he remembered the girl who had made an effort to save his life is quite evident," Muna continued. " . . . for this fact is where the pearls come in."

* * * * *

The marriage of the Prince had served its purpose. He gathered his troops and continued his pursuit of peace for the tribes of Al Hasa. Then, one day a messenger arrived at the camp of Sheikh Abdullah and presented him with a package. It contained a veil with silver studs, some rice and coffee for the family and a most valuable pearl necklace strung with one large black pearl, the rarest of all varieties found in the Gulf. Although the mother kept the pearls in her trunk of personal treasures, the necklace was given to Hessa as the Prince's bride, for it was the Amir who had sent the most generous of gifts.

The weeks went by, and the Sheikh noticed Saiyda's pregnancy, unaware she had been the Amir's bride. Her life must be sacrificed to restore family honor.

Hessa could keep silent no longer. Filled with horror and guilt, she told the truth of that night. " . . . it was I, not Saiyda, who betrayed the family," she confessed.

But even that did not make the problem any easier to resolve. Hessa had been exploited as the Prince's bride; yet Saiyda carried his true *welad*. Mother made the decision, as she did in most family situations, to be corroborated by the elders. Hessa retained the pearl necklace as the rightful bride of the Amir. Saiyda's fate would be dealt with when the camp moved on. How could she be condemned to death when she nourished the Amir's child?

"Asa, our eldest son, will take her into the territory of the Ajman and there abandon her," Sheikh Abdullah said. "If Allah wills she shall be found—if not, that, too, is the will of God."

Learning the terrible fate of her innocent sister, Hessa took the pearl necklace from her mother's trunk and gave it to Saiyda, thinking that whoever found her sister would keep her for the value of the pearls that rightfully belonged to her.

It was not Asa but Jamil who took Saiyda on camelback into the *dirrah* of the Ajman. There he left her in sight of a distant campfire. He promised to find her one day, and taking the camel, left her alone in the darkness. Saiyda's instinct for survival led her to the glow of light, as blinded by tears and sadness she reached the tent. Exhausted, she rested against a camel. The beast swung his neck at her and hissed, disturbing the shepherd curled up near a smoldering fire. There were no hyenas tonight to threaten the herd, and he dropped off to sleep.

Saiyda pushed past the camels to join a group of sheep huddled together in front of the tent face for warmth.

The shepherd found her there next morning. He aroused Rafha, the woman of the tent, who took Saiyda inside. She noticed the girl's condition, fed her and gave her warmth at the tent fire. Her son had told of seeing a strange camel's tracks, indicating two people arrived but only one returned. Rafha knew the ways of the desert well. It meant the girl had been abandoned. She would not question her too closely, for Saiyda said only that she became lost and would not give her tribal name.

Rafha kept the girl against her husband's wishes. She had no daughter, and this one could help with the work of the tent. "Even an enemy is given shelter for three days," Rafha reminded her husband. The three days stretched into months.

The family was on the move when Saiyda's time came to deliver her child. She allowed her camel to graze until it lagged far behind the others. With the pains ever stronger, she slipped to the ground. Her strength had been given to help Rafha who had saved her life. Now none was left when she needed it most. A cry under her skirts—a rush of blood—and a child was born. A girl. Saiyda tried to pack herself with sand to stop the bleeding, as she had seen her mother do. But life slipped away. She raised a hand to touch the veil about her neck.

Rafha found her as dawn lit the sky. She wrapped the infant in her heavy shawl and released Saiyda's clenched fingers from her throat. The cloth parted and the pearls glowed pink and gold, as beautiful as the morning sunrise. Rafha was shrewd. The ways of the desert were hers. The girl wore a dowry no Bedouin ever owned. She decided to keep the infant, to hide the pearls and to guard the secret she had discovered.

* * * * *

Muna stopped speaking. She had told how the family first received the pearls. But what of the years that followed? What did Rafha do with the necklace? How did it return to the Al Abdullah family so that Duha could wear it tonight?

"What happened to the black pearl?" Sara asked.

Muna shrugged. "We can only guess," she said. "Perhaps Rafha sold it to a shopkeeper when they needed supplies. Perhaps as time went on she became more curious about the little girl she claimed as her own—perhaps even guilty for not searching out the child's birthright."

"How could she do that?" Duha asked.

"The Bedu can do many things. They know what the desert holds . . ." Muna said with a smile for her daughter.

"And the baby was my grandmother . . ." Duha said.

"Yes—and my mother . . ." Muna added. "She married into the Ajman and it appears Rafha gave her the necklace at that time. When my mother knew she was dying, she told me some details of her birth, as I have told them to you. I wore the pearls when I married Duha's father, bringing them back into the family of the Al Saud."

"That's quite a story," I said. " . . . though there are some parts missing."

Latifa looked at me and smiled. "Isn't that true of all stories?" she said. "Look at the pleasant time we will spend imagining the rest!"

As I do about you, I thought. Isn't it enough to enjoy your friendship? To begin to understand this country where I live? To be privy to secrets of tradition and custom?

"I bet I know what happened . . ." Linda said, leaning forward with some excitement. "It was Jamil . . . he said he'd find her, and I bet he did. He'd know who the baby was. Did your mother ever mention his name?"

"No—not that I recall . . ." Muna said.

"My brother is called Jamil . . ." Duha added.

"Just a coincidence," Muna said. "Remember it's only a story, and there will always be many more."

I hadn't thought about the lateness of the hour until Azziza returned, accompanied by the woman in the scarlet dress. We would have coffee again, and when the incense burner was passed around, the time for departure would be near. It was difficult to unfold my legs, for I had been sitting on the floor and was glad of a moment to stretch. My gaze followed the lady in the scarlet dress, for she kept looking at me as she walked among us.

"Do you know her?" I asked Latifa. "Is she Bedu?"

"She very well could be," Latifa admitted. "A house like this holds many people—distant relatives, even among the Bedu. It's too confusing to speculate who anyone might be. Maybe in time I'll find out."

Azziza was in earnest conversation with Fahada, a fact that didn't go unnoticed by Latifa. "There must be some problem with the cars again," she told me. "Azziza seems to be making arrangements. I must leave with the others. Will you visit with me again? I'd like that very much."

Her tone was so sincere, I knew it to be a promise, and that there would be a place for me in her life. There was so much I wanted to know about her. Now was the moment to seek an answer to an incident I could not forget.

"May I ask you something . . .?" I asked.

"Please do . . ."

"I wouldn't want to offend you . . ." I said.

Latifa laughed. "I assure you that you won't. I had many questions to ask—and I still do—for I am always learning something new about this life."

"Did our visit cause an embarrassment?"

"Certainly not. Why do you ask?"

"Someone was in the house. It seemed to upset you. I wouldn't want to do that—ever." I said.

Her eyes twinkled with amusement. "Oh—well, it was my husband. He had returned from the Amirate early and forgot you were coming to visit. Usually men do not interfere with our social activities. I hope you weren't concerned."

A FAMILY OF THE DESERT

"I'm glad it was just that. I suspected it was the Prince—maybe wanting to be sure we were suitable people to be visiting you."

"He already knew that," she laughed. "I want you to meet him. He is quite charming."

At that moment I could not foresee the future that entwined our lives ever closer. The tranquility of her Dollhouse became my haven, too. Many were the times His Highness joined us for coffee and cakes, and I realized how much he treasured his wife and daughters. His kindnesses to me over the years were many, and I wondered at his dedication to family that included raising the orphaned child of a servant as his own. And I realized, I, too, had stories to tell of a way of life isolated and unknown.

The hour approached for us to say goodnight. Amira Azziza confessed she had been listening to all the problems of relatives that comes with being the wife of the Amir and hoped we had not been bored. I expressed my thanks for her hospitality. Far from being bored, we had enjoyed every minute.

"We must go now," Azziza said. "There will be a car to take you to Ras Tanura. *Masalamah*."

I watched Latifa leave with her, Haifa following. Umm Naiyf, in *abbaya* and veil waited near the door. Soon we would be alone in the once vibrant room with only the servants scurrying about.

Duha's mother sat silently on the straight chair. The story was over but not forgotten. It would be told again and again to those who would listen. She seemed to be waiting with the lady in the scarlet dress to see us off. Again we would be riding with Fahada.

"Sara," I called "Are you coming with us?" But Sara would not return. She had been invited to spend the night with Juad at her father's villa in Dammam. Then, final goodbyes ". . .thank you—may Allah go with you . . ." and we were on our way—through a door of welcome—not one to be closed behind us. And I knew we would see them all again.

We were half way down the steps, when the lady of the scarlet dress hurried after Fahada, displaying much urgency and calling in a loud voice. Fahada gave her a cursory answer and continued on to the gate. The G.T.O. was waiting. We got in and drove away. The streets were black save for a dim oil lamp hanging from a nail in a small coffee shop, where men contentedly smoked their waterpipes and conversed late into the night. Fahada alighted at her villa, instructing the driver to take us to Ras Tanura.

"Good night," she said. "I shall see you soon—and a safe journey."

I heartedly seconded her wishes, and hoped I would be able to control the speed of the car. It was a long way to Ras Tanura over a dark rough road.

A final thought crossed my mind.

"What did she want?" I asked. " . . . the lady in the scarlet dress? She seemed quite intense when she looked at us."

"Oh, that . . ." Fahada answered. "She wanted to know if you could get her a Sears catalogue . . ."

The misfit didn't strike me at first.

"Is she Bedu. . . ?"

"She is Samir Al Abdullah's wife . . ."

Chapter Thirty-One
TRADITIONS ARE STRONGEST

Living in the Kingdom required us to take a long or short vacation every year. With a local leave approaching, Russ and I decided to spend three weeks in the Lebanon. We could visit Linda at the American School in Lugano and enjoy the beautiful country of Lebanon.

Cyndy had elected to stay home in R.T. with Fran Richards.

"It's boring at the hotel," she had said. "And I want to practice with our Blue Devil Marching Band for the County Fair." Cyndy played the piccolo.

And, so, Russ and I took off for Beirut.

Beirut, Lebanon—Paris of the Middle East: Five Points, Suq Taweela, Rue Al Hamra and Pigeon Rock; the core of banking and finance, of French finery, gold *suqs*, Sarkis and syrupy pastries. Russ and I stayed at the Excelsior Hotel and spent our nights at the Caves du Roi, nightclub extraordinaire, famous for pepper crusted steaks, tall red tapers flickering from every table and a French combo that invited late hour dancing to the swell of "I Love Paris In The Springtime".

I loved Beirut—every moment of it. No matter the elevators didn't always work—electricity in the sixties was fitful—or that water pressure declined almost every day. Beirut was life, laughter, excitement—everything Arabia lacked. We haunted Aldo's American Long Bar, only one in the Middle East. With persuasion this personable Italian would concoct the essence of gin disguised in plum and raspberry juice bottles to evade Saudi customs. A drop or two turned homemade alcohol into the world's most authentic gin.

Beirut—home of the American University, Khayyat's bookstore, St George and the Dragon and Neechamal's on the Corniche where we bought jewels by candlelight. It would satisfy our appetites for another year to come.

On our return, Ali's taxi brought Fran and Cyndy to meet us at the Dhahran Airport. The long ride back to Ras Tanura caught us up on local happenings during our absence. It was good to be home. "I Love Paris In The Springtime" became a song in my heart to override the limited pleasures of every day.

"You know Elaine," Cyndy said. "Well, she really got in trouble."

"How's that?" I was more interested in having her close than in the escapades of a classmate.

"She sneaked out of her bedroom window and met Jimmie on the beach."

"Oh, no!"

"And Doug threw a tomato at Mrs. Johnston's house. It made a big mess."

"Whatever for?" I feigned interest.

"She gave him an F in art," Cyndy went on. "Boy, Elaine was sure glad Dad wasn't around in the Rover . . ."

Somehow our young teens suspected Russ of snooping on them. The Jerboa was to be avoided at all costs! At least such an idea served as a precaution for unauthorized activities teens could get into. Better that, than formal Company restrictions.

"She was absolutely delightful!" Fran enthused when she could get a word in. "I'll take her any time."

I knew Cyndy wouldn't be any trouble. She could be so helpful, always a "good citizen" and lots of fun.

"With Sandy gone, Cyndy was a real life saver." The Richard's daughter was at school in England.

"How's the tonette band doing?" I asked Fran. She volunteered her musical expertise to teach classes at the Senior Staff School.

"I'm really encouraged," Fran said. "And speaking of school, Sara's leaving."

Did I hear right? Sara? Leaving?

"Turned in her resignation yesterday," Fran continued.

No—it couldn't be. Had the inevitable happened? I must contact Sara as soon as possible. The affairs of my Arab friends had touched me once again. I only half heard Fran rambling on about the horses and school until I caught the name "Fahada".

"You're not listening," she chastised. "I want to know who Fahada is. You didn't tell me you had Saudi friends. I tried to pump Cyndy but she clammed up."

"Gosh—I don't know. So many people have the same name, like Ali . . . Mohammed . . ."

"But Fahada?" Fran twisted the needle.

"Isn't she the little daughter of Brahim who works for Russ? I invited her to a birthday party but she didn't come."

"Hmmm . . . Dick knows him, too. Did you meet his family?"

"Once," I said.

" . . . nothing like the Royal Hareem?" Fran goaded.

" . . . nothing."

"That's all?" She knew me pretty well.

"What else? Nothing to it."

Her eyes expressed utter disbelief. "Oh, you . . ." was all she said.

I'd have to caution the girls further, for if Fran knew about my relationship with the Governor's family, the news would be all over town. A brisk canter along the beach in the morning should silence curiosity, at least for the time being.

I caught up with Sara a few days later. She seemed cheerful

enough, but mention of Fahada brought complete dejection.

"I'm leaving for Beirut in a week," she said. ". . . and I'm not coming back."

"Why, Sara! Whatever for?"

"It's Hammad. He's married."

The tears fell as I knew they would. Glistening pools of moisture had been threatening to spill from the corners of her troubled eyes. Punctuated with sniffles and swipes of tissues, I learned that Hammad had returned from Taif, and Sara had extracted from him the fact that he had married his cousin. It didn't change anything, he had assured her. That it was just something he had to do. Sara had his true love.

"Oh, these women!" Sara exclaimed in the telling. "They are so strong! They say what is to be in a family! I know! And I will never be a second wife!"

How could I comfort her? Sara had come too far to change her priorities now.

"Hammad says he's going away soon—maybe to America to begin training for an astronaut. He wants me to join him."

"And will you?"

"No," she sighed. "I told him traditions were strongest for him, and I must keep my standards." She wept bitterly.

"You can't fight the whole family," I said.

"It's the women . . ."

"Maybe you should be glad," I said, wanting to turn a bad situation into a better one. "You could never be one of the forgotten wives of Royal Princes who are neither truly married nor divorced. They live a collective life of loneliness in the Women's Palace in Riyadh."

"I love Hammad. But I will leave him."

"What will you do in Beirut?" I asked.

"First I shall wait for Fahada. She wants me to go to Paris with her to select a wedding gown."

"Fahada?" I exclaimed.

"She is married."

"Married!"

"To the King's brother. And she will be a left wife, because Prince Bandar is the King's advisor and goes everywhere with him."

"Don't be so bitter, Sara. You can't change what will be. It's not as bad as you think. You're just upset, and I don't blame you."

She wiped away another tear, then took a deep breath, as if to recharge a fighting spirit. "Fahada agreed only when she got what she wanted." A look of triumph dammed the overflow. A small gain in a process already set. "Bandar divorced his wife as Fahada insisted. Also, she will be allowed to continue her education and will receive half a million *riyals* on her wedding day."

"Alimony in advance," I said. "Good for her!"

Was she fighting the system in the small way she could? No, that was my viewpoint. Fahada was the true daughter of warriors and would hold to family loyalty and tradition. In unity lay strength—the world acknowledged that—the Saudis lived it.

"I told her you were back, and she wants you to visit her— Azziza, too,—when she returns from Paris."

"What does Latifa say to all this?" I needed to know about her.

Sara shrugged in a disinterested way. "Well—I never see her. She is first wife now with the Governor—that's all right with Azziza and Umm Naiyf—they say they are getting too old . . ."

"I shall miss you, Sara," I said. " . . . and I respect your decision. When will you leave?"

"When I get an exit visa."

"In a week, maybe?" It took Russ several days to obtain emergency visas for families with a death in the States, or for a crisis concerning children at boarding schools in Europe and the Lebanon.

It was difficult wishing Sara the best of all worlds. Somehow I felt she would come out on top, and that her friendship with the Al Abdullahs would not terminate with her departure from the Kingdom.

About a month later, Amir Turki brought me an invitation to visit the villa in Dammam. I didn't know it would be a prenuptial event for close family members.

"I may be late," I told Russ.

The few women gathered at the villa were all ladies I had met before. Though I recognized my non-relationship, I felt no sense of being an intruder. Amira Azziza and Princess Hussa greeted me with cordiality, together with affectionate interludes from Amsha, Lulu and Alia. In spite of their light heartedness, I missed their joviality I had come to know.

A feeling of conclusion, quiet anticipation, flowed from the fanning skirts and soft toned voices. I missed the Princess Fahada and asked after her.

"She will come shortly," Hussa answered in English, using every opportunity to expand her knowledge of our language. "I would learn it perfectly in six months," she once declared. "If I could go to New York!" Proud of her heritage, Hussa often explained unfamiliar situations to me.

"You see," she began, " . . . marriage formalities have taken place. Fahada is now—what do you say?—very shy. She remains in seclusion most of the time. It is our custom until she meets her husband."

It was difficult for me to imagine the out going and vivacious Princess confined by time honored humility.

Hussa continued. "For us the marriage has already taken place—the contract between families signed in the presence of the *qadhi*."

I had to say it. "And the bride? Has she met him?"

"She will meet her husband the night of their union—a celebration in their honor! Arrangements are being made for the party." Then, with a note of amusement: " . . . we saw the Prince once on TV."

I knew such formalities preceded a wedding—a contract between the bride and groom, though neither was present. Both families signed the contract in the presence of a *qadhi*, verifying the bride would be taken care of and that the groom would receive a virgin wife, thus assuring the comfort and well being of their children and the continuance of family honor. All was as it should be.

"Is she happy with these events?" I had to ask.

"Well—let Fahada speak for herself. Here she comes."

Loving relatives surrounded the Princess, who accepted their voluble outpourings with little emotion. The daughter of the Al Abdullahs followed her destiny to the letter. I was fascinated by her every move—pride and determination coloring every glance, every half smile. The once rebellious teenager had accepted the role of bride of a Royal Prince—her inner self held in check by the demands of family loyalty.

Automobiles had driven up, and animated male voices resounded from the porch. Fahada's quiescent attitude changed to one of excitement, as she stepped outside to greet several young men. I recognized Prince Naiyf. The others were undoubtedly close relatives, for she greeted them warmly and without a veil.

"Mrs. Nicholson . . ."

I knew the voice. It was Sara. My surprise at seeing her needed no questions asked.

"I returned with Fahada from Paris," she said by way of explanation. "I promised not to leave until after the wedding."

"I'm glad," I said, pleased she had set aside her own troubles to support a friend. Here was the true Sara I had recognized long ago. "How was the shopping?"

"Great! You must see some of her gorgeous clothes!"

"And THE dress?"

"That's a secret!" She whispered it had been designed by

AN 7W ⊗
4/5/22

Shopping List

Pads — (6) Don't use those thot-where
they without do not then a ⊠ where
the patts no paying ing in center

— for tips

the most famous couturier in Paris.

"I can't wait to see it," I said without thinking.

The informal invitation to the wedding some months before, may have been mere politeness. Today Azziza's reminder of the event was for real. The festivities would take place in four weeks, and she would let me know the exact day. Meantime, I must deliver the black and silver net as soon as possible, if the seamstress was to complete my dress in time.

"Today the Princess Fahada receives best wishes from her closest friends," Azziza said. "She will remain in seclusion long after the union. The bride's commitment to marriage requires adjustment to activities she has not experienced before."

I thanked her for telling me. Perhaps she wanted to explain their customs, as I had been asked to do with ours. There would be no honeymoon to Niagara Falls. Their way was right for them.

"You will come to the wedding?" Azziza invited.

"I'll be delighted!"

"Then tell Fahada, for here she is . . ."

I looked up as Fahada freed herself from Lulu's effusive grasp and came my way. The simplicity of her plain cotton dress, unadorned by any finery, complimented the repose of her face.

"I was so glad Sara decided to stay and help me," she said, taking a brief moment to sit with me. "I was lost in Paris without her."

"I wish you many years of happiness with *welad* (children) to flower the gardens of the Al Saud."

"It is frightening, I confess," she whispered. "My aunt married another of the King's brothers. I shall take strength from her."

"Will you live in Riyadh?"

"Yes. The Prince has his own villa."

She gestured with her hands, and I noticed the palms were

marked with several dots that appeared to be henna. I traced them with a finger, and she pulled back with a laugh.

"The marks indicate a drawing," she said. "Before the wedding, an artist will paint the crossed swords and palm tree on my hands."

". . .the insignia of the house of Al Saud," I said. "Do all brides do that?"

"No," she said. "It indicates I am marrying a Royal Prince of the Al Saud, and I am myself a Princess."

I felt humbled to share a small part of the private life of a Princess.

"One day I must sit in State," Fahada continued. ". . . wearing traditional clothing and smothered with the jewels of my family. This is to show my worth to the groom's family." She sighed. "I think it would be easier to do like Linda would—run off with the man you love and have a simple wedding . . ."

"That is right for us," I said. "You live your family's history—something we cannot do, for Americans have few traditions." I reached for her hand. "You are the daughter of a noble Arab family with an ancestry that is always behind you. Can you see that you are never alone? That you are the past and the future . . ." I was glad for Sara to explain my thoughts, though a scowl told me they were not altogether hers.

"Yes . . ." she sighed. "I may never forget who I am . . ." an involuntary lift of her proud head " . . . nor do I wish to."

The Princess Fahada got to her feet, observing newly arrived ladies anxious to greet her.

She turned to Sara. "I am sorry our way didn't work out for you . . ."

"*Ma'laish,*" Sara said. It doesn't matter. "I live in two worlds and wanted one more than the other . . ."

The Princess faced me with all sincerity. What she might have said, I'll never know.

What she did say concealed a sense of longing. "Thank you for coming. I wish Linda was here, but your friendship will remain with me. Now, I must go." Her half smile held re-membrances of unique associations, soon to be lost as the bride of a Royal Prince.

Chapter Thirty-Two
THE WEDDING

I saw the lights blazing through the trees long before the taxi reached the garden entrance to the private grounds of the Amirate. Princess Fahada Bint Sultan Al Abdullah Bin Mohammed Al Saud tonight would celebrate her marriage to His Royal Highness Bandar Bin Abdul Azziz Bin Abdul Rahman Bin Faisal Al Saud of the Kingdom of Saudi Arabia.

The event had been postponed for three months, since the groom accompanied the King on trips throughout the Arab world to advise him on political issues with Middle Eastern rulers. Today His Royal Highness would come to the guesthouse on the Amirate grounds in Dammam, a three-story structure near the garden gate, where the celebration would take place. Protocol prescribed the groom claim his bride in her family home and later escort her to his villa in Riyadh.

Ties of friendship bound me to Princess Fahada and her family. Tonight, as any parent, I shared joys and concerns for her days to come. She had chosen the way that was correct for her: a marriage of tradition ensuring the bonding of a family and the security of a daughter.

The narrow dirt road Ali had stumbled on months before had been graded and oiled to receive the chauffeur driven limousines bearing female guests. A double array of soldiers policed the gate, scrutinizing each guest's right of passage. Now and again someone of note was allowed to drive through, to be ceremoniously greeted under the hundreds of strings of lights that created a canopy of brilliance over the buildings and surrounding trees.

There would be no blackout tonight, as when electricity first sparked in the Eastern Province some ten years before. ARAMCO personnel would attend the extra generators needed to carry the load.

The path from the gate had been swept of pebbles, uneven ruts filled with sand and the whole covered with dark green carpeting. Borders of sweet jasmine added fragrance to the night. Escaped tendrils crept up intermittent pedestals carrying large basins of flowers shipped in from Baghdad in Iraq and Beirut in the Lebanon.

The plain guesthouse, haven for Heads of State and Tribal Leaders over past years, had been transformed into a Royal Palace. Its weather beaten facade, freshly scrubbed and woodwork polished, came alive under the strings of white lights that dipped from every inch of the flat roof to surrounding trees and ivy covered archways. Above them radiant stars in a deepening desert sky would guide the steps of a Princess to her predestined future.

Distant from this occasion, yet part of it, I joined lithe figures in black hoods and cloaks hurrying along the garden path, offering a glimpse of sparkling gowns, as jeweled fingers raised the intrusive silk covering to ascend steps into the house. My simple black net dress and silver cloth coat, acquired in Hong Kong, offered no competition to the array of exquisite gowns revealed when servants collected cloaks from arriving guests.

Across the broad garden, male guests gathered at the Central Amirate entrance. They would escort the Governor and dignitaries to the East side of the Guest House. Here the lights dipped above a heavy worsted tent, erected for the men's separate celebration. Layers of brilliant silk lined the roof, and luxurious rugs covered the sandy floor. Velvet divans and piles of cushions, interspersed with small tables, offered comfort for male guests. A Saudi attendant prepared to serve coffee from a large brass stockpot near the coffee hearth, and after midnight a sumptuous dinner would be served. Sometime during the evening the men would perform the Ardah. The traditional line dance, which told of valor in battle, tonight would sing of love and fulfillment.

Beyond the brilliant lights, the garden stretched in shadow. The soft glow of oil lamps, barely different from the stars, illuminated the walkway of a minaret hidden behind the black bulk of trees. And beyond that, in the forbidden darkness, would be the Dollhouse. Princess Latifa had shared this secret with me over past months. Amira Latifa. Would she be here tonight?

Once again I walked through the Lion Gate. Its replica outlined in flashing lights arched in front of the main doorway, the curly headed lions proclaiming the domain of the Al Abdullah family. I needed to stand aside and absorb the effect of wealth and oil glittering from brass filigree lamps along the hallway, where their glow on women's beaded skirts flashed jets of light, reminiscent of refinery flares.

I deposited my coat and prepared to follow guests into the salon, just as Lulu hurried toward me.

"You're wanted upstairs," she said, beckoning to a servant in long Arab dress of Saudi green topped with an embroidered apron.

I followed the woman up the stairs. On the landing a door burst open, and a puff of white organdy skirts slipped into a room, followed by Reema who beckoned me inside.

And there they were—a line of little girls—Alia, Aysha, Haifa, Muna and cousins—sitting between the legs of the child ahead, one in front of the other, removing pins and curlers from each other's hair. Tumbling locks received a brushing equal to the one the bride would receive from her Paris hairdresser. Chattering voices accompanied fingers urged on by excitement and the need to finish the job.

"It won't stay on!" Aysha cried. "Where does it go—here or here?" In desperation she handed me the white satin bow fastened to a large clip. "Do something . . ."

I pulled strands of hair from each side of her face and anchored them with the clip. Then I knelt behind the last child in line and unwound the hair curlers, careful not to crush her white organdy skirt, identical to the one each wore. Alia was satisfied with her sweep of curls and jumped up on the bed, unmindful that Reema had covered herself with a cotton *shershif* and squeezed her ample body between the bed and a wall closet to catch up on prayers she had missed. This was no deterrent to Alia. The child crawled to the edge of the bed, and leaning over Reema's bowed head, pulled open the upper closet door. With both hands she reached for a large box, pulled it from the shelf, dropped it on the bed, and lifted the lid. Immediately many small hands dove inside the box, spilling gold chains and bracelets, pearl necklaces and rings, while noisy voices made decisions about a choice to wear.

"I want this," Aysha said. " . . . to dance at the wedding."

A child's headdress lay at the foot of the bed. Aysha reached for it and pulled it over her head. The garment, heavily embroidered with red, gold and green sequins, bugle beads and gold thread on black net, fit snugly under her chin and against her forehead, leaving the face exposed. It rippled over her shoulders and down her back, as her youthful body swayed into an impromptu dance.

Fahada—Amira Azziza—Umm Naiyf—Hussa—where were they? Busy preparing for the evening, I felt sure. And Sara—I would look for her downstairs.

Music floating up from the salon reminded me that time was passing. I checked the bow on Aysha's head, noted that Reema was still praying and the little girls occupied with selecting jewelry, so I stepped out into the hall.

Servants rushed from room to room. Would Latifa be in one of them? The music drifted louder, a warning to return to the salon. I was about to descend, when a voice called my name, and Princess Latifa walked toward me, holding Haifa by the hand.

"I hoped to see you," she said. "In all the confusion Haifa was the one who knew where you were."

"That was lucky for me," I said. "I wondered if you would be here."

"Allah's goodness answered our wishes." She hesitated before continuing. "I can not stay—please forgive me—it seems my shoes have yet to be found." A smile brightened her face, " . . . I wanted to let you know my husband has arranged for me to visit my parents."

"He agreed?"

"Yes."

"I am so glad."

VILLAGE MEN PREPARE TO PERFORM THE
ARDAH

She laughed—as though it had been a simple thing to side step tradition, and gain identity for herself. Then, on a serious note, "I shall leave for Europe next week."

I remembered the conversation we had had on one of my visits to the Dollhouse and spoke up as I might have to my own daughters.

"Enjoy what you have missed . . ."

She smiled. "I shall try." She started to leave, then turned back. "We had an unexpected visitor last night. Prince Bandar. He came to pay his respects to my husband."

"And did you like him?"

"Oh, yes—young and handsome—quite intelligent—and most of all a kind man."

"Did Fahada see him?"

"She was shy at first, but he made her feel at ease. Yes—he was really very kind."

"I am glad for her."

"Of course, my husband had met him several times before. Now we are all glad to have seen him."

"Then, it will be a good match."

"Fahada's parents always knew that. Now, I must go. I will call you when I return."

For some time I had been privy to her personal phone number.

I watched her leave and enter a room down the hall. If I never saw her again, I would remember the self-assurance in her step and the swing of her lime silk gown, adorned only by the rose hued pearls about her neck—both treasures from the Gulf.

I descended to the hall and mingled with ladies heading for the salon. My long dress in the Arab style with silver yoke and wide sleeves seemed lost in the luster of shimmering gowns, as more and more artfully coiffured and jewel bedecked ladies filled the salon. The room was awash in lavender, Princess

Fahada's favorite color. Divans against the walls, table lamps, and wall draperies all blended into an artful display of lavender.

I looked around for Sara. She had promised not to leave the Kingdom until after Fahada's celebration. In my effort to locate her, I surveyed the ladies parading their finery and pausing to chat with friends. One of them invited me to join her table. A servant offered delicacies from her tray. Selecting a French pastry, I was careful not to catch my sleeve on the red juice oozing from pomegranate seeds that promised fertility.

Immersed in the thought that a genie had created the impossible, I wondered at the elegance collected in one place. Where had it all come from in this desert setting? The vats of Ali Baba—or the oil wells of the Eastern Province?

I was more excited than ever to see Fahada, but the bride was not expected to appear before midnight. It was close to eleven P.M., and a quiet restlessness settled over the room. To allay the waiting, several ladies appeared in front of the stage. The women began to dance. I recognized Princess Hussa as one of them. She looked at the tall velvet chairs the royal couple would soon occupy, then broke into unchoreographed movements, the expression of a free soul. She had topped her pale pink gown with an airy overdress, rose colored and shimmering with gold and lavender sequins—the traditional dress from the Gulf, light and delicate as butterfly wings.

I wondered whether the dancers would free their hair in true Arabic fashion, but at that moment Sara caught up with me.

"I've been looking for you," she said. "Have you seen Princess Latifa?"

"Yes."

"She sent out a search party."

"You mean—Haifa . . ." I couldn't help but smile. "What a delightful little girl."

I could tell Sara was not in the best of humor. Usually vivacious, she seemed quite subdued.

"I just left Fahada—a dream in her wedding dress." She sighed, " . . . if only . . ."

"Don't think about it, Sara. Fahada can handle the situation. It's not new in her family—she is the Governor's niece."

There was no comment, so I directed her thoughts elsewhere. "Latifa told me she met the groom and was quite pleased." Still no response. "Come on, Sara, enjoy this celebration. Have you changed your mind about leaving the Kingdom?"

"No."

"Will you return for a visit with me—or to see Fahada?"

"No."

"Because of Hammad?"

" . . . because . . ." She cut her words short.

I knew she was struggling with her emotions.

"Sara, this is such a joyous occasion, share it with Fahada—wish her happiness."

A servant offered more sweets. Who could be downhearted in the midst of such hospitality?

"Are you sure you want to leave?" I asked.

"Yes."

"When. . . ?"

" . . . very soon . . ."

I couldn't change Sara's mood, so I turned my attention to the activities in the salon.

Female musicians, imported from Beirut, entertained with popular Arabic tunes from the bistros of Cairo, and haunting melodies from postwar Europe. The hour was truly one of perfection, the ultimate in luxury the Kingdom could produce in the sixties, each guest a participant in the joyous wedding of the Al Abdullah daughter.

"Sara—see the lady standing in front of the stage, the one in the apricot satin dress—do you know who she is?"

"An aunt of the groom," Sara said. I met her upstairs."

AMSHA CELEBRATES PRINCESS FAHADA'S
WEDDING IN A GULF GOWN

"The gown—what a beautiful color."

"She is wearing cinnamon stones—the closest jewel to match her dress."

I touched the star ruby necklace set in heavy gold that Russ had given me a long time ago. Not a match for my dress, but a promise that living in Saudi Arabia would be an adventure, coming true tonight.

In a dramatic moment, to catch the attention of the guests, the music ceased and the lights dipped. A hush descended over the hall, and all eyes concentrated on the walkway in the center of the room. The finest of Persian rugs would guide the light step of a bride to meet her groom.

The trilling notes from a flute, like birds in flight, accompanied six little girls in white organdy dresses, as they walked down the aisle. They struggled to keep their eyes straight ahead and compressed their lips to keep from smiling, as they passed the tables where their parents were sitting. The children ascended the steps to the stage and stood on each side of the flower-decked chairs.

The lights had risen slightly for the entrance of the bridesmaids. Now they dimmed almost to darkness, to quickly rise to full glory, as the violins vibrated the theme of an Arab love song, punctuated with bell tones from the flute—the voice of a bulbul from Shiraz.

And there she was!

The bride! Walking alone to meet her destiny. Why, at that moment, did I think of Saiyda, holding her torn veil over her face in a *bait ash sha'ar*, as she awaited her Prince those many years ago? Daughters of warriors honoring their families.

There the similarity ended, for the Princess Fahada walked in a dream of beauty. The exquisite finery of the guests, the haunting song of the violin, the fragrance of lilies bowed in humble servitude to the magic of the bride.

Her sedate and even steps, hidden under a luxury of

white satin and lace skirts, heavily embroidered with pearls and crystal beads, gave her the appearance of floating. Wisps of dark hair escaped from a veil of French lace that draped her head and shoulders, allowing no glimpse of her face and withholding whatever emotions walked with her. The widespread train, artfully designed into the gown so as not to hide her slender figure, was constructed of lace over damask silk and decorated with tiny star jasmine. As it swept the carpet behind the bride, it seemed to brush away her life that had gone before.

All sound became a stillness in the presence of ultimate excellence. The violin and the flute bowed to a vision of loveliness, more intoxicating than their love song, as the bride reached the end of the walkway and took her seat on the stage. She sat perfectly still, oblivious of all around her. A spotlight augmented the sheen of pearls encrusted on a chain yoke about her throat and others laced to the backs of her hands. A profound silence held the guests in awe of the vision that had walked in beauty before them.

I felt a surge of excitement as a loud fanfare announced the arrival of his Royal Highness Prince Bandar, accompanied by male members of both families. He strode down the aisle with alacrity, eagerly awaiting the pleasures to come. I noted a gleam of expectation lighting his eyes, and a friendly grin fringed a neatly groomed beard. An embroidered white *qaffiyah* draped his head and shoulders, held in place by a rope of gold, the *egal,* shining like the sun on his proud head. His white *thaub* of rich silk, fastened by gold buttons on a chain anchored by a cluster of pearls, was topped by a cloak of sheer white wool. He ascended the stairs with dignity. Turning to take his seat, his cloak brushed Aysha's face. She put up a hand to stifle a giggle, and he leaned over to pat her on the head.

The arrival of the Prince's entourage, with males from both families, prompted a flurry among some ladies, who felt obliged to cover their faces with a square of lace they had brought for that purpose. Congratulations were offered the bridal couple from both families, and then the men discreetly withdrew.

Immediately, the musicians filled the hall with Arabic songs, and the dancing began in earnest. Amsha increased her tempo. She had slipped a Gulf dress over her gown, a divine wisp of chiffon and sequins that surrounded her in waves of gossamer. Dancers began to unpin their hair. It floated around their shoulders, as they bent low, thrust their heads upward, whirling their tresses around in a shower of crowning glory. Hussa signaled Lulu to join in, her filmy costume the aqua of the Gulf, a reminder the bride would take with her to the desert fastness of Riyadh. Caught up in the excitement, Hussa removed her overdress and tossed the shimmering rose garment to Muna to continue the family tribute—to dance on and on in endless repetitive movements, conveying feelings no words could express.

"The blessings of Allah be with you . . ."

The bridal couple prepared to leave the salon. They descended the stage. The music dropped to a low key, and a different note broke through—the voices of men. Their vigorous chanting from the garden vibrated through the room, accompanying the bride and groom, as they left the hall.

"Do you hear it, Sara?" I called.

There was no answer.

"Sara, it's the men. . . ?" She did not answer.

The singing grew louder. The rhythmic pace increased, and the salon filled with the sound: the Ardah of the men, chanting love poetry to send the bridal couple on their way.

I turned to face Sara. "Listen . . . can't you hear it? The men have joined the women . . ."

There was no response. I stood up, but Sara was nowhere to be seen. She had chosen her moment to depart. She had already gone.